John Gregory

Centennial Proceedings and Historical Incidents of the Early Settlers of Northfield

John Gregory

Centennial Proceedings and Historical Incidents of the Early Settlers of Northfield

ISBN/EAN: 9783337425579

Printed in Europe, USA, Canada, Australia, Japan

Cover: Foto ©ninafisch / pixelio.de

More available books at **www.hansebooks.com**

1776.  1876.

Centennial Proceedings

AND

HISTORICAL INCIDENTS

OF THE

EARLY SETTLERS

OF

NORTHFIELD, VT.,

WITH

BIOGRAPHICAL SKETCHES

OF

PROMINENT BUSINESS MEN

WHO HAVE BEEN AND ARE NOW RESIDENTS OF THE TOWN

By Hon. JOHN GREGORY

Montpelier, Vermont:
Argus and Patriot Book and Job Printing House,
1878.

INTRODUCTION.

PROCEEDINGS PROVIDING FOR, AND RELATING TO, A HISTORY OF THE TOWN OF NORTHFIELD.

At the annual town meeting held March 5th, A. D., 1878, Dr. P. D. Bradford offered the following resolution, which was read and adopted, to wit:

Resolved, That the Selectmen, together with a Committee of three, who shall be appointed by the Selectmen, be directed to procure the publication of one thousand copies of the History of the town of Northfield, said copies to be furnished to our citizens for such price as will cover the actual cost of the same. And the Selectmen are hereby authorized to draw an order on the Treasurer sufficient to pay any deficiency that may arise from the sale of said History, not exceeding five hundred dollars. *Provided*, that the Committee above named shall serve without compensation.

Agreeably to the provisions of the foregoing resolution the Selectmen appointed Philander D. Bradford, John P. Davis, and George H. Crane, as such additional Committee, and at the first meeting of the Committee, which was called the 14th day of March, 1878, by George Nichols, Chairman of the Board of Selectmen, the Committee organized by the appointment of George Nichols, Chairman, and George H. Crane, Secretary.

On motion,

VOTED. To elect John Gregory as Historian.

VOTED. To appoint George Nichols, Philander D. Bradford, and James Morse, a Committee on Printing.

VOTED. To adjourn, subject to the call of the Chairman.

At a meeting of the Committee held on the 13th day of April, A. D., 1878. On motion,

VOTED. To appoint John Gregory, Philander D. Bradford, and George H. Crane, a Committee on Engravings.

VOTED. To receive sealed proposals for printing and binding 1000 copies of the History of the town, and that the contract be awarded the lowest bidder therefor.

VOTED. To adjourn till Saturday the 20th instant.

At an adjourned meeting held on the 20th day of April, A. D., 1878. On motion.

VOTED. To authorize John P. Davis to confer with Hiram Atkins, Esq., of Montpelier, with reference to the details of publication, and make report thereof at a future meeting of the Committee.

VOTED. To adjourn, subject to the call of the Chairman.

At a meeting of the Committee held on the 1st day of June, A. D., 1878, Mr. Davis made a report agreeably to the instructions given at a previous meeting, and thereupon the Committee, on motion,

VOTED. To execute a contract for the publication of the History of the town, with Hiram Atkins, Esq., agreeably to the terms of his proposal for such work.

VOTED. To adjourn without day.

A true Copy of record,

GEORGE H. CRANE, Sec'y.

PART I.

The following "Joint Resolution" of Congress explains itself:

FOURTH OF JULY.

WASHINGTON, May 25, 1876.

The within resolution was issued to-day by the President of the United States.

A PROCLAMATION.

WHEREAS, A joint resolution of the Senate and House of Representatives of the United States, and was duly approved on the 1st day of March last, which resolution is as follows: Be it

Resolved, By the Senate and the House of Representatives of the United States of America, in Congress assembled: That it be, and is hereby, recommended by the Senate and House of Representatives, to the people of the several States, that they assemble in their several counties and towns on the approaching Centennial anniversary of our National Independence, and that they cause to have delivered on such day a historical sketch of such county or town, from its foundation, and that a copy of said sketch be filed, in print or manuscript, in the Clerk's Office of said County, and an additional copy, in print or manuscript, be filed in the office of the Librarian of Congress, to the intent that a complete record may be thus obtained of the progress of our institutions during the first centennial of their existence. And,

WHEREAS, It is deemed proper that such recommendation be brought to the notice and knowledge of the people of the United States: now, therefore, I, ULYSSES S. GRANT, President of the United States, do hereby declare and make known the same, in the hope that the object of such resolution may meet the approval of the people of the United States, and that proper steps may be taken to carry the same into effect.

Given under my hand, at the City of Washington, the 25th day of May, in the year of our Lord, 1876, and of the Independence of the United States the 100th.

BY THE PRESIDENT:

U. S. GRANT.

HAMILTON FISH, *Secretary of State*.

Agreeably to the foregoing resolution, a meeting of the citizens of Northfield was called, at which the subject was discussed, and the following gentlemen were appointed a Committee of Arrangements for said purpose, to wit:

George Nichols, Philander D. Bradford, Orvis D. Edgerton, Heman Carpenter, John Gregory, William H. Boynton, Carlos D. Williams, John L. Moseley, Jasper H. Orcutt, Joseph W. Gould, John P. Davis, E. K. Jones.

The Committee subsequently selected the Hon. John Gregory to deliver an Historical Address, and adopted the following programme of exercises for the occasion:

1776. 1876.

Northfield Centennial.

JULY 4th, 1876.

PROGRAMME OF THE DAY.

Firing of cannon, and ringing of bells at sunrise. The procession to be formed on the common, Depot Village, at 10 o'clock A. M., in the following order: Marshal of the Day, Capt. W. H. Boynton, mounted; Northfield Cornet Band; Ye Ancients, with Fife and Drum; New England Guards; Cadets of Norwich University; Post Johnson, No. 23, G. A. R.; Fire Companies; Mount Zion Commandery, K. T.; Masons; Odd Fellows; Good Templars; Sovereigns of Industry; Children of the several Sunday Schools; 39 Young Ladies, representing the States and District of Columbia.

Officers of the Day.

President, Hon. Philander D. Bradford. *Vice Presidents*, Hon. Heman Carpenter, Hon. David W. Hadley, Hon. Moses Robinson, William Parker, Esq. *Orator*, Hon.

John Gregory. *Chaplain*, Rev. William S. Hazen. *Toast Masters*, Hon. George Nichols, and George M. Fisk, Esq.

Town Authorities, Clergy and citizens generally.

ORDER OF EXERCISES,

In front of the Congregational Church: 1st, Music; 2d, Prayer by the Chaplain; 3d, Ye Ancient Choir, "Hail Columbia;" 4th, Reading of Declaration of Independence, by Rev. R. A. Green; 5th, Reading of Lincoln's Proclamation, by Frank Plumley, Esq.; 6th, Ye Ancient Choir, "My Country, 'tis of thee I sing;" 7th, Historical Address, by Hon. John Gregory; 8th, Recitation, Poem, "Green Mountain State," by Miss Flora Averill; 9th, Dinner, Toasts and Speaking; 10th, Band, "Yankee Doodle."

At sundown, ringing of bells and firing of cannon.

THE CELEBRATION.

This was a great day for Northfield; indeed, it was said to excel any celebration ever held in town in her palmy days, and called forth praises from at least five thousand people. The people felt their independence, and went in for a good time. Grandly was the old Fourth spent intellectually, and never will it be effaced from the memory of those present.

The procession was formed promptly at the hour, escorted by the New England Guards, Captain C. D. Williams, moving up Central, through Washington, down Main, and through the principal streets on the North and West sides of the village. The speaking was from a stand erected on the grounds of the Congregational Church, and commanded undivided attention. Considering that this celebration was gotten up by our own citizens, without any foreign aid, it must be acknowledged that it was a grand success. All honor to those who planned and carried forward this long-to-be remembered Centennial Celebration.

HISTORICAL ADDRESS

OF THE

HON. JOHN GREGORY.

FELLOW CITIZENS:

The occasion that has called us together is one fraught with great interest to the inhabitants of Northfield, for although it is not quite a century since the first settlers organized this town, yet it comes so near to it, and all are engaged in reviewing the past in this Centennial year of our nation, that I think we shall be justified in examining the old landmarks, and gathering encouragement and wisdom for the future. It is indeed a glorious period in the history of our country, and deserves well the consideration of every American citizen. We hope the great Centennial at Philadelphia will be a success, and that the expectations of those engaged in it will be more than realized. Already it is pronounced by good judges to exceel in many particulars the World's Exhibitions at London, Paris and Vienna, showing the growth and excellence of our free institutions, though our nation is but a stripling in years, compared to the nations of the Old World. All who can spend the time, and can bear the expense, should make a trip to Philadelphia the present summer, for never again shall we have an opportunity of witnessing so gigantic an exhibition.

PRIVATIONS OF OUR FOREFATHERS.

It was originally my design to confine myself in this address wholly to the early history of Northfield, but as this is the Grand Centennial Day of the nation, I will spend a little time in the commencement in reviewing the history of our fathers in their struggle for civil and religious liberty. Referring to that time when they came to this country to make for themselves *homes*, far from the polluting and jarring interests of the Old World, we shall see what discouragements they had to encounter and overcome, and how, under the fostering care of God, "they made the wilderness to bud and blossom as the rose." We can afford to pause awhile, amid the cares and scenes of life, and reflect on those to whom we are indebted for the great privileges we enjoy, "looking to the Rock from whence we were hewn," and feeling in our hearts great reverence and admiration for the noble men and women of that early period.

How appropriate are the words of the Great Teacher to us, in our prosperity: "And herein is that saying true, one soweth and another reapeth." Enjoying, as we richly do this day, the blessing of Civil Government, let us be thankfully impressed with a sense of obligation to our ancestors for the privileges we have inherited from them. We have, indeed, entered into their labors, and recreant is that son or daughter who will not "render unto Cæsar the things that are Cæsar's."

Let us briefly consider our origin. On the opening of the sixteenth century, the vast territory which now embraces the population of these United States was one immense forest, broken only by the silent bosom of the lake, or the lonely pathway of the river, inhabited by the savage and his game. At this time Great Britain claimed authority over it, disputed in the title only by the States General of Holland. By all in that nation it was regarded with great interest—by the King as an accession to his dominions, by the capitalist as a source of profitable investment, and by the adventurer as a source of hardy and industrious enterprise. Divided into North and South Virginia, and held by the two companies of Plymouth and London, by patent from the King, it was prepared for the reception upon its soil of the adventurous colonist, who from any motive might choose to fix his residence here, and plant the germ of a rising empire.

A colony of Englishmen under the auspices of Sir Walter Raleigh first landed as settlers in South Virginia. To North Virginia the Puritans, exiled from their native land, or harrassed in it, came, bearing in their breasts the sacred love of Liberty and Religion. I confine myself to these, for their history is briefly the history of all, and soon merges itself in that of all. These adventurers, while their ship was yet hovering on the coast, and before they disembarked, appointed a day of Thanksgiving to God who had conducted them safely across the ocean, and formed on that day a civil compact with each other that they should be ruled by the majority, by which latter act they founded the liberties of a representative Republic. When they landed, the germ of all our present prosperity lay concealed in their little society. Theirs was the spirit of liberty, of hardy enterprise, the desire of virtuous freedom, which was to be developed on the theatre of this Nation, and to mark the character and bless the destiny of a numerous posterity, the effect of which we feel to-day, even in the Green Mountain State, in the peculiar privileges which the God of Heaven and earth has secured to us as our fair inheritance.

But what in brief is the history of our Puritan fathers? Go back and survey the adventurers landed upon our unexplored coast on the eve of a bleak and desolate winter, with a vast ocean on the one side separating them forever from their homes, and on the other a boundless forest filled with savage beasts, or with men as wild and savage. They are to unlock the stores of temporal wealth which the God of the whole earth had concealed beneath these valleys and mountains. They are to protect, extend and perpetuate those civil and religious liberties which had been inspired in their breasts; yet, please consider at what toil, with what privation and suffering, through what perils and dangers, to be endured and surmounted only by the guiding and protecting care of Heaven! To God they commit their infant interests, and go forth strong in heart and vigorous in nerve to the perilous encounter. They fell the forest, they build their houses, they erect their sanctuaries, they sow their plantations, and over their harvests they raise their pious thanksgivings.

And now, fellow citizens, behold the result. Look abroad upon this great land, with its spreading population. See what a country is yours—washed by the oceans, and stretching from the arctic to the torrid zone. Note its immense resources, its mountains reaching to the skies, its villages nestling in the bosom of sunshine, its rivers upon which a nation's traffic may be borne, and its lakes on which the navies of the earth might ride! Mark its capacities in their as yet incipient state of development, its varied fertility, its mineral wealth, its gigantic support for future generations. Survey the people of this Union, peruse their several branches of enterprise and industry, with none to hinder or molest. Ponder the statistics of your country's growth. See the iron rods of communication along which the electricity of life is transmitted from the Atlantic to the Pacific shores! Examine the architecture of that social order under whose security you live, simple yet firm, a grand model for other communities in its principles, and a blessing to ourselves in the protection it extends over us, all the protection—but no more—that a freeman needs. And when you have filled your contemplation with the spectacle presented by your own beloved Republic, then bless the Lord for His goodness and His wonderful loving kindness, for it is He who has given us this ample heritage! If ever men were bound to own that God is good, it is the people of the United States. If ever a community on earth should be distinguished by religious sensibility, it is this grand nation, of which we are a part.

Time would fail me to speak of all that might be said of our *fathers*. In truth, we may say:

They to life's noblest ends
Gave up life's noblest powers,
And bade the legacy descend
Down, down to us and ours.

And of our *mothers* may we say:

But not alone, nor all unblessed,
Our Fathers sought a place of rest;
One dared with him to break the knot
That bound her to her native spot,
In life, in death, with him to seal
Her kindred love, her kindred zeal."

I do not wonder that the *women* living in a section of the State where they could enjoy the luxuries and blessings of civilized life should have some misgivings about coming into this wilderness to assist in establishing new homes for themselves and their families, but judging from the following vote of the Proprietors, on the 5th of August, 1788, as an inducement for them, I think such was the case:

"Voted, that the Proprietors of Northfield will give to the wives of Stanton Richardson and William Ashcroft, each, one Lot of land in the second division of Northfield, to be to them, their heirs and their assigns forever; on condition that the said Stanton and William shall continue to live in Northfield five years each, and the above women to have an equal share in the second division."

An eloquent orator speaking at a centennial celebration in Massachusetts, remarked, "There is a *legend* most worthy to be remembered, that of all the band of Pilgrims who landed from the Mayflower it was a woman's foot that first pressed the rock of Plymouth, that it was a woman from that glorious company who, with high constancy and firm faith, began in an act of adventurous heroism the settlement of this mighty empire; as it has been, in every subsequent period of its history, the fortitude and perseverance of the sex, and the purity of their domestic character, which have encircled it with glory."

With admiration we view the women of our early history, forgetting self, and uniting their destinies with the noble men to whom we are indebted for our growth and prosperity as a town and as a people. May they be held in grateful remembrance, and considered co-workers, equal in *rights* and *privileges*, in laying the foundation of our representative Republic!

I have spoken briefly on the character of the principles by which the first settlers of New England were actuated: of their original enterprise, of their fidelity on which, under the smiles of a beneficent Providence, their success was founded, and to the same order of principles have traced the prosperity of our towns. In their growing and flourishing condition, New England has been honored; with the matron of old, presenting them as her offspring, she has been ready to exclaim, "These, these are my jewels."

On a day like this, a day that no mortal eye present shall ever behold again, when the children of this our household have gathered home, when, with a filial reverence and glowing affection, we have come to sit once more by the family hearthstone and to enjoy the social pleasures of the fraternal birthday, when we have come to mingle our gladness and our grief together in many of the proud and happy, no less than the tender and affecting, remembrances of the past, let us never forget our birthright! Honorable and inspiring are the reminiscences that rise up before me! One hundred years have passed away since the foundation of our Federal Government was laid in blood and tears, and nearly one hundred years since our town felt the tread of the early settler. Oh, what joyful scenes, and what sorrowful ones, have come and gone in all her habitations! Generation after generation have followed each other, like wave rolling upon wave, alike swallowed up together, but time and its changes have never stopped for them, nor have the divine appointments been altered or set aside. The cradle, with its infant smiles watched over by parental fondness: the bridal, with its garlands and hopes, each of them rosy and bright; the grave, with its breaking hearts and tearful eyes; sickness, with its own pains and the watchful solicitude of those who have bent over it; merry gladness and withering gloom knocking side by side at countless doors; prayers of thanksgiving, and prayers imploring comfort, ascending from the same and different scenes; sunny prosperity, and times that tried the soul: battle and peace, with all their terrors and rejoicings, who, who shall recount all these? In what thronging numbers do these affecting remembrances thicken around us? As we turn to the scenes of home, to the cemetery, to worshiping courts, where in all their varied character they have been acted out, how do they rise to our imaginations, as, through the dim aisles of the past, fancy pictures to us the retreating footsteps of the passing generations?

What remains for us, descendants of the early fathers, in helping forward all *reform* movements so auspiciously begun? On our fidelity to principle, everything that is grand and ennobling depends. Nothing great or noble lives, the roots of which have been planted in the lower propensities of man. Everything triumphs at last, which is based upon right and religion and truth. The appearance of the passing hour, the shouts of the multitude, may give a temporary prosperity to the wrong: black night may shut down for a while around the righteous cause, but, by the omnipotence of truth and the fidelity of human endeavor, the final consummation is sure, and the steady progress toward it is certain. Fathers of New England, may your sons learn this of you. Let the inheritance of your children be your trust in God, your never faltering faith in the capacities of man.

"Thou carriest Caesar," said the world's conqueror to the trembling boatman, as he ferried him in fear through the perilous tempest; "never despair with such a burden." Thou art bearing forward the purposes of God, is a nobler reflection, yet appealing to the same sentiment, to inspire and sustain our souls. He who despairs with such a burden deserves not to know what he carries. Let self-patience, perseverance and diligence be in all times to come, as in all times past, the cardinal virtues in the land of the Pilgrims. Blessed with the memory of the great and the good who have lived and labored for our benefit, measuring justly what man is and what he has done, watching the steady growth of the ages, worshiping the divine power of truth, and still more adoring Him who gives truth its power, thus may we, and those who come after us, aim to catch some ennobling sense of the true destiny of our race. Springing beyond the fences of our own time, without fear to the advancing generations, to the irresistible laws and the presiding care of God, let us be men.

And let us remember also that the human race constitutes one great *brotherhood*, and ask in the language of Joaquin Miller:

Is it worth while that we jostle a brother,
  Bearing his load on the rough road of life?
Is it worth while that we jeer at each other,
  In blackness ahead? that we war to the knife?
  God pity us all in our pitiful strife.

God pity us all as we jostle each other;
  God pardon us all for the triumph we feel
When a fellow goes down 'neath his load on the heather,
  Pierced to the heart! Words are keener than steel,
  And mightier far for woe or for weal.

Were it not well, in this brief little journey,
  On over the isthmus, down into the tide;
We give him a fish instead of a serpent,
  Ere folding the hands to lie and abide
  Forever and aye in dust at his side?

Look at the roses saluting each other,
  Look at the herds all at peace on the plains—
Man, and man only, makes war on his brother,

And laughs in his heart at his peril and pain,
Shamed by the beasts that go down on the plain.

Is it worth while that we battle, to humble
Some poor fellow soldier down into the dust?
God pity us all! Time oft soon will tumble
All of us together, like leaves in a gust,
Humbled indeed down into the dust.

Time will not permit me to follow this history further; but had I time I would notice the Indian War instigated by Philip the brave, the Revolutionary War, then the War of 1812, and last our Civil War, in which we have been preserved, as we must believe, by the kind Providence of God, and made *one* people. Let us never forget the trials and sufferings our fathers endured for the prosperity of the land of their adoption. They were noble, large-hearted men! The branch which they planted, under the fostering care of Heaven, rose extended and invigorated. It acquired strength by oppression, and gained importance by the means used to crush it. Possessing souls magnanimous as the cause in which they enlisted, they knelt at the shrine of freedom, and upon the altar of God swore eternal hostility to every form of tyranny and usurpation. They unfurled the "Star Spangled Banner" to the breeze and the storm, and struck their harps to victory and triumph upon New England's mountains of freedom. And now we can exclaim with Lord Byron:

One great clime, in full and free defiance,
Yet rears her crest unconquered and sublime.

Preserve, O, preserve the ark of your nation's safety. I charge you to transmit it to posterity unimpaired. In the language of the patriot Tell:

———I have laid me flat along,
And as gust followed gust more furiously,
Threatening to sweep me o'er the horrid brink,
I've thought of other lands,
Where storms and summer flaws compared to mine,
And, for a moment, I have wished me there;

The thought that mine was free has checked
The wish, and I have raised my head,
And cried in thraldom to that furious wind,
"Blow on, blow on, this is a land of Liberty!"

And now, fellow citizens, surrounded as we are to-day, on this grand Centennial year of our nation, by this bright array of beauty and intelligence, representing the thirty-nine States of this free and independent country,, let us take fresh courage, and save it from every encroachment of power, so that we can hand it down to posterity with not one star effaced, having ever for our motto "E Pluribus Unum," significant of a united people. That above and beyond all party considerations we have a duty to perform for the benefit of those who shall come after us, and that is, united in *love*, united in *strength*, united in *principle*, we shall be strong in our affection for the dear old flag that has cheered us in our many fiery trials, so that we shall stand "towering and sublime, like the lofty Appenine, around whose summit the lightnings may play, and at whose base the thunders may roll, unharmed by the ravages of time!"

SETTLEMENT OF NORTHFIELD.

At the time of the adoption of our Declaration of Independence, this town was an unbroken wilderness, with not a white man settled within its limits. And the hearer will please consider that up to 1784 no measures were taken to settle this township, although a charter was granted in 1781. We have no record of any settlers in Northfield previous to Elijah Paine, who came soon after 200 acres of land had been offered him if he would build a saw mill, and 200 more if he would build a grist mill, an inducement to make a beginning, as we shall subsequently show; and that he built a grist mill and a saw mill in the same romantic region a deed to Abel Keyes will confirm. Some have doubted that Judge Paine built a saw mill in conjunction with a "corn mill," as it was called, although he took 400 acres from the Proprietors as a compensation for the buildings, but said deed will establish the fact.

Commencing at a late day to gather historical incidents, the compiler has been somewhat embarrassed by finding them so meagre, and it has been only by interviewing some aged people and consulting the town records that he has been enabled to collect as many as he has. Had this matter been attended to sooner, many interesting facts would have been rescued from oblivion. Joel Brown, John Green, Oliver and Jesse Averill, and Elijah Smith, could have given an account of many interesting scenes that should have been preserved.

THE CHARTER OF NORTHFIELD.

I have before me a literal copy of the Charter as originally written, which is as follows:

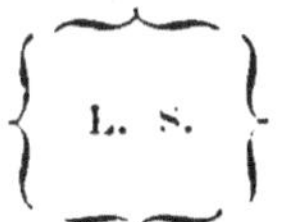

"The Governor, Council and General Assembly of Representatives of the Freemen of Vermont.

To all People to whom these presents shall come Greeting. Know ye that Whereas it has been represented to us by our worthy friends Major Joel Matthews and company to the number of sixty-five, That there is a tract of vacant land within this State which has not heretofore been granted, which they pray may be granted to them; We have therefore thought fit, for the due encouragement of settling a new plantation within this State, and other valuable Considerations as hereunto moving. And, do by these Presents and in the name and by the Authority of the Freemen of Vermont give and grant unto said Major Joel Matthews, and the several persons hereafter named his associates; viz, Capt. William Gallup, Micheal Flin, Oliver Williams, Amos Bicknal, Benjamin Cox, Zabulon Lyon, Timothy Grow, Benjamin Emmons, Steel Smith, Samuel Smith, Samuel Patrick, Zebina Curtis, Elias Taylor, Ebenezer Smith, John Smith, Elisha Smith, Edward Hazen, John W. Dana, Zebulon Lee, Sylvester Smith, James Cady, Joel English, Resolved Sessions, Edmund Hodges, Abel Emmonds, Thomas Chittenden, Joseph Parkhurst, Calvin Parkhurst, Moses Kimball, Paul Spooner, Amasa Spooner, Jeremiah Richardson, Daniel Gilbert, Amos Robinson, Elias Thomas, Ebenezer Miller, Barnabas Strong, John Throop, Bariah Green, Joseph Kimball, George Dennison, Oliver Gallup, John Payne of Pomfret, Amasa Payne, Elijah Payne, Jacob Clark, Abida Smith, Barkus Green, Elisha Smith B. A., David Fuller, William Gallup, Junr., Jesse Safford, Thomas Lawton, Willys Hall, Samuel Matthews, Benjamin Burtch, Oliver Taylor, John Sergeants, Phineas Williams, Shubal Child, Ebenezer Parkhurst, William Andrus, James Andrus, and Perias Gallup, together with five equal Shares or Rights to be appropriated to the Public uses following; viz, One share or right for the use of a SEMINARY or COLLEDGE within this State; one Share or right for the use of the County Grammar Schools throughout this State; one Share or Right for the first settled Minister of the gospel in said township, to be disposed of for that purpose as the Inhabitants thereof shall direct. [One share or right for the support of the Ministry.] One share or right for the benefit and support of a School or Schools within said Township. The following Tract or Parcel of Land, BEGINNING at the North and most Westerly Angle of Williams Town, then South thirty degrees West in the Line of Williams Town, about six miles to an Angle thereof, then North Sixty-one degrees West in the Line of Lands heretofore granted, six Miles; then Northerly to the South-westerly Corner of Berlin, then Easterly in the Line of Berlin to an Angle thereof, then Southerly to the Bounds begun at. PROVIDED it be not before intersected, and the same be and is hereby incorporated in a Township by the name of NORTHFIELD, and the Inhabitants that do or shall hereafter inhabit said Township are declared to be enfranchised and intitled to all the priviledges and Immunities, that other Towns within this State do by Law exercise and enjoy.

TO HAVE AND TO HOLD the said granted premises as above expressed and all the priviledges and appurtenances thereunto belonging to them and their respective Heirs and Assigns forever under the following conditions and reservations: viz. that each Proprietor of said Township of NORTHFIELD, his Heirs and Assigns shall plant and cultivate five acres of Land and build a House at least Eighteen foot square on the floor, or have one family setled on each respective right or share of Land in said TOWNSHIP within the Term of Three Years next after the Circumstances of the war will admit of it with safety on pain of the forfeiture of his respective share or right of Land in said Township, and the same to revert to the Freemen of this State to be by their Representatives regranted to such Persons as shall appear to settle and cultivate the same. That all Pine Timber suitable for a Navy shall be reserved to and for the use and benefit of the Freemen of this State.

IN TESTIMONY WHEREOF We have caused the seal of this State to be hereunto affixed the Tenth day of August, in the year of our Lord, One Thousand Seven Hundred and Eighty-one, in the fifth year of the Independence of this State, and the sixth of the United States.

N. B. [The words one share or right for the support of the Ministry, were interlined before execution. The name of Daniel Benton erased and Benjamin Emmons entered in his room.]

THOS. CHITTENDEN.

By His Excellency's Command,

JOSEPH FAY, Secretary.

N. B. *Elisha Payne* was altered to *Elijah Payne*, and *Amos Robertson* to *Amos Robinson* by order of the Governor and Council. Oct. 25th, 1785.

Attest, THOS. TOLMAN, Secretary.

PROPRIETORS' FIRST MEETING.

I find by examining the records of the Proprietors of land in Northfield, before any settlements were made, that their first meeting was held in Hartford, Vt., on the 11th day of November, 1783. They also met at different times at Windsor, Hartland and Pomfret, making arrangements for surveying and laying out the Town into lots; and this continued until 1794, when a sufficient number had moved into Northfield to organize and officer it with suitable persons.

The following is a vote passed by the Proprietors in those days, that I presume was characteristic of the times:

"Voted that Mr. Marston Cabot be allowed 27 days in surveying Northfield

	£	S.	D.
At 9s 1 per day - - - - - - -	12.	3.	0
And 18s expense money - - - - -	0.	18.	0
And for three gallons of West India rum at 8| per gal. and one of New England ditto at 5|6 per gallon, - - - - - - - - -	1.	9.	6
	14.	10.	6

It was thought necessary in that early day to have a little "New England." to make labor easy. Now, behold the change! It would be a curiosity to find a man carrying the "ardent" into the field to give him *strength* and *endurance!*

We give a list of the Proprietors of Northfield as they stand in the charter, with each Proprietor's lot, and the range, as they were drawn by Mr. Marston Cabot, (a disinterested person) beginning with the first on the charter, etc., (as the law directs) together with a true copy of the chart of the first division lots presented to the Proprietors at the before mentioned meeting, by Mr. Marston Cabot, and attested by the rest of the Committee.

Attest, OLIVER GALLUP, CLERK.

	LOTS.	RANGES.
Maj. Joel Matthews, - - - -	10	6
Capt. William Gallup, - -	1	1
Michael Flin, - - -	7	2
Oliver Williams, - - - - -	4	5
Amos Bicknal, - - - -	6	7
Benjamin Cox, - - - - -	2	3
Zabulon Lyon, - - - -	1	5
Timothy Grow, - - - - -	7	4
Benjamin Emmons, - - -	8	5
Steel Smith, - - - - - -	3	6
Samuel Smith, - - - -	10	5
Samuel Patrick, - - - - -	9	4
Zebina Curtis, - - - -	5	1
Elias Taylor, - - - - - -	3	2
Ebenezer Smith, - - - -	9	3
John Smith, - - - - - -	10	1
Elisha Smith, - - - -	1	2
Edward Hazen, - - - - -	8	2
John W. Dana, - - - -	6	5
Zebulon Lee, - - - - - -	8	1
Sylvester Smith, - - - -	2	4
James Cady, - - - - - -	5	2
Joel English, - - - -	1	7
Resolved Sessions, - - - - -	8	3
Edmund Hodges, - - - -	6	3
Abel Emmonds, - - - - -	6	6
Thomas Chittenden, - - -	10	2
Joseph Parkhurst, - - - - -	7	5
Calvin Parkhurst, - - -	3	3
Moses Kimball, - - - - - -	8	7
Ebenezer Parkhurst, - - -	3	1
William Andrews, - - - - -	4	4
James Andrews, - - - -	2	6
Paul Spooner, - - - - - -	8	6
Amasa Spooner, - - - -	10	1
Jeremiah Richardson, - - -	2	1
Daniel Gilbert, - - - -	7	6

	LOTS.	RANGES.
Amos Robinson, - - - - - -	9	6
Elias Thomas, - - - - - -	5	6
Ebenezer Miller, - - - - - -	7	7
George Dennison, - - - - - -	2	2
Barnabas Strong, - - - - - -	5	3
John Throop, - - - - - -	7	3
Bariah Green, - - - - - - -	1	3
Joseph Kimball, - - - - - -	3	5
Oliver Gallup, - - - - - - -	1	4
John Payne, of Pomfret, - - -	8	4
Amasa Payne, - - - - - - -	3	4
Elijah Payne, - - - - - -	9	2
Jacob Clark, - - - - - - -	5	5
Abida Smith, - - - - - -	4	7
Barkus Green, - - - - - - -	2	7
Elisha Smith, B. A., - - - -	9	1
David Fuller, - - - - - - -	6	4
William Gallup, Jr., - - - -	4	3
Jesse Safford, - - - - - - -	4	6
Thomas Lawton, - - - - - -	4	2
Willys Hall, - - - - - - -	4	1
Samuel Matthews, - - - - -	6	1
Benjamin Burtch, - - - - - -	2	5
Oliver Taylor, - - - - - -	5	7
John Sergeants, - - - - - -	1	8
Phineas Williams, - - - - -	10	4
Shubal Child, - - - - - - -	6	2
Perias Gallup, - - - - - -	9	5
College Right, - - - - - - -	3	7
Right for the County Grammer School,	7	4
First settled Minister's Right,	1	6
Right for the support of the Ministry,	2	8
Town School Right, - - -	5	4

Number of acres comprising the township 18,515.

We thus see that provision was made for *public schools* and *religious teachings; land* being set apart for that purpose, showing that our fathers had an interest in the moral and religious welfare of their kindred--realizing that without *virtue* and *education* no people could succeed in any undertaking.

The first town meeting held in Northfield was at the house of Doctor Nathaniel Robinson, who lived a little north-west of the Poor Farm, and who held the office of Town Clerk for many years, until he died. The meeting was called by Cornelius Lynde, Esq., of Williamstown.

The Justice says: "In consequence of a petition from a number of respectable inhabitants of Northfield, who are legally qualified to vote in Town Meetings, are hereby warned to meet at the dwelling-house of Doctor Nathaniel Robinson, in said township, on Tuesday, the 25th day of March, inst., at 9 o'clock, forenoon, to choose such Town Officers as the law directs, and transact any other legal business.

CORNELIUS LYNDE, Justice of Peace.

Williamstown, March 12, 1794."

Then follows an account of the meeting as follows:

"At a meeting of the inhabitants of Northfield, legally warned, and holden March 25, 1794:

Cornelius Lynde, Esq., was chosen Moderator.

1st. Voted, and choose Nathaniel Robinson, Town Clerk.
2d. Voted, and choose Stanton Richardson, 1st Selectman.
3d. Voted, and choose Amos Robinson, 2d Selectman.
4th. Voted, and choose Ezekial Robinson, 3d Selectman.
5th. Voted, and choose Amos Robinson, Town Treasurer.
6th. Voted, and choose David Denny, 1st Constable.
7th. Voted, and choose William Ashcroft, 1st Lister.
8th. Voted, and choose Stanton Richardson, 2d Lister.
9th. Voted, and choose Ezekial Robinson, 3d Lister.
10th. Voted, and choose David Denny, Collector of Taxes.
11th. Voted, and choose Aquilla Jones, 1st Highway Surveyor.

12th. Voted, and choose Samuel Richardson, 2d Highway Surveyor.

13th. Voted to dissolve this meeting.

Attest. NATHANIEL ROBINSON, Town Clerk."

In 1800, the first votes were cast in Northfield for Governor, Lieut-Governor, Treasurer, and twelve Councillors, and resulted as follows:

For Governor,		Isaac Tichenor,	had 12 votes.	
For Lieut. Governor,		Paul Brigham,	"	"
For Treasurer,		Samuel Mattocks,	"	"
For Councillors.		Samuel Spafford,	"	"
"	"	Timothy Toda,	"	"
"	"	Abel Spencer,	"	"
"	"	John Strong,	"	"
"	"	Solomon Miller,	"	"
"	"	Ebenezer Marvin,	"	"
"	"	Luke Knowlton,	"	"
"	"	Benjamin Burtch,	"	".
"	"	Stephen Jacob,	"	"
"	"	Elisha Ellis,	"	"
"	"	Elijah Robinson,	"	"
"	"	Wm. Chamberlin,	"	"

The voters in that day seem to have been better united on their candidates than our citizens are now; for all received 12 votes, which must have been near the number of legal voters in town.

Seven years after the organization, (in 1801) three school districts made returns of the number of scholars that attended school within their limits. Taking school district No. 1, which is now called the "Loomis district," in the north part of the town, we find the following:

Ebenezer Fox, - - - - - -	1
John Coates, - - - - - - -	1
James Paul, - - - - - - -	3
David Hedges, - - - - - - -	2

Ithamir Allen, - - - - -	6
Ezekiel Pierce, - - - -	4
William Tubbs, - - - -	3
	23

In school district No. 2, in the "Robinson neighborhood," there were forty scholars, and this was the principal part of the town at that early day. Here was the first beginning:

John Kathan, - -	1
William Coates, - - -	2
Aquilla Jones, - - - - -	2
Amos Robinson, - -	6
Ezekial Robinson, - - - - - -	5
Nathaniel Robinson, - - - - -	6
Abraham Shipman, - - -	3
Oliver Cobleigh, - - - - - -	2
John Emerson, - - - - - -	3
Abel Keyes, - - - - - -	3
William Ashcroft, - - - - - -	5
Justus Burnham, - - - - - -	2
	40

Also same year, (1801) a return was made from School District No. 3, the school-house being near where Mr. Guild now lives, on the main road to South Village:

Stanton Richardson, - - - - - -	5
Samuel Richardson, - - - - -	5
Eliphus Shipman, - - - -	5
Isaac Lynde, - - - - -	4
Isaiah Bacon, - - - - - - -	5
Amos Starkweather, - - - -	3
Thomas French, - - - - - -	2
Justus Burnham, - - - - - -	2

Roswell Carpenter, - - - - - -	1
Elisha Brown, - - - - - - -	1
	33

Two years after, (1803) in District No. 5, what is called "South Village," the following return was made:

Isaac Lynde, - - - - -	5
Eliphus Shipman, - - - - - -	5
Amos Starkweather, - - - - -	2
David Denny, - - - - - - - -	5
Justus Burnham, - - - - -	4
Elisha Brown, - - - - - -	1
	22

We have named these four school districts to show when the settlements were made, and by whom. Many will be able to recognize the section where their ancestors first pitched their tents. You will also see by this account how quickly the town was settled; for our fathers believed in the divine injunction to "be fruitful, multiply and replenish the earth." They were of good old Massachusetts and Connecticut stock, were all of industrious habits, and just the men to clear up and subdue the wilderness, turning the forest into a land of fertility and profit. You will notice also that their first settlements were upon the hills, judging that the mountain land was better adapted to raising wheat, an article frequently used for paying debts, as money in those times was not as plenty as are the greenbacks of to-day.

A vote was passed in March, 1784, by the Proprietors, which reads as follows: "Voted that the above mentioned two dollars tax be paid, one-half in money, and the other half in good merchantable pork or wheat; pork at eight pence per pound, and wheat at six shillings per bushel."

Every man had to labor in order to secure a living. No rich dividends of bank or railroad stocks had they to fall back upon. They knew no other way to gain an honest living but to till the earth, and make it yield commodities "for man and beast." The noble men of that day knew they could not grow rich without industry, and valiantly did they make the wilderness resound with the echoes of toil, as the tall old trees came crashing down upon the right hand and left, laid low by the sturdy woodman's axe! Even with their privations, they were measurably comfortable and happy.

A COPY OF A RECORD OF A TOWN MEETING HELD IN NORTHFIELD, MARCH 7TH, 1826.

1.	Voted and chose Amos Robinson, *Moderator.*	
2.	Voted that the meeting be opened with Prayer.	
3.	" " Elijah Smith, Jr., *Town Clerk.*	
4.	Voted and chose Elijah Burnham,	*Selectmen.*
5.	" " John West,	
6.	" " Charles Paine,	
7.	" " Albajence Ainsworth,	*Listers.*
8.	" " Elijah Smith, Jr.,	
9.	" " Jesse Averill,	
10.	" " Harry Ainsworth,	
11.	" " John Starkweather, *First Constable.*	
12.	Voted the remainder of the officers be chosen by nomination.	
13.	Voted and chose John Starkweather, *Collector of Taxes.*	
14.	Chose John Fisk, *Grand Juror.*	
15.	Chose William Jones,	*Highway Surveyors.*
16.	" Amos Robinson,	
17.	" Joel Winch,	
18.	" Michael Shaw,	
19.	" William Wales, Jr.,	
20.	" Alva Henry,	

21.	Chose Curtis Wright,	*Highway Surveyors.*
22.	" Isaac F. Hardin,	
23.	Voted to excuse I. F. Hardin.	
24.	Chose Hezekiah Williams,	
25.	" Samuel Dunsmoor,	
26.	" Titus Rice,	
27.	" William Case.	
28.	" Horace Fullerton,	
29.	" Elijah Smith, Jr.,	
30.	" John Fisk,	
31.	" Jacob Amidon,	
32.	" Jacob Keyes,	*Fence Viewers.*
33.	" Oliver Averill,	
34.	" John Braley,	
35.	" John West, *Pound Keeper.*	
36.	Voted to excuse John West.	
37.	Chose David Robinson, *Pound Keeper.*	
38.	" Elijah Smith, Jr., *Sealer of Leather.*	
39.	" Joseph Keyes, *Sealer of Weights and Measures.*	
40.	" David Stiles,	*Tything Men.*
41.	" Justus Burnham,	
42.	" Asa Sprout,	
43.	Voted to excuse Asa Sprout.	
44.	Chose Justus Burnham,	*Hay-Wards.*
45.	" Suel Keyes,	
46.	" James Nichols,	
47.	" John White,	
48.	" Albert Stevens,	
49.	" Nathaniel Jones,	*Committee to settle with Overseer of the Poor.*
50.	" Amos Robinson,	
51.	" John West,	
52.	" Oliver Averill,	*Committee to settle with Treasurer.*
53.	" Henry Knapp,	
54.	" John Fisk, *Overseer of the Poor.*	
55.	Voted to adjourn half an hour.	
	Met agreeable to adjournment.	

56. Chose William Cochran, ⎫
57. " Nathaniel Jones, ⎪ *Committee to divide*
58. " Samuel Whitney, ⎬ *the Ministerial*
59. " Oliver Averill, ⎪ *Money.*
60. " Henry Emerson, ⎭

61. Voted to excuse William Cochran.

62. Chose Elijah Smith.

63. Voted to accept of the nomination for Grand Jurors:

Amos Robinson,	Nathaniel Jones,
Nathan Green,	Benjamin Fisk,
David M. Lane,	Joseph Williams.

64. Voted to accept the nominations for Petit Jurors, which are as follows:

Jesse Averill,	Ezekiel Robinson,
Eleazer Loomis,	Anson Adams,
Daniel D. Robinson,	Joel Winch,
Samuel Dole,	Oliver Averill,
John West,	John White,
Albajence Ainsworth,	Abel Keyes.

65. Voted to accept of the report of the Committee to settle with the Overseer of the Poor.

66. Voted to allow Benjamin Porter $9.87, it being for doctoring Samuel Richardson's and Ebenezer Fox's families.

67. Voted to accept of the report of Committee that was appointed March, 1824, to settle with Town Treasurer.

68. Voted to accept of the report of the Committee to settle with Town Treasurer.

69. Voted to allow Langdon, Smith & Co., $2.75 for one set of grain measures.

70. Voted to raise one cent on a dollar on the Grand List for Town expenses the ensuing year.

71. Voted to pass over the 5th, 6th and 7th articles in the warning.

72. Voted to set up the compiled Laws at auction; lowest bid to be $2.00 a book.

73. Voted that Amos Robinson be Auctioneer. Eight Books sold for $16.16.
74. Voted to annex the highway Districts in which Roswell Carpenter and Oliver Averill live.
75. Voted to appoint a Committee of three to examine into the situation of the District in which John Hinckley lives, and report some future time.
76. Voted to choose Elijah Smith, Jr., John Starkweather, and John Fisk, Committee.
77. Chose Seth P. Field, District Trustee.
78. Voted to adjourn this meeting until the first Monday in April next, at one o'clock P. M.

A true Record, Recorded March 8, 1826.

Attest, ELIJAH SMITH, Jr., Town Clerk.

REPRESENTATIVES CHOSEN FROM THE SETTLEMENT OF NORTHFIELD.

From 1794, when the town was organized, until 1801, no Representatives were chosen. Beginning with that year, we record the following named gentlemen as having been elected:

1801–09. Amos Robinson.
1810. Gilbert Hatch.
1811–14. Amos Robinson.
1815–17. Gilbert Hatch.
1818–19. Abraham Shipman.
1820–21. Josiah B. Strong.
1822–23. Joel Winch.
1824–25. Abel Keyes.
1826–27. John Starkweather.
1828–29. Charles Paine.
1830–31. Lebbeus Bennett.
1832–33. John Averill.
1834. David Robinson.
1835. Moses Robinson.
1836. Anson Adams.

1837–39. Jesse Averill.
1840. Lebbeus Bennett.
1841. Moses Robinson.
1842. Nathan Morse.
1843. David W. Hadley.
1844. John L. Buck.
1845–46. David W. Hadley.
1847–48. Heman Carpenter.
1849. George B. Pierce.
1850–51. John Gregory.
1852. No choice.
1853–54. Moses Robinson.
1855–56. Wilbur F. Woodworth.
1857–58. Isaac B. Howe.
1859–60. Jasper H. Orcutt.
1861. Moses Robinson.
1862. Edward F. Perkins.
1863. Charles Barrett.
1864. George M. Fisk.
1865–66. Samuel Keith.
1867–68. Edwin K. Jones.
1869. George B. Warner.
1870. David W. Hadley.
1872–73. Edmund Pope.
1874–75. Elbridge G. Pierce.
1876–77. Andrew E. Denny.

NOTE.—The last two years have been added since the address was delivered.

THE SENATORS CHOSEN FROM NORTHFIELD WERE THE FOLLOWING:

1846–47. Moses Robinson.
1856–57. John Gregory.
1862–63. Philander D. Bradford.
1866–68. Jasper H. Orcutt.
1870–73. Heman Carpenter.

SELECTMEN CHOSEN FROM 1794 TO 1878.

1794. Stanton Richardson, Amos Robinson. Ezekiel Robinson.
1795. Amos Robinson, David Denny, Ezekiel Robinson.
1796. Stanton Richardson, James Paul, William Ashcroft,
1797. Stanton Richardson, James Paul, Oliver Cobleigh.
1798. Aaron Partridge, Oliver Cobleigh, David Denny.
1799. Oliver Cobleigh, Abraham Shipman, Ezekiel Robinson.
1800. Oliver Cobleigh, Abraham Shipman, David Denny.
1801. Abraham Shipman, Ithamir Allen, Nathaniel Robinson.
1802. Nathaniel Robinson, Ithamir Allen, Stanton Richardson.
1803–04. Amos Robinson, David Denny, Ithamir Allen.
1805. Abraham Shipman, Daniel Edson, James Paul.
1806. Abraham Shipman, David Denny, Elijah Smith.
1807. Abraham Shipman, Joseph Nichols, Charles Jones.
1808. Gilbert Hatch, Joseph Slade, Thomas Slade.
1809. Joseph Nichols, Gilbert Hatch, William Jones.
1810. Gilbert Hatch, Amos Robinson, James Morgan
1811. Ezekiel Robinson, Oliver Averill, Stanton Richardson,
1812. Oliver Averill, Stanton Richardson, William Jones.
1813. Charles Jones, Abrahm Shipman, Elijah Smith.
1814. James Morgan, Amos Brown, Seth Smith.
1815. Ezekiel Robinson, Abraham Shipman, Jesse Averill.
1816. Jesse Averill, Eleazer Loomis, Joseph R. Williams.
1817 Jesse Averill, Gilbert Hatch, Charles Jones.
1818. Joseph R. Williams, Elijah Smith, Nathaniel Jones.
1819. Joseph R. Williams, Charles Jones, Oliver Averill.
1820. Gilbert Hatch, Jesse Averill, Nathaniel Jones.
1821. Jesse Averill, Joseph R. Williams, Richard Hedges.
1822. Richard Hedges, Joel Winch, Joseph R. Williams.
1823. Joel Winch, David M. Lane, Daniel Parker.
1824. David M. Lane, Elijah Burnham, Abel Keyes.
1825. Elijah Burnham, Abel Keyes, Benjamin Fisk.
1826. Elijah Burnham, John West, Charles Paine.
1827. Gilbert Hatch, Jesse Averill, David M. Lane.
1828. Elijah Burnham, Jesse Averill, Anson Adams.
1829. Anson Adams, Daniel D. Robinson, John West.
1830. Charles Paine, Joel Brown, Jesse Averill.
1831. Charles Paine, Jesse Averill, Erastus Parker.
1832. Harry Ainsworth, David Partridge, John Averill.
1833. Elijah Burnham, John Averill, Jesse Averill.
1834. Jason Eaton, Samuel Fisk, Eleazer Nichols.
1835. Jesse Averill, Elijah Burnham, Joel Parker, Jr.
1836. Jesse Averill, D. W. Hadley, Hiram Dwinnell.

1837. Elijah Burnham, Samuel U. Richmond, James W. Johnson.
1838–39. Elijah Burnham, Samuel U. Richmond, Lebbeus Bennett.
1840. Jesse Averill, Oliver Averill, David W. Hadley.
1841 Nathan Morse, Nathaniel King, Jr., David W. Hadley.
1842. David W. Hadley, Luther S. Burnham, Nathaniel King, Jr.
1843. Nathan Morse, David W. Hadley, Hiram Dwinnell.
1844. Nathan Morse, David W. Hadley, Nathaniel King, Jr.
1845. Nathan Morse, David W. Hadley, Moses Robinson.
1846. David W. Hadley, Moses Robinson, James Palmer.
1847. Nathan Morse, Samuel Fisk, Emanuel Sawyer.
1848. Nathan Morse, Moses Robinson, Joel Winch.
1849. Nathan Morse, Ara V. Rawson, Moses Robinson.
1850. Moses Robinson, Ara V. Rawson, Anson Munson.
1851–52. Moses Robinson, Heman Carpenter, S. U. Richmond.
1853–54. Moses Robinson, Nathan Morse, Marvin Simons.
1855–56. Moses Robinson, D. W. Hadley, Marvin Simons.
1857. Marvin Simons, Aaron D. Metcalf, S. U. Richmond.
1858–59. Moses Robinson, D. W. Hadley, F. A. Preston.
1860–61. Marvin Simons, Samuel U. Richmond, W. C. Woodbury.
1862. Marvin Simons, William C. Woodbury, A. J. Braley.
1863. Marvin Simons, D. W. Hadley, I. W. Brown.
1864. D. W. Hadley, I. W. Brown, A. S. Williams.
1865–67. Marvin Simons, J. H. Orcutt, E. K. Jones.
1868. William Winch, Samuel Keith, Reuben Smith.
1869. William Winch, Samuel Keith, Joseph Gould.
1870–71. D. W. Hadley, Edmund Pope, D. T. Averill.
1872. D. W. Hadley, George Nichols, E. C. Fisk.
1873. George Nichols, E. C. Fisk, John A. Kent.
1874–75. D. W. Hadley, E. K. Jones, O. D. Edgerton.
1876–78. George Nichols, James Morse, R. W. Clark.

Note.—The last two years have been added since the address was delivered.

THE LISTERS OF NORTHFIELD FROM THE ORGANIZATION IN 1794, WITH THE GRAND LIST EACH YEAR.

		£. S. D.
1794.	Stanton Richardson, Ezekiel Robinson, William Ashcroft,	295. 5. 00.
1795.	William Ashcroft, Stanton Richardson, Ezekiel Pierce,	671. 15. 00.
1796.	William Ashcroft, Stanton Richardson, Ezekiel Pierce,	433. 10. 00.

		DOLLS. CTS.
1797.	Stanton Richardson, Nathaniel Robinson, Samuel Pierce,	1,738 35
1798.	David Denny, Abel Keyes, James Paul,	2,126 75
1799.	Aaron Partridge, Oliver Cobleigh, Daniel Hedges,	2,551 47
1800.	Oliver Cobleigh, Abraham Shipman, John Emerson, Elisha Brown,	2,776 74
1801.	Amos Robinson, Gilbert Hatch,	3,000 96
1802.	Oliver Cobleigh, Justus Burnham, Ezekiel Pierce,	3,153 16
1803.	James Paul, Ezekiel Robinson, Gilbert Hatch,	3,230 88
1804.	Oliver Cobleigh, Elisha Brown, Ethan Allen,	3,804 92
1805.	Ethan Allen, Elisha Brown,	4,201 84
1806.	Joseph Nichols, James Morgan, Amos Robinson,	4,391 31
1807.	Joseph Nichols, Abel Keyes, Charles Jones,	5,203 15
1808.	Joseph Nichols, Oliver Cobleigh, William Jones,	5,285 75
1809.	Joseph Nichols, Oliver Cobleigh, Charles Jones,	5,632 34
1810.	Nathaniel Richardson, Ezekiel Robinson.	5,907 32
1811.	Nathaniel Richardson, Jesse Averill, Ethan Allen,	5,735 00
1812.	Gilbert Hatch, Seth Smith, Charles Jones,	5,942 65
1813.	Oliver Averill, Nathaniel Jones, Eleazer Loomis,	6,027 83
1814.	Gilbert Hatch, Oliver Averill, Eleazer Loomis,	6,147 12
1815.	Eleazer Loomis, Solomon Dunham, Nathaniel Jones,	6,238 50
1816.	Gilbert Hatch, Thomas Slade, Nathaniel Green,	6,267 25
1817.	Josiah B. Strong, Oliver Averill, Dyer Loomis,	6,607 50
1818.	Gilbert Hatch, Josiah B. Strong, Jesse Averill,	6,003 00
1819.	John Starkweather, Elijah Smith, Jr., Daniel D. Robinson,	6,994 00
1820.	Nathaniel Green, John Hinkley, James Morgan,	7,441 96
1821.	John Starkweather, Charles Jones, John Hinkley,	5,748 54

		DOLLS. CTS.
1822.	John Starkweather, Charles Paine, Joseph Keyes,	5,305 42
1823.	Charles Paine, Daniel D. Robinson, Joseph Williams,	6,458 81
1824.	Benjamin Porter, Samuel Gilson, Henry Knapp, John West, David M. Lane,	8,036 56
1825.	Joel Winch, Samuel Gilson, Henry Knapp, John West,	7,701 75
1826.	Elijah Smith, Jr., Jesse Averill, Harry Ainsworth,	6,480 99
1827.	Nathaniel Jones, Joseph Williams, Eleazer Loomis,	6,802 95
1828.	Charles Paine, Daniel D. Robinson, Amos Robinson,	5,635 23
1829.	Elijah Smith, John Averill, Harry Ainsworth,	7,620 02
1830.	John L. Buck, Erastus Parker, Allen Patch,	8,159 95
1831.	David Partridge, Nathaniel Richardson, Daniel Parker, Jr.,	8,064 12
1832.	Elijah Smith, Jr., Elijah Burnham, Joel Winch,	9,743 80
1833.	George K. Cobleigh, Samuel Denny, Numan R. Dryer,	9,977 66
1834.	Samuel Denny, George K. Cobleigh, Joel Winch,	10,197 18
1835.	Elijah Smith, Jr., John Averill, David W. Hadley,	10,270 20
1836.	Joel Winch, Numan R. Dryer, Elijah Smith, Jr.,	11 017 97
1837.	Elijah Smith, Jr., Jesse Averill, David Robinson,	11,337 17
1838.	David Robinson, John Averill, John Starkweather,	11,280 80
1839.	Hiram Dwinell, Moses Robinson, David W. Hadley,	11,311 82
1840.	Moses Robinson, Samuel U. Richmond, Harvey Tilden,	11,821 52
1841.	Moses Robinson, Samuel U. Richmond, Harvey Tilden,	12,834 74
1842.	Nathan Morse, Jesse Averill, Joel Winch,	3,906 23
1843.	Harvey Tilden, Moses Robinson, James Gould,	4,281 25
1844.	Moses Robinson, William Nichols, Daniel P. King,	4,226 36

		DOLLS.	CTS.
1845.	Samuel U. Richmond, Marvin Simons, Jesse Averill,	4,286	80
1846.	D. P. King, G. P. Randall, Samuel U. Richmond,	4,400	32
1847.	Moses Robinson, Moses Thurston, Samuel U. Richmond,	4,776	50
1848.	Samuel U. Richmond, Daniel P. King, Moses Robinson,	4,744	70
1849.	Moses Robinson, D. W. Hadley, Richard H. Little,	5,035	96
1850.	Samuel U. Richmond, Joseph Denny, Joseph Gould, Hiram Henry,	5,205	05
1851.	D. W. Hadley, Marvin Simons, William Gold, Jr.,	5,440	07
1852.	D. W. Hadley, William Nichols, Marvin Simons, William Gold, Jr., Samuel U. Richmond,	7,408	16
1853.	Marvin Simons, D. W. Hadley, Samuel U. Richmond,	7,341	28
1854.	D. W. Hadley, Marvin Simons, Henry Jones, Jr.,	7,857	09
1855.	D. W. Hadley, A. D. Metcalf, F. A. Preston,	8,285	97
1856.	William Gold, Jr., F. A. Preston, W. C. Woodbury,	8,144	97
1857.	Moses Robinson, William Nichols, F. A. Preston,	8,187	71
1858.	Marvin Simons, William C. Woodbury, E. B. Pride,	8,848	12
1859.	Moses Robinson, D. S. Burnham, F. A. Preston,	8,848	12
1860.	D. W. Hadley, George Robinson, F. A. Preston,	8,695	70
1861.	Moses Robinson, I. W. Brown, Freeman Thresher,	8,875	94
1862.	Moses Robinson, Freeman Thresher, I. W. Brown,	8,798	42
1863.	Moses Robinson, Freeman Thresher, A. D. Metcalf,	8,642	08
1864.	Moses Robinson, William C. Woodbury, J. C. Gallup,	8,569	26
1865.	J. C. Gallup, Joel Winch, William H. Loomis,	8,467	30
1866.	J. C. Gallup, William H. Loomis, Joel Winch,	8,428	48

		DOLLS. CTS.
1867.	George Nichols, William S. Smith, William Gold,	9,041 37
1868.	William Gold, A. A. Preston, William R. Tucker,	9,212 45
1869.	William R. Tucker, A. A. Preston, T. L. Salisbury,	9,415 70
1870.	George Nichols, F. S. Kimball, A. A. Preston,	8,148 32
1871.	George Nichols, Fred. Parker, Ira A. Holton,	9,422 20
1872.	Ira A. Holton, William H. Loomis, Fred Parker,	9,288 33
1873.	Ira A. Holton, Royal Clark, James Morse,	8,640 40
1874.	J. C. Gallup, James Morse, Ira A. Holton, Royal W. Clark, A. D. Metcalf,	8,569 01
1875.	Ira A. Holton, A. A. Preston, Francis Wright,	8,314 37
1876.	Fred. Parker, E. H. Howes, O. P. Winch,	8,871 14
1877.	Freeman Thresher, J. H. Ransom, E. H. Howes,	8,561 91
1878.	John L. Moseley, C. A. Tracy, J. C. Gallup,	8,530 57

NOTE.—The two last years have been added since the address was delivered.

LAWYERS AND PHYSICIANS WHO HAVE LIVED AND PRACTICED IN NORTHFIELD.

LAWYERS,

John L. Buck,
B. F. Chamberlain,
Heman Carpenter,
F. V. Randall,
A. V. H. Carpenter,
A. C. May,
Charles H. Joyce,
George M. Fisk,
C. N. Carpenter,
James N. Johnson,
E. J. McWain,
Frank Plumley,
C. D. Joslyn,
Cyrus M. Johnston.

PHYSICIANS,

Nathaniel Robinson,
Jeptha White,
Edwin Porter,
P. D. Bradford,

Benjamin Porter,
Julius Easterbrook,
John Work,
Clifton Claggett,
Numan R. Dryer,
Samuel W. Thayer,
Washington Cochran,
Jared Barrett,
Edward H. Williams,
Joshua B. Smith,
George Nichols,
Samuel Keith,
M. McClearn,
Daniel Bates,
P. E. O. Chase,
S. H. Colburn,
M. F. Styles,
G. W. Colton,
J. Draper,
H. C. Brigham,
Leonard Thresher,
W. B. Mayo.

THE PAPER CARRIER.

Henry Dewey, of Randolph, was the *first* regular *paper carrier* that accommodated the people of this town, by bringing the weekly news, and Ambrose Nichols the *second.* The paper carrier was always a welcome visitor. When the tin horn sounded his approach, the children were on tip-toe, and would rush out to the highway to get their papers, which were read with great avidity, and perhaps what they read was remembered longer than what we read from our multitude of *weeklies* and *dailies.* A paper once a week was considered a very great blessing. Now, in our days of *steam* and *telegraphs,* if we do not see one or more dailies in every twenty-four hours, we consider we are "behind the times." Perhaps the people of another century will surpass us in getting news; but should this history of Northfield be *preserved* and *transmitted* to that remote period, we would like to have the future historian tell his readers how much improvement has been made upon the following *item,* during the past one hundred years:

"The Queen of England's speech" (in Parliament) "consisting of eight hundred words, was telegraphed to Russia in seven minutes after its reading, and consumed twenty-three minutes and ten seconds in delivery at the

Czar's palace. To Alexandria, Egypt, it was conveyed in thirty-three minutes and twenty seconds; to Constantinople in forty minutes, while Paris and Berlin had it in fourteen minutes. New York received it in fifty-four minutes after it was read in Parliament, and before the British public knew its tenor."

NORTHFIELD IN 1824.

Thompson, in his Gazeteer of Vermont, speaking of Northfield in 1824, says: "There were considerable revivals of religion here in 1802, 1807, 1811, and 1821. There are three ordained preachers, viz.: Elder Joel Winch, and Nathan B. Ashcroft, Methodists, and Elder James Morgan, Freewill Baptist. The epidemic of 1811 12 was very mortal here, and the dysentery swept off about thirty children in this town in the fall of 1823. The physicians are Benjamin Porter and Julius Easterbrook. The principal stream, in this town is Dog River, which runs through it in a northerly direction, and affords a great number of valuable mill privileges. The timber is principally hemlock, spruce, maple, beach and birch, intermingled with fir, pine, ash, etc. The soil is generally good, and in many places is easily cultivated. A range of argillaceous slate passes through the township from south to north. The surface is considerably uneven, but it forms a convenient centre, in which is a small village, containing a meeting house, one tavern, two stores, one saddler, one hatter, two blacksmith shops, one physician, one tannery, and seventeen dwelling-houses. This is a place of some business, and is rapidly increasing. The second house was erected in this village in 1814. There is a small village a mile and a half south of the one above mentioned, containing two saw mills, one grist and one fulling mill, one carding machine, one cider mill, and several machine shops. One mile north of the meeting house (Depot Village) is an extensive woolen factory, containing two hundred and thirty spindles and eight looms. There are also here some other mills and machinery. There are in town nine school districts, seven school houses, one company of militia, one of artillery, eight saw, three grist, and two fulling mills, one carding machine, one woolen factory, two stores, two taverns, two tanneries, and four blacksmith shops."

Green Mountain Song.

Recited by Miss Flora Averill.

Ye may sing, ye may sing of the mild Southern breeze,
  The climate of gentle repose,
Of the land where the Vine and the Olive unite,
  And the sweet-scented Orange bud blows.

We will tell, we will tell of the life-giving North,
  With its noble old forest trees great,
And where, never waning, mid beauties sublime,
  Beams the Star of the Green Mountain State.

Ye may sing, ye may sing of the charms of the West,
  With its wide spreading prairies of green,
Where the buffalo ranges in freedom along,
  And the Father of Waters is seen.

We will tell, we will tell of the region where Stark
  Brought of yore the invader his fate;
Where Allen found soldiers, all made to his hand,
  In the wilds of the Green Mountain State.

Yes, hurrah for Vermont! 'tis the land of the free!
Hurrah for Vermont, ever steady and true!
What foeman can ever deprave?
Her fair are for worth and for beauty renowned,
Her mountain boys "EVER ARE MEN!"
Her soil is unrivalled, her breezes are pure,
Hurrah for Vermont, once again!

Ah! other bright scenes may entice us away,
  In other lands oft may we roam,

Our Guests From Abroad:—Northfield extends a cordial welcome to those who have honored the town and the occasion with their presence.

The President of the Day:—Though an adopted son of our worthy town, he brings to her aid and advancement the best efforts of his nature. The success that attends his administration on this the great Centennial Anniversary of our national existence, renders him worthy of more exalted executive duty. May he ever receive the plaudit—"Well done, good and faithful servant."

Response by Hon. P. D. Bradford.

The Militia:—The right arm of a nation's defense. Upon none more than our good company F can we confidently rely for support in the hour of danger. May its colors never be trailed in the dust, or its steps be other than in perfect accord with the music of the Union.

Post Johnson, Grand Army of the Republic:—"First in war, first in peace, and first in the hearts of their countrymen."

The Clergy:—The Salt of the earth. May God grant that this Salt may never lose its savor.

The Orator of the Day:—Happy in his conceptions, chaste in his style, and elegant in his diction, we thank him for the history of our town so eloquently rendered on this the great centennial of our nation. In the declivity of life, may the remembrances of to-day serve as golden links to bind him to the past, and constitute the great beacon light to guide him to a glorious future.

Response by Hon. John Gregory, by reciting the following Poem, written for the Great Centennial at Philadelphia:

A National Centennial Hymn.

One hundred years! We celebrate
  Our nation's birth with glad acclaim.
Among the powers she stands as great
  As any realm of proudest fame.
Her eagle soars and spreads his wings
  O'er realms as broad as empires are;
He lifts his pinions, soars and sings,
  Ascendant still through heavenly air.
Then hymn your praises, good and brave,
To freedom's throne, who lives to save;
One hundred years! one hundred years!
Ten million more through endless spheres.

One hundred years! What works of grace,
  Divinest art, and skill, and taste,
Sweet freedom, wrought in every place,
  Her hand has touched, her fingers chased!
Behold the grouping of her skill,
  In marble forms and paintings fine;
Behold her genius ascending still,
  In gems of gold and silver mine!
Then hymn your praises, freeman good,
To freedom in her beauty-hood,
One hundred years! one hundred years!
Ten million more through endless spheres.

Behold her works in shining steel,
  Her implements of husbandry,
Now Ceres aids our human weal
  By every means of industry;
Her engines, strong as fire and steam,
  Abroad, ahead, in every land;
Behold the flash on flash and gleam
  Her cannon make at her command!
Then shout, ye sons, for freedom's day,
Aloud to fly on winds away;
One hundred years! one hundred years!
Ten million more through endless spheres.

Behold her fabrics, woolen ware,
  Centennial silks and robes of fur,
Her laces wrought Parisian air,
  Excelling *them* as freedom *her*;
Behold her work of jewelry,
  Chronometers and telescopes,
Divinest proofs of liberty,
  In all the arts of horoscopes.
Hurrah for freedom's day of birth,
So sweet and dear through all the earth.
One hundred years! one hundred years!
Ten million more through endless spheres.

Behold her schools for all her youth;
  The germ of life is nurtured here
  To know its worth, the *false* to fear.
The black and red, the yellow, white,
  Are trained to think, and *thinking* know
The sweets of freedom's happy light,
  And how to crush fair freedom's foe.
Then three cheers now in freedom's name,
Forever more we'll shout the same—
One hundred years! one hundred years!
Ten million more through endless spheres.

Behold the nations o'er the sea—
  A line of beauty fair and strong—
To scan the facts of liberty
  They come, they come, with joy and song;
Ye sons of freedom's soil awake,
  Extend the welcome hand of greeting.—
Receive so glad their joyous shake,
  Cementing a most happy meeting.
Then shout in chorus, blessed sweet,
And cast your flowers at freedom's feet;
One hundred years! one hundred years!
Ten million more through endless spheres.

THE MARSHAL OF THE DAY:—A noble leader of a marshalled host. At the head of the column, or in the social circle, alike distinguished for gallant bearing and pleasing address. May he ever be as ready to lead as he is to follow.

THE FARMERS OF NORTHFIELD:—While their flocks and herds attest their kindness and skill; their productive fields and full granaries, their industry; their bank stock, their economy: their out-hanging latch-strings, and open doors, are no less indicative of their hospitality.

Response by D. T. Averill, Esq.

WOMAN:—God's best gift to man—created to stand, not *alone or below*, but by his side—his *equal*. May it ever be our fortune to enjoy the sunshine of her smiles, and the glad recognition of her approval.

Response by Rev. W. L. Himes.

MASONRY:—Ancient in its origin, sublime in its teachings, and glorious in its results. As George Washington honored it by his profession, let no one hesitate to unite in its perpetuation.

Response by Hon. Charles H. Heath.

OUR YOUNG LADIES WHO TO-DAY REPRESENT OUR NATION:—Though wanting in some of the sterner qualities that make a nation's strength, yet possessed of all the innate spirit that loves freedom and true independence that has ever characterized womanhood in America, and stamped itself upon her noblest minds, from the days of the Pilgrim Fathers to the present. May their loveliness of mind, their purity, and the spirit of their heroism, come to be more and more the inspiration of every American citizen.

BROTHER JONATHAN:—May he continue to grow, both in strength and true manliness, and live to enjoy a *thousand Centennials*, like the one we celebrate to-day.

THE GOOD TEMPLARS:—We bid them God speed in their benevolent work.

THE JUVENILE TEMPERANCE BAND OF NORTHFIELD:—
"Just as the twig is bent the tree is inclined."

Ye Fifers and Drummers of ye Olden Time:—May they long live to cheer the monotony of the hour by the soul-stirring strains they have this day so impressively discoursed; and may their steps continue elastic till the last note of the fife and the last roll of the drum shall have died with its own echoes.

CONCLUSION OF PART I.

For want of room we draw this part of our History to a close; having given but a few particulars of the early settlement of Northfield. In the Biographical Sketches many interesting facts of the early settlers, in the different parts of the town will be found, giving a correct idea of its steady growth and prosperity.

PART II.

Biography and Portrait.

Biography and Portrait, with which this work abounds, will be a source of great pleasure to those who love to contemplate the features of loved friends, made dear by the recollections of the *past*, and the associations of the *present*. It is by the combination of those that we reap the utmost degree of utility and pleasure. As in contemplating the portrait of a person, we long to be instructed in his history, so in considering his actions, we are anxious to behold his countenance. So earnest is this desire, that the imagination is ready to coin a set of features, or to conceive a character to supply the painful absence of one or the other. So it is of things of great antiquity—of far off distances of time; they invest the character of even a common mind with a glory beautiful as a picture, and as enchanting as an angel! And so we love to gaze upon the lineaments of our friends with whom we have been familiar, and living over again in their presence we derive a sweet satisfaction in the contemplation, for though *dead* or *living* they yet speak to us.

We confess a sort of pride and pleasure in being able to grace this volume with so many good likenesses of friends departed and friends living; and trust that all interested in this work will appreciate the propriety of their reproduction. It will be a *souvenir* dear to many hearts.

"Lives of great men all remind us,
We can make our lives sublime;
And departing, leave behind us
Foot-prints on the sands of time."

Biographical Sketches.

HON. ELIJAH PAINE, LL. D.

The leading spirit that came to Northfield at an early day, and induced others to follow, was Elijah Paine, and although he settled in the edge of Williamstown, on the main thoroughfare to Boston, which was known afterwards as "Judge Paine's Turnpike," yet he built a grist mill, a saw mill, and a factory in this town.

He was a remarkable man, full of energy and enterprise, and just the man to clear up and settle a new country. As he had so much to do with the beginnings of Northfield, I have taken considerable pains to collect facts, incidents and anecdotes of him that will show the character of the man, and add to the interest of this history.

The *American Cyclopedia* says:

"Elijah Paine was born in Brooklyn, Conn., January 21st, 1757, and died in Williamstown, Vt., April 28, 1842. He graduated at Harvard College in 1781, and removed to Vermont in 1784. Mr. Paine was a scholar, a well read lawyer, and also a farmer, a road maker, and a pioneer in the manufacture of American Cloths, for which purpose he constructed an establishment in Northfield. He was a member and Secretary of the Convention to revise the Constitution in 1786; member of the Legislature 1787-91; a Judge of the Supreme Court 1791-5; United States Senator 1795-1801, and United States Judge, "appointed by President John Adams," in 1801. In 1789 he was one of the Commissioners to settle the controversy between New York and Vermont; President of the Vermont Colonization Society, of which, as well as to Dartmouth College, and the "University of Vermont," he was a liberal benefactor, and Fellow of the American and Northern Academies of Arts and Sciences. In 1782 he pronounced the first Oration before the Phi Beta Kappa Society of H. U., and was elected its President in 1789.

"Mr. Paine built a factory in Northfield to make broadcloth when it was a wilderness, at a cost of $40,000. This factory was one hundred and eighty feet long, forty-two feet wide, and contained six sets of Woolen Machinery, employed from one hundred and seventy-five to two hundred workmen, and indirectly several hundred more."

At a meeting of the Proprietors of Northfield, held in Hartford, Vt., at Burtch's Inn, on the second Tuesday of November, 1784, I find the following vote recorded:

"Voted, that Mr. Elijah Paine shall have the privilege of pitching two hundred, or four hundred acres of land in said Northfield, at his option, *provided* and on *condition* said Paine doth build one good saw mill in said Northfield within eighteen months from this date, and one good grist mill in one year from this date."

Judge Paine built the Mills in what is called the "Mill Woods," on the road to Williamstown, and persons having the curiosity to know where they were located, can see the remains to this day lying in the water near the bridge as they cross over to the poor farm. The ravine is certainly one of the wildest and most romantic places we know of, and the very last place (with our abundance of water power) that would be selected at the present day for that purpose. For many years this place was the only one in town where milling was done. Customers who came quite a distance frequently brought their grists upon their backs, or on horseback. Vehicles were few in those days. Occasionally a "one horse shay" was seen, (no buggy wagons) and the early settlers did not think it beneath their dignity to go to mill or meeting in an ox cart.

Judge Paine cleared the *first land* in Northfield, near his mills, which was subsequently owned and occupied many years by John Averill, Esq., and then by D. T. Averill, Esq.

Judge Paine had rare executive ability. He could manage a gang of men with success, making every thing count to his advantage and profit. In farming at that early day, when the country was new, he kept from fourteen to fifteen hundred sheep, and received quite a revenue yearly from wool, which he worked into flannel and broad-cloths. In the haying season it was no uncommon thing to see thirty or forty men in the field, all busy as bees, for the owner was round with his eyes wide open, seeing that they earned their wages. Many clever anecdotes are told of him, some of which we will record.

In the early days of Northfield it was customary to carry liquor into the field in the forenoon and afternoon. The Judge would parade his men near a spring of water, take from his pocket a glass, and pour out for each a dram of good dimensions. And he had a singular practice peculiar to himself. When his men began to drink he would turn his head half way round, so as not to see them. One day a wag of a fellow thought he would play a joke upon him, and so when his head was turned the joker stepped below the next man ready for another swig, but the Judge was too quick for him, for seeing the man about to indulge the second time, cried out: "See here, sir, haven't you drank once?" At another time the men were permitted to drink out of a stone jug that had an uncomfortable nozzle. One of them resolved that he would destroy it, so as to get a better one, and while holding the jug up for a drink he managed to stumble over a stone heap and break it. "Never mind, never mind," cried the Judge, "I have another one at the house."

Very exacting was this remarkable man with those

who owed him, and equally prompt was he in paying to a cent what he owed others.

There are not many people living in Northfield but what have heard of the "Paine pasture," near the North corner of the town. At one time the wood had been cut from this one hundred acre lot, and it had been sown to wheat. Between thirty and forty of Judge Paine's men were reaping, when, having been to Montpelier, and calling to see how they were getting along, lost a package of money that he had taken from the Bank, of which he was President. That evening, after his men had taken their supper, he called them together, and addressed them thus: "Men, I want you all to be on hand to-morrow morning ready to go into the field when I come, but don't a man of you get over the fence before I do. If I am not there as soon as you are, sit down by the fence and wait." So when the men and the Judge had arrived, he placed them a few feet from each other, and directed them not to get ahead of him, but look on the ground and see if they could find a package which he had lost in that field the day before. When all was ready, he gave the order "March," and soon one of the men cried out that he had found it. "That is mine," said the Judge; "there is $400 in that package."

Judge Paine's *punctuality* was proverbial. On a time when the inmates of his house had all retired, and were asleep in the soft embraces of Morpheus, he remembered he had not paid a note due Mr. Ainsworth, of Williamstown, on that day, and going to the chamber door he cried out, "John, John," meaning John Green, "get up and harness my horse."

The order was obeyed, and before twelve at midnight the note was paid. Upon Mr. Ainsworth's saying, "You need not have taken the trouble to come to-night, to-morrow would have answered," the Judge replied, in his quick, nervous style, "Did I not promise to pay it to-day?"

Hon. Daniel Baldwin, when a lad, lived in Berlin, on Dog River, and remembers going to mill on horseback in the

"Mill Woods," when but few buildings had been erected on the route. When he had become a merchant in Montpelier, Judge Paine called upon him, and requested the loan of $1000 for a few days. He said that amount was due him at Washington for his services as United States Judge, and that he had expected it every day for some time, and would return it as soon as he could get it from the Government. Baldwin told him he would loan it to him if he could be sure and have it at a given time, as he should then want it to buy goods with in Boston. The Judge promised he should have it, and received it, but not hearing anything from him up to the day previous, Baldwin made arrangements to go after his goods, thinking he would call on him on his way, and get his money. As he was about taking the stage he looked out of his store, and saw the Judge hurrying along to be "on time." He had the money, and made the following explanation: He had waited for it until the day before, but not receiving it, as expected, he mounted his favorite horse and went to Woodstock, some forty miles, and obtained it and paid Baldwin according to agreement, going without sleep and riding all night, traveling not far from eighty miles in order to keep his word good, so persevering and punctual was he in his business transactions. What a noble lesson for the rising generation!

Elijah Paine married Sarah Porter, of Plymouth, New Hampshire, June 7, 1790, and had seven children:

Sarah, b 1792; Martyn, b 1794; Elijah, b 1796; Charles, b 1799; Caroline, b 1801; Sophia, b 1803; George, b 1807.

All born in Williamstown.

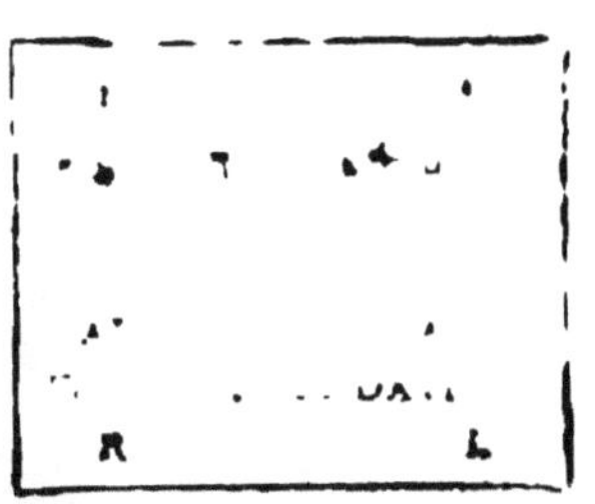

Truly yours

Chas. Peirce

Governor CHARLES PAINE.

Charles Paine was born in Williamstown, Vt., April 10, 1799. At an early age he was sent to Harvard College, Mass., where his father graduated, and afterwards became one of the most eminent men in Vermont. Indeed we are indebted to him for our beautiful Depot Village, which was the center of the first railroad projection in our Green Mountain State, by his wisdom and energy. This being the headquarters for the "Vermont Central," the shops were here located by his influence, and had Providence lengthened his life to this day, we can imagine what great prosperity would have blessed our town. Well may Northfield consider Charles Paine her great benefactor! No other man in Vermont could have interested Peter C. Brooks, Harrison Gray Otis, and others, men of great wealth, to favor the project of building a railroad in this Mountain State. Having been the Chief Magistrate of Vermont, and becoming acquainted with these leading minds while in college, he carried an influence that but few if any, could, and which brought him directly into intimate relations with the best men in New England, and the road was built.

Many citizens of Northfield will remember with what rejoicing, ground was broken near the Depot by Gov. Paine, for the Vermont Central Railroad, the spade he used being still preserved by the Railroad officials. This occurred January 8, 1847, and the first train came into Northfield Depot, October 11, 1848, at 20 minutes past 9 o'clock, P. M., conducted by Charles Paine Kimball.

Gov. Paine felt an interest in education and religion, and donated the land on which was built our Academy, and $500 in money, and also gave the Institution an excellent apparatus. His executors donated the land occupied for the Roman Catholic church and cemetery, and gave the land for Elmwood cemetery, according to his expressed desire before he went to Texas. He built the church in the Depot Village now occupied by the Congregational Society, from his own funds, wishing to have a convenient place for the people to attend meeting. By this we see the *desire of his heart* for the welfare of his race.

I shall be excused for quoting at some length what a number of distinguished citizens said in memoriam of this, our *friend* and *benefactor*. The Rev. Ezra Gannet, D. D., of Boston, remarked in preaching his funeral sermon: "The early life of Charles Paine was passed under circumstances suited to prepare him for the part he afterwards filled. Born almost on the commencement of a century remarkable for its control of mechanical agencies, and the development of popular institutions, he entered on the period of his vigor, at a time for the favorable exercise of his peculiar abilities. His father, the late Judge Paine, was one of the most honorable citizens of the State, and merited the respect which was awarded him. The influence of his home doubtless laid the foundation of that character which in subsequent life raised the son to a not less conspicuous position. Amidst the green hills of his birth-place, he breathed the air of a manly freedom, and a virtuous energy. Nature spoke to him in her clear and sweet tone, and he listened in the uncorrupted delight of youth. Surrounded by a yeomanry that have ever maintained a frank independence, in union with honest industry, intelligent, brave and hospitable, free from the vices of suburban communities, and strong in their local attachments, he acquired the traits which ripened into a wise and noble manhood. The love of his native State, the inborn passion of every son of Vermont, lost none of its fervor as his judgment grew more mature. He loved her mountains and her streams, her history and her people! At the age of 17, he became a member of Harvard College. It was there my acquaintance with him began, and there that the bonds of friendship, which four years of various fortunes served but to strengthen, were knit between him and his fellow students! Among them was not one who regarded him with any other feelings than those of respect and esteem. Thirty-five years after," added Mr. Gannet, "they first met in the halls of Cambridge; nearly one-half of the surviving members of his class were assembled, by his invitation, around the board, which was spread with an ample hospitality. I recall that scene with special interest, for it shows me the host and friend happy in the sympathy of an occasion which he made delightful to others. I see his erect form, his open face, his princely demeanor. I hear his words of cordial greeting, and feel no painful obligation, since I am sure his enjoyment of the re-union, for which we were indebted to him, whose hand we shall never grasp again, for the ineffable recollections of that day.

"Governor Paine was not a man of professions. His words were not many, and they never were uttered to secure admiration or to forestall an impartial judgment. It is not strange, therefore, that he said little on the subject of religion. But such actions as speak more loudly than words attest both the reality and the character of his faith. This edifice is a memorial of the value he set on the institution of public worship, and an unsectarian administration of religious truth. On this point he was strenuous and consistent. The most emphatic disapproval of dogmatic exclusiveness which he could have left, as well as the most decisive testimony to his faith in the great Christian truths, is given in the paper by which he makes a final disposition of his property.

"This remarkable document contains also unimpeachable proof of that disinterested concern for the good of others, and that desire to see all classes of the people enjoying the means of knowledge, virtue and happiness, which, I think, gave to his character its largest claim on our fond remembrance. As a testamentary provision I should not be surprised to learn that it is without a parallel. Brief but distinct in its language, it is as peculiar for the modesty as for the liberality which it evinces. Leaving all details to the friends in whom he reposes the utmost confidence, and avoiding any suggestion that might have the effect of connecting his name with the uses to which his bequests may be put, he only requires of those whom he appoints as Trustees, that, after assisting such persons as they may think have any claim arising from consanguinity, friendship, or obligation incurred by him, they 'use and appropriate whatever property he may die possessed of for the best good and welfare of his fellow men, to assist in the improvement of mankind; recommending that they do it without sectarianism or bigotry, according to the intention of that God whose will is found in the law of the Christian religion, in which,' he adds, 'I believe and trust.' What could be more characteristic, or more admirable?

"The manuscript from which I have quoted bears a date somewhat distant from the present time. But if evidence were needed that he retained the same feelings to the close of his life, it is furnished, to say nothing of other facts, by an incident which I am permitted to relate. A short time before his departure for Texas, Mr. Paine was reminded by a friend that he had never made an explicit declaration of his religious belief, and was requested to say what doctrinal tenets he had adopted. After a moment's hesitation he took from his pocket a slip of paper bearing the stains of age and use, which he gave to his friend, and said, 'There is my creed.' It contained the well-known lines of Leigh Hunt, which, familiar as they may be, no one will probably complain of my repeating in this connection:

Abou Ben Adhem—may his tribe increase—
Awoke one night from a deep dream of peace,
And saw within the moonlight in his room,
Making it rich, and like a lily in bloom,
An angel writing in a book of gold.
Exceeding peace had made Ben Adhem bold,
And to the presence in the room he said,
'What writest thou?' The vision raised its head,

And, with a look made all of sweet accord,
Answered, 'The names of those who love the Lord.'
'And is mine one?' said Abou. 'Nay, not so,'
Replied the angel. Abou spoke more low,
But cheerily still and said, 'I pray thee, then,
Write me as one that loves his fellow men.'
The angel wrote, and vanished. The next night
It came again, with a great wakening light,
And showed the names whom love of God had blest,
And lo! Ben Adhem's name led all the rest."

This admirable sermon, from which I have largely quoted, concludes in the following eloquent language: "A gloom hangs over the village in the warm summer's day. The sky is clear, and the air is healthful: yet every aspect of nature is sad, and the scene around us impresses us like a funeral monument. And such it is. Our hearts cast their own shadows upon the landscape. We have come to lay the remains of him whom we loved in the grave. He died far away from us, and far from the spots that were dear to him, but we could not leave his dust in that distant land. The hope, tenderly expressed in their first anguish of bereavement, is realized:

That noble form, so proud, so calmly bold,
Shall make its last sad resting place amid
The scenes he long had loved and cherished,
Within the vine-clad State o'er which he was
A Ruler.

Here will we lay his mortal frame in the grave which he would have chosen, in front of the temple which he built to the glory of God, and in the midst of the proofs of what he had done for man. The associations of this hour shall henceforth invest the spot. Business and travel shall own its sanctity, and time shall guard it with watchful reverence."

Hon. Heman Carpenter said in his eulogy on him, at a meeting of the citizens of Northfield, upon receiving intelligence of his death: "By his influence and his energy the Charter of the Vermont Central Railroad was obtained, and to him we are indebted for the accomplishment of this stupendous work! THERE IS HIS MONUMENT!

And when we are dead and forgotten, then fresh in the memory of the future will be his name, and as long as the iron horse shall traverse our State his name will be remembered and cherished by the honest and hardy sons of the Green Mountain State. He also gave an impetus to other railroads.

"To me," said Mr. Carpenter, "this dispensation of Providence is overwhelming. Language fails to express the deep emotions that thrill through every nerve. He was my friend when I needed a friend. For seventeen years I enjoyed his intimate and uninterrupted acquaintance and confidence. I see him now as I last saw him, when a few friends took him by the hand and bade him good bye, with tears in their eyes, as he left the station here in the cars for his journey South. The words of one of the friends, as the train left, have made an impression upon my mind that time will never efface. 'That car carries more men from Northfield than it will ever bring back.' That was the fearful belief of us all when he left, and sadly true it has proved indeed. It carried the living man, it can only bring back his earthly remains. It carried him in whom human nature can stand up before all the world, and say, 'He was a man!'"

Hon. John Wheeler, of Burlington, formerly President of the University, said of Gov. Paine: "On his return from college he showed no inclination for professional study, but asked to enter upon the employment of practical life, both to lesson the labors of his father, and to advance his interests. This he was allowed, without much thought that he would do otherwise than soon grow weary of it, and call for a different mode of employment. 'I was greatly surprised' said his father, 'at the readiness with which he took hold of labor, the energy with which he followed it, and the capacity and completeness with which he finished it. I found he could do as much and as well as I could in my best days.' Those of us who live in Vermont know that such a parent could give scarcely higher praise."

Charles Paine was elected Governor of Vermont in 1841 and 1842, and, in the language of Hon. E. P. Walton: "The youngest man, I think, in the Gubernatorial office in the State, I am sure there never was any man who more highly esteemed the claims of age and wisdom and experience, or was more ready to distinguish and encourage whoever among the young gave hopeful promise of an honorable and successful public career.

"What, then, shall I say to you who have known him: to you, who have been the witnesses of his life; to you, who have esteemed him beyond all other men; to you, who feel that you have lost more than a father or a friend—both—lost all? I can only say it is right now for you to weep. Grief is the necessary burden of this day, and of many days to you; but when the fountain of your tears shall fail, when you shall become weary and worn, because of your great grief, then will it be fit for you to rejoice that one has lived so briefly, yet so well, and so honorably, so unremittingly, and so successfully labored in important services for his neighborhood, his State and his country—that you feel his death is an irreparable loss, and a public calamity. Weep now. It is good to weep.

* * * * * * *

"His ambition in that great undertaking, (building the Vermont Central Railroad) was of a character which the world justly esteems to be noble; he aimed to win for himself an honorable public name, by rendering a great public service. However much of direct personal advantage he naturally and properly may have expected from it, I am sure his chief purpose was to win an honorable name. In the brightest days he looked joyfully to this reward, and in the darkest, when every other hope seemed to fail, this remained to solace him. It was on one of these darkest days, and at a time when courage, hope and health were all failing, that he said to me, in his familiar mode of conversation, 'Well, Walton, whatever may become of the corporation, they cannot rob us of the road! It is done; it will be run; and the people will, at any rate, reap the blessings which we designed. Oh! if it were not for that. I really believe I should die.' "

In Governor Paine's first Message to the General Assembly, in 1841, there is one topic presented for their consideration that I wish to preserve, showing that he was a warm friend to *education*, and sought to elevate and protect the laboring classes.

He says: "Education is a subject which cannot fail to command your earnest attention. It is true that no community can boast of more widely and universally diffused instruction than ours, and it might therefore appear useless to urge the topic upon your consideration. But we must continually bear in mind that it is not the result of accident that the people of this State, with so few exceptions, can all read and write, and have enjoyed the benefit of at least a good English education. They owe their happy and enviable condition in this respect entirely to the unceasing solicitude and wise legislation of our forefathers. While our State was yet almost a wilderness, those who themselves felt the want of education were most careful that their children should not be grown up in ignorance, and the efforts they made to establish and support Common Schools and Seminaries for the higher branches of learning, must forever command our gratitude and admiration."

Such sentiments are "like apples of gold in pictures of silver," and show the character of the man! He took an interest in the education of all our people, and did not fail to speak an encouraging word when it would do good.

Governor Paine took an interest also in AGRICULTURE. Desiring to improve the stock of cattle in this vicinity, he imported a full blood Durham into town, and for many years the milking qualities of the dairy were improved to a good degree. It was by his influence that the Washington County Agricultural Fair was held one year in Northfield, on what is now called Central Street, and it was one of the most successful fairs ever held in this County. He loved good cattle, and good horses.

Governor Paine built and kept in good order a *fish pond*, near his hotel, where he lived, and took great delight in feeding the speckled tribe from his hand. The little fellows would jump at times almost out of the water, to get little pieces of meat offered them. The people came far and near to see this display of the finny race, and Governor Paine's celebrated *fish pond* was one of the curiosities of the Depot Village. Its dimensions were ten rods long and eight rods wide.

Governor Paine built the Hotel in the Depot Village, and before its alteration the cars came across the common from both directions, and would stop at the south end of the building for refreshments. In the days of William Rogers and E. A. Webb it was a popular resort, and in good times, when the Vermont Central and Northfield were in their days of prosperity, it was no uncommon thing to have from fifty to one hundred guests at this house at a time.

VERMONT CENTRAL RAILROAD COMPANY,
IN DIRECTORS' MEETING, August 25, 1853.

Resolved, That this Board has with deep sorrow received intelligence of the death of the Hon. Charles Paine, late President of this Company, and in consideration of his indefatigable and important services in originating and sustaining the corporation, and of his honorable character as its chief officer, we deem the event a suitable one for the official action of the Board.

Resolved, That in token of our individual respect and regard, and the high estimation in which we hold the character and memory of the deceased, we will in a body attend his funeral obsequies.

Resolved, That the President be empowered and requested to furnish *free passes* to the relatives and friends of the deceased, for the purpose of attending his funeral at Northfield, on the 1st inst.

E. P. WALTON, JR., Clerk.

The "Committee of Arrangements" acknowledged the receipt of letters from the following gentlemen, tendering their sympathies to the relatives and friends of the Hon. Charles Paine, and regretting that imperative duties must occasion their non-attendance at his funeral obsequies: His Excellency, Erastus Fairbanks; R. Bruce, Esq., Secretary to the Governor General of Canada; Pliny H. White, Esq.; Hugh Henry, Esq.; James M. Ferries, Esq.; John L. Buck, Esq.; Ex-Governor H. Hubbard.

SAMUEL W. THAYER, Jr.,
JOHN GREGORY,
MOSES ROBINSON,
HEMAN CARPENTER,
PERLEY BELKNAP,
ELIJAH SMITH, Jr.,
} Committee.

Northfield, December 16, 1853.

By examining the granite monument placed over the Governor's remains in our beautiful Elmwood, by the *generosity* and *munificence* of his friend, Benjamin P. Cheney, Esq., of Boston, at a cost of $1,000, we learn that he died in Waco, Texas, July 5th, 1853, aged fifty-four years. Inscribed thereon are the following words, containing sentiments of love and affection:

Happy in his parentage, a youth of preparation
Was followed by an early maturity of usefulness.
Invigorated by many virtues, and adorned
By many manly acts;
Devoted to his native State, he applied
His talents, his wealth, and his strength to the
Advancement of her great public works,
And the encouragement of her Institutions of learning.
Having bestowed upon Vermont benefits of which
The value cannot yet be justly appreciated.
He considered the wants of the world and the age,
And, while seeking a path which should unite
The Atlantic with the Pacific coast, he died
In a distant land, far from those who loved him.
Having merited well of the Commonwealth
And his kind, his remains were here interred,
Hallowed by public honors, and private tears.

PAINE

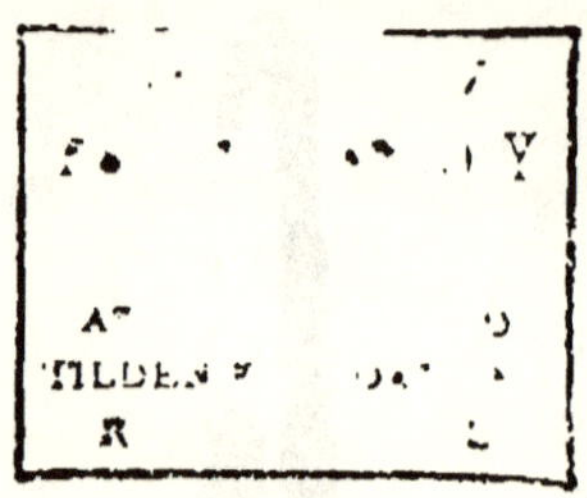

Esquire AMOS ROBINSON

Was born in Providence, R. I., August 19, 1762, and next to Elijah Paine was the most influential man of that early day. He made the first settlement where his son, Hon. Moses Robinson, now lives, in May, 1785, nine years before the organization of Northfield. He had great influence with his fellow townsmen, and induced a number of his friends and relatives to move from Westminister, Vt., to this town.

Mr. Robinson held a number of offices in town. He was the first Representative, chosen in 1801, and was re-elected for the years 1802-3-4-5-6-7-8-9-11-12-13 and 14, the succession of thirteen years being only broken by the election of Gilbert Hatch in 1810. He was a Justice of Peace for many years, and was a large-hearted, honorable man, well qualified for a leader in a new settlement.

Mr. Robinson married for his first wife Batheny Jones, and they had eight children:

Polly, b 1786; *Kezia, b 1787; Amos, b 1789; Patty, b 1791; Alman, b 1794; Judge, b 1795; Loretta, b 1796; Elijah, b 1799.

Mr. Robinson married for his second wife Mrs. Submit Holden, and they had three children:

Moses, b 1804; Sophronia, b 1810; Caroline, b 1815.

We regret we have no likeness of this pioneer man, nor of any of the *first* settlers, save Elijah Paine. They lived before daguerreotypes and photographs were taken.

Mr. Robinson died March 13, 1840.

---

* The first child born in Northfield. She married Ira Sherman, of Waterbury, Vt., and died in 1877.

Hon. MOSES ROBINSON

Was the son of Esquire Amos, and lives on the old homestead where he was born. Mr. Robinson has been honored with a number of offices in town. He was chosen Selectman in 1846-49-50-51-52-53-54-55-56-58-59, and elected Representative in 1835-41-53 and 61. He was chosen State Senator for Washington County in 1846-47. He was frequently Moderator of the Town Meetings, was Lister for 1839-40-41-43-44-47-48-49-57-59-61-62-63-64, and in all these offices he filled them with credit to himself, and to the acceptance of his fellow citizens.

Mr. Robinson is one of our fore-handed farmers, and has succeeded in acquiring a large property. He is very retiring, being seldom seen at the village, and never goes there unless he has some business that demands his attention.

Mr. Robinson married Jane, daughter of Samuel Dole, and they had one child:

Mary, b 1853.

Judge ROBINSON,

Son of Amos, settled near the Roxbury line in the south part of Northfield, and was a farmer by occupation. He married Sophia Tyler, of Claremont, N. H., and they had several children, three of whom lived to grow up, and settled in Stowe, Vt., Albert, Amos, and Maria. We have taken considerable pains to ascertain the particular history of this family, but have failed.

MOSES ROBINSON.

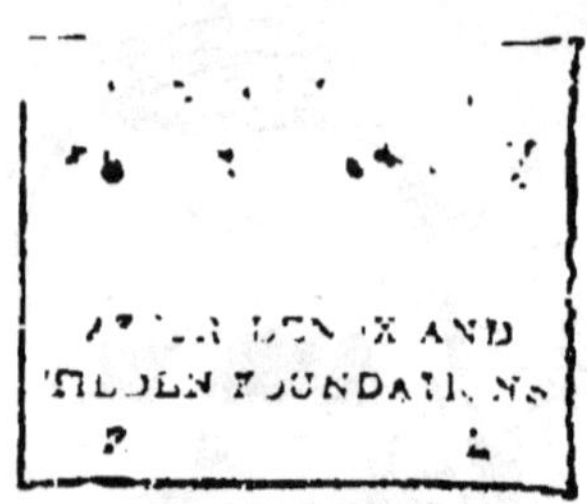

Col. EZEKIEL ROBINSON

Was born in Providence, R. I., July 15, 1764, and came to Northfield from Westminster, Vt., in May, 1785, nearly ten years before the town was organized. He settled on the farm now occupied by John Henry on the East Hill. He held a number of offices in town, such as Moderator, Selectman and Collector. He was a brother of Amos Robinson, Esq. He married Dinah Doubleday, who was born in Palmer, Mass., April 28, 1761. Mrs. Erastus Parker, a daughter of Col. Ezekiel, now living in Waterbury, Vt., says in a written letter: "I have heard father and mother tell much about their living in a log house without a board or door about it, until they had two children: when the first was born in January 26, 1788, father went over the hills of deep snow, with snow shoes and a hand sled, almost down to Farewell village, (nine miles he called it,) to get a midwife. She went home with him, some of the way on a sled, and some on foot. Those were perilous times.

"I was quite young, but remember the talk about father being called a 'Fed,' and Uncle Amos Robinson a 'Whig.' Father held the common offices in town, and was a surveyor through all its early history. He used to get great pieces of peeled hemlock bark for his bed, then make a rousing fire to keep the wolves off—they used to follow him home, many a time close to his horse's heels. The bears were kept from the cabin the same way, by great fires."

They had seven children:

Lucinda, b 1788; Daniel, b 1789; Reuben, b 1791; Sylvanus, b 1793; Anna, b 1796; David, b 1799; Weltha, b 1806.

All born in Northfield.

Mr. Robinson died in 1834; Mrs. Robinson died in 1851.

Doctor NATHANIEL ROBINSON

Was a brother of Amos, and came to Northfield from Westminster, Vt., soon after him. He settled on the East Hill, a little way back of the poor farm, where the first town meeting was held. This occurred March 25, 1794, and frequently after the meetings were held at his house.

Mr. Robinson was a very good physician, and was the first one that practiced in town. He was the first Town Clerk, and held that office until he died, from 1794 to 1813. He was frequently elected to other offices, and was decidedly popular with the people.

Mr. Robinson married Lucy Cushman, and they had eight children:

Lydia, b 1784; Peggy, b 1786; Betsey, b 1789; Nathaniel, b 1791; Lucy, b 1794; Philetus, b 1797; Weltha, b 1800; Adaline, b 1802.

All born in Northfield, except Lydia and Peggy, who were born in Westminster.

Mr. Robinson died in 1813, with the *measles.*

PHILETUS ROBINSON,

Son of Doctor Nathaniel, married Betsey Reed, of Williamstown, and three of their children are recorded in the Town Records:

Fanny, b 1816; Sally M., b 1818; Nathaniel, b 1820.

All born in Northfield.

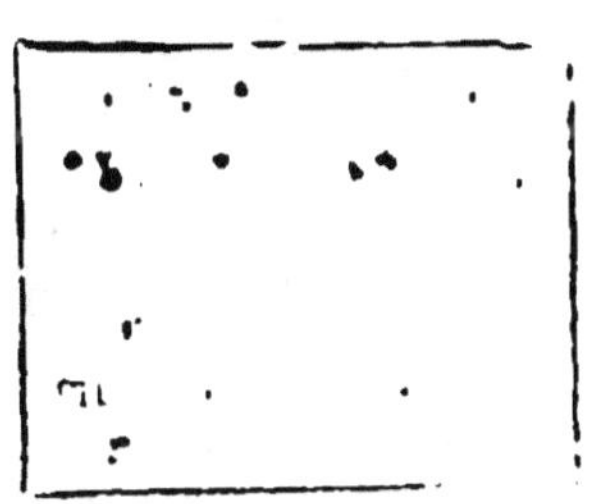

GEORGE ROBINSON.

DAVID ROBINSON, Esq.,

Son of Colonel Ezekiel Robinson, was born in Northfield in 1799. He was identified with the early history of Northfield, and partook of the zeal of its first settlers. He was a man of industry and sterling integrity. His enterprise led him to engage in the first manufacturing interests of the Falls Village, with James Gould, Walter Little, and David Fletcher, about 1835. They made woolen goods.

Mr. Robinson beginning life as a farmer, with comparatively nothing, his industry and economy secured for him success, and at his death, aged forty-two years, was in independent circumstances.

Mr. Robinson married Sarah Denny, of Northfield, in 1820, and they had ten children:

George, b 1821; Mary, b 1823; Ezekiel, b 1825; Charles, b 1827; John, b 1829; Martin, b 1831; Ezekiel, b 1833; Franklin, b 1836; Sarah Ellen, b 1838; David, b 1841.

All born in Northfield.

GEORGE ROBINSON, Esq.,

Was the son of David, and grand-son of Colonel Ezekiel Robinson. When young he went to Randolph, with his father, and was brought up on a farm. For a time he was in trade with Joseph Denny, at the Centre Village, and subsequently carried on the same business there and at the Depot Village. He was one of the company and agent for the Brookfield Fork Factory.

Mr. Robinson is one of those substantial men who make

but little noise in the world, but is noted for his genial good nature and kindness of heart. He loves his native town, and is interested in its welfare.

Mr. Robinson married Cynthia Davis, of Brookfield, in 1849, and they had two daughters:

Francese M., b 1850; Gertie L., b 1856.

Born in Northfield.

Mrs. Robinson died in 1866, and Mr. Robinson moved to the West in 1867, and now resides, with his daughters, in Fairbault, Minn., and is engaged in the grain trade.

THOMAS AVERILL, Senior,

Was born in Westminster, Vt., in 1745, and his wife, a sister of Amos Robinson, by the name of Elizabeth, was born in Providence, R. I., in 1751.

Mr. Averill came to Northfield from Westminster, with his two sons, Jesse and John, in 1805. Oliver, another son, came from the same place two years later. They settled on the East Hill, the only part of the town that had much settlement, but a little distance from the *first clearing*, and were all industrious, enterprising farmers. Mr. Averill was a strong minded man, and well calculated for a pioneer settlement. He was terribly afflicted with that awful disease, a *cancer*, which shortened his days, perhaps, a few years. His house was used occasionally for holding the town meetings.

Mr. and Mrs. Averill had ten children:

John, b 1775, died young; Betsey, b 1777; Amos, b 1779; Oliver, b 1782; Nabbie, b 1784; Jesse, b 1786; Lucy, b 1788; Lavina, b 1790; John, b 1794; Keziah, b 1798.

All born in Westminster, Vt.

Mr. Averill died in 1823, aged 78 years; Mrs. Averill died in 1840, aged 88 years.

OLIVER AVERILL.

Col. OLIVER AVERILL,

After living on the East Hill a number of years, working at farming, and the blacksmith business, removed to the Center Village, engaging in the same branches of trade. He was a public spirited man, and received many town offices, which he filled with fideiity and trust. He was elected to the office of Town Treasurer many times, and such was the unbounded confidence his fellow townsmen reposed in him that they did not require a bondsman. He was Postmaster many years, holding the office until 1842.

Colonel Averill was a characteristic man. He was of a nervous temperament, very decisive, and did not wait for others to form an opinion before he expressed his on any particular subject. He had good sound common sense, and was not afraid to express his views of theology or politics at any time or place. He was a man of whom it might be said, "in him there was no guile." In his old age he was remarkably active, and retained his natural buoyancy of spirit almost to the close of his life.

Mr. Averill married Polly Hopkins, who was born March 7, 1780. They had four children, among them Volney H., who for many years was Town Clerk, and filled the office to good satisfaction. His children were:

Volney H., b 1804, died 1871; Riley, b 1807, died 1863; Rolan, b 1813; Mary, b 1824.

All born in Northfield, except Volney H., who was born in Westminster.

Mr. Averill died April 11, 1870, aged 88 years; Mrs. Averill died October 5, 1847, aged 67 years.

Captain JESSE AVERILL.

No man in the town of Northfield had more to do with its public business from the year 1815 to 1840. In examining the Town Records we find he was elected Selectman for the years 1815-16-17-20-21-27-28-31-33-36 and 40. During this period of twenty-five years he held almost every office that the town could confer upon him, not only Selectman, but Representative, Justice of the Peace, Lister, Moderator, School Committee, and such offices in the gift of the people. He commenced his public career when quite young, and was deservedly popular with both parties. His sound judgment and quiet, unostentatious manner endeared him to the people, and his sterling honesty and firmness of mind, always seeking to do right, and particularly being the friend of the poor and unfortunate, led him to be appointed Administrator in the settling of estates.

Mr. Averill was one of those men who never sought office, but office would frequently seek him, and when the voters had a severe contest over some candidate, and found they could not elect him, they would say, "Let's send Captain Jesse; we can elect him!"

Mr. Averill married Polly Loomis, of Hinsdale, Mass., sister to Eleazer and Dyer Loomis, who was born November 28, 1783, and had five children, all of whom are now living:

Clark, b 1812; Maria P., b 1814; Russell, b 1816; Thomas, b 1820; David T., b 1823.

All born in Northfield.

Mr. Averill died July 25, 1860, aged 74 years; Mrs. Averill died October 17, 1855, aged 72 years.

JESSE AVERILL.

JOHN AVERILL.

JOHN AVERILL, Esq.,

Was the youngest brother of Amos, Oliver and Jesse, and carried on the blacksmith business, with farming, on the East Hill. He bought one hundred acres of land formerly owned by Judge Paine, including the first clearing. He, too, like his brothers, was elected to a number of offices, Representative, Selectman, Lister, Justice of the Peace, and Overseer of the Poor, honoring his trusts with fidelity. He still lives near the Center village, at the advanced age of eighty-four years, having sold his farm a number of years ago to his nephew, D. T. Averill, Esq. He has probably seen more years in Northfield, with the exception of one or two, than any man now living. His recollection of past events is very good, and I am indebted to him for many reminiscences in the lives of the early settlers; more than to any other man.

Mr. Averill remembers when a lad of attending the raising of Judge Paine's factory, in the Factory Village, and it is vivid in his memory that they had pork and beans for dinner, cooked in a five pail kettle.

Mr. Averill married Loretta, daughter of Amos Robinson, and they had six children:

Albert J., b 1819; Charles, b 1823; George, b 1827, died 1856; Loretta C., b 1831; Edwin, b 1835, died young; Henry, b 1837. All born in Northfield.

ELIJAH SMITH

Was born in Putney, Vt., May 29, 1763. He married Polly Nichols, who was born August 22, 1761. They were married in Northfield in 1785, but lived in Putney until 1803, when they returned to Northfield, and spent here the remainder of their lives. They had eight children:

Polly, b 1796; Sally, b 1789; Susanna, b 1791; Elijah, b 1795; David, b 1799; Betsey, b 1801; Fanny, b 1803; Emily, b 1808. All born in Putney.

Mr. Smith died in 1840, aged 77 years and 4 months; Mrs. Smith died in 1844, aged 80 years and 3 months.

ELIJAH SMITH, Jr., Esq.,

Was born in Putney, Vt., in 1795, and came to Northfield with his father, in 1803. He married Anna, daughter of Colonel Ezekiel Robinson, who was born in Northfield in 1796. They were married December 17, 1818, and had ten children:

Edward A., b 1819; Julia A., b 1821; Louisa, b 1823; Amanda, b 1825; Ann Maria, b 1827; Charles E., b 1829; Frederick E., b 1830; Caroline M., b 1832; Erastus P., b 1834; John E., b 1834. All born in Northfield.

Mr. Smith died July 7, 1863, aged 68 years; Mrs. Smith died July 27, 1875, aged 79 years and 5 months.

Many now living will recognize Esquire Smith in the likeness that stands at the head of his Biography. He was of a tall, commanding figure, manly and dignified in his deportment. He was for many years Governor Paine's chief clerk, and enjoyed the respect and esteem of all who knew him. He succeeded Gilbert Hatch, Esq., as Town Clerk, and held the office quite a number of years. The ability he brought to that office showed him to be a man thorough in his business. His elegant and precise penmanship stands out in bold relief all through the Town Records during the years he held the office. He was an obliging and accommodating man, and the writer has been pleased to notice the reverence and respect our citizens have for his memory.

Elijah Smith Jr.

ELEAZER LOOMIS.

The prominent characteristic of his life, which distinguished him, and gave him success, was his high sense of public virtue, his spotless and irreproachable integrity. Against him the tongue of calumny never dared to whisper a breath of suspicion. Through all his private life and public services there shone the lustre of a noble manhood, a pure and unsullied name.

GILBERT HATCH, Esq.,

Was born in Preston, Conn., August 14, 1761. He married Sally Nichols, who was born January 22, 1767. He came to Northfield between the years 1790 and 1800. He settled on the William Gold farm, and held the office of Town Clerk from 1813, when Doctor Robinson died, for many years. He held other offices in town, and was highly esteemed by all who knew him. He had seven children by his first wife, viz:

Polly, b 1801; Sarah, b 1802; Amos S., b 1803; Elizabeth, b 1805; Edward N., b 1806; Sidney S., b 1808; Sarah Ann, b 1810. All born in Northfield.

Mrs. Hatch died in 1817.

Mr. Hatch married for his second wife Martha Royce, and they had three children, viz:

Sidney, b 1818; Gilbert M., b 1822; Marion F., b 1824. All born in Northfield.

Mr. Hatch died in 1835.

ELEAZER LOOMIS, Esq.,

And his brother Dyer, at the respective ages of nineteen and seventeen, came to Northfield, and settled on the mountain, near where Hopson Baker now resides. Eleazer was born in Hinsdale, Mass., in 1785, and married Polly Buck, who was born in Connecticut in 1787. They had good success in raising wheat, it being the staple commodity for paying debts, raising one year three hundred bushels. Living opposite where our railroad depot now stands, they could look down into the valley of Dog River, where not a stick of timber had been cut.

These pioneer men had many privations, many struggles for a foothold in the forest, but, like other early settlers, they had brave hearts and willing hands, and success crowned their labors. At times they were alarmed at the howling of wild beasts, as they often said, making their hair stand on end, for the country abounded with bears, wolves and catamounts. One morning Eleazer went out to a corn crib, back of his house, it being made of rails, to get some corn for his hens, when a huge bear, that had been helping itself without invitation, jumped down from the crib, which so alarmed the young man that he ran round on the other side to escape its presence, when Bruin and he met face to face; then both being frightened ran round again, both trying to escape, the company not being agreeable.

After a few years the brothers moved over on the east side of the mountain, and located at what is called the "North Corner," where Eleazer's son, William H. Loomis, Esq., now resides. Eleazer held a number of offices in town without seeking them, and was a hard working, industrious man, and well liked. He had seven children:

Roxanna, b 1809; Eleazer, b 1811; Louisa, b 1813; Cynthia, b 1814; William, b 1818; Mariette, b 1824; Adaline, b 1825. All born in Northfield.

Mr. Loomis married for his second wife Louisa Bullock, of Berlin.

Mr. Loomis died in 1866; Mrs. P. Loomis died in 1835.

DYER LOOMIS

Removed from the North Corner to Middlesex, Vt., in 1824. He was born in Hinsdale, Mass., in 1787. He married Lucy, daughter of Thomas Averill, Esq., in 1810. He was quite successful in acquiring property, it being done by *farming*, and not by *speculation*. He was of industrious habits, and realized, in the language of the old adage, that

He that would thrive
Must rise at five.

And again, that

He that would thrive
Himself must either hold or drive.

Following these maxims, he was prosperous.

Mr. Loomis had the following children:

Salmon, b 1811; Mary, b 1813; Infant son, b 1815; Betsey, b 1816; Mary A., b 1818; Lucy, b 1821; Vienna, b 1823; Infant son, b 1825; Lucina, b 1826; Weltha, b 1828; Marinda, b 1831.

The first seven were born in Northfield, and the last four in Middlesex.

Mr. Loomis died in 1875; Mrs. Loomis died in 1877.

AQUILLO JONES

Was born in Westminster, Vt., in 1745, and came to Northfield soon after Esquire Amos Robinson. He married Prudence Wise, who was born in 1742, and they settled on the farm known afterwards as the "Bennett place." They built the common log house, and were *industrious* and *eccentric* people. Mrs. Jones possessed an indomitable courage, and when she came to Northfield she came on horseback, and used for a riding stick a twig of a

"Balm of Gilead," which she stuck into the ground on her arrival by her log house, and it grew and became a great tree, so that the fowls of the air occupied the branches. She was indeed a help-meet to her husband, and worked out of doors occasionally, lending a helping hand in those early days to keep the wolf away from their doors. She could turn her hand to almost any kind of business—the *cradle*, the *loom*, the *sugar place*, and the *barn yard*. It was said by those who worked for them that she would get up mornings, in the spring of the year, by two or three o'clock, and go to the barn to see if the cows were cared for, and in judging of the value of *neat stock* Esquire Amos Robinson used to say he would give more for her judgment in that direction than for any man's in Northfield.

Mrs. Jones was a very persevering woman. At one time the saw mill stopped on account of the saw breaking, and the men were so busy in their farming operations that they could not go to Westminster to get another, and so Mrs. Jones volunteered to go and get one, bringing it in her arms while riding on horseback. Such a feat would test the patience and strength of a good stout man.

Aquillo was a man full of trouble of what would become of his earthly tabernacle after he had "shuffled it off," and he declared often that he would not be buried on "Cobble Hill," as he called a little burying ground near where he lived, for he said it looked "so cold and dreary." On being questioned about his son Charles buying a farm in Randolph (where they were all going to live) he guessed he had not got cheated, for they had a good *burying ground* in that town.

Mr. and Mrs. Jones had five children:

William, b 1778; Charles, b 1779; Polly, b 1781; Nancy, b 1783; Sally, b 1784. All born in Westminster.

Mr. Jones died in 1830, aged 82 years; Mrs. Jones died in 1824, aged 82 years.

WILLIAM JONES

Came to Northfield with his father, and, after a few years, settled on Judge Paine's turnpike, near the toll gate, and commenced keeping tavern in 1811 on the farm now occupied by Timothy Holland. This was quite a public place of resort in those early days of staging: horses used on the through line to Boston were changed here.

Mr. Jones married Sally Babbitt, born in 1773, and had thirteen children:

Charles, b 1805; Lucy Ann, b 1807; Louisa, b 1809; Emery, b 1810; William, b 1812; William, Jr., b 1814; Lamira, b 1816; Sarah, b 1818; Rebecca, b 1820; Prudence, b 1821; Seth, b 1823; Harriet, b 1825; Luther, b 1827. All born in Northfield.

Mr. Jones died in 1840, aged 63 years; Mrs. Jones died in 1829, aged 44 years.

CHARLES JONES

Settled on the old homestead, and built the two story house near "Bennett's Pond," now owned by Edward Howes. He married Lucinda, daughter of Colonel Ezekiel Robinson, and had six children:

Alba, Daniel, Lucinda, Caroline, Daniel 2d, and Weltha.

Mr. Jones died at Menasha, Wis., in 1871, aged 91 years, where he located in 1855.

ABRAHAM SHIPMAN, Esq.,

Came from Westminster at a very early day, and was quite a prominent man in the settlement of Northfield. He was a Selectman eight years, and represented the town in the Legislature. His first wife's name was Annis Rice. They had six children:

Azubah, b 1791; Hiram, b 1793; Orran, b 1796; Ophir, b 1801; Orphia, b 1805; Sardis, b 1807. The first three were born in Westminster, and the last three in Northfield.

Mrs. Annis Shipman died in 1809. Mr. Shipman married for his second wife, Peggy, daughter of Doctor Nathaniel Robinson. They had two children:

Annis R., b 1811; Phidelia C., b 1815. Both born in Northfield.

A story is told, in which "Uncle Abraham" plays a prominent part, that is worthy of preservation. In the month of April, nearly fifty-two years ago, when our townsman, David T. Averill, Esq., was in small clothes, his father, Captain Jesse, started for the cows near evening, in a pasture that lay south of his house, not knowing that the little fellow was following him. After his return he learned that the boy was missing. Great alarm prevailed for fear that he would wander into a piece of woods near by, and perish before morning. These woods were not far from a mile in length, and a stream of water ran through them. At "Uncle Abraham's" the lights were burning, and all but the old people had retired; they, as usual, were smoking, preparatory to going to bed, when a noise was heard at the window, and two little hands came pat upon the panes of glass. Aunt Peggy was alarmed, and the fire flew from her pipe across the room. Uncle Abraham went out, and brought in the lost child, when he was cared for, by stripping off his wet clothes, and wrapping him up in a warm blanket, soon he fell asleep. Soon the shell was sounded, and the news flew along the line where the men were in search of the lost one, that he was found. Colonel George K. Cobleigh, being quite excited, had been riding up and down the road some time, on hearing the good news, cried out with a stentorian voice, "THE CHILD IS FOUND; HE IS SAFE IN ABRAHAM'S BOSOM!"

ELIPHUS SHIPMAN

Was a brother of Abraham, and came to Northfield about the same time. He lived and died in a little log house near where James Morse, Esq., now lives. He married one of the four sisters (Sally Doubleday,) who came to this town together, being the first women seeking a new home in the wilderness of Northfield. They had eight children, viz.:

Phebe, Electia, Caleb, Levi, Daniel, Edmund, Cynthia, and Polly. All born in Northfield.

ELEAZER NICHOLS, Senior,

Was born in Putney, Vt., October 18, 1762. He married Betsey Goodwin, who was born in Putney, June 30, 1773. He came to Northfield in 1809, and located where Doctor Benjamin Porter subsequently lived in the Centre Village. Their children were:

Ambrose, b 1791; Eleazer, Jr., b 1793; James, b 1796; Patty, b 1798; Polly, b 1800; William, b 1802; Betsey, b 1804; John G., b 1807; Lucy, b 1811; Laura, b 1817. All born in Putney, Vt.

Mr. Nichols died in 1831, and Mrs. Nichols in 1853.

AMBROSE NICHOLS, Esq.,

Was born in Putney, Vt., in 1791, and came to Northfield in 1809. He married Sally Hutchinson, of Braintree, and located upon the farm afterwards owned by Moses Lane. He built the "Red House," so called, now occupied by Miss Maria Howes, which was the second house erected on the road leading from the Centre to the "Factory village," as it was then known.

In addition to the care of his farm, he was for many years, and until his death, the "Postman" of this section. His route included the towns of Berlin, Barre, Williamstown, Brookfield, Randolph, Braintree, Roxbury, and Northfield, and the well-known sound of "Uncle Armus'" horn, calling his patrons to the road-side for their weekly news, was always greeted with a kindly welcome.

Mr. and Mrs. Nichols had three children:

Ambrose, Jr., b 1825; Sarah, b 1828; George A., b 1834.

Mr. Nichols died in 1835, and his widow in 1853.

ELEAZER NICHOLS, Jr.,

Came to Northfield with his father, when he was sixteen years old. He is now in his eighty-fifth year, having lived in town sixty-eight years. Though feeble and lame, his mind retains its memory to a good degree. Mr. Nichols has until lately had in his possession the ballot box used at the first town meeting held in Northfield, March 25, 1794, at the dwelling house of Doctor Nathaniel Robinson. It is said to have been made by Seth Smith. It is five inches long inside, and two inches wide, and two and a half inches deep, and was dug out of a pine block. It was presented to the town for safe keeping.

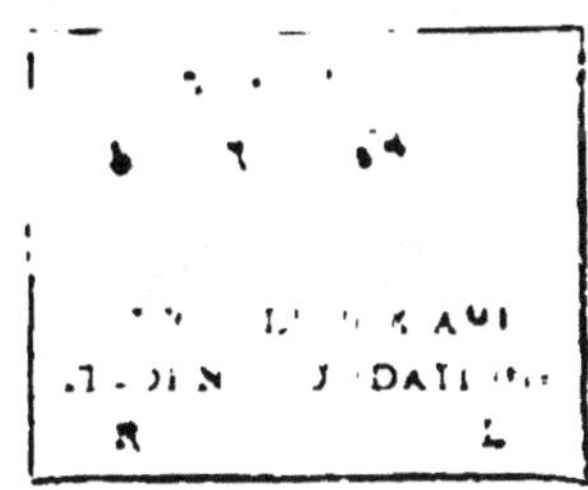

JAMES NICHOLS.

WILLIAM NICHOLS.

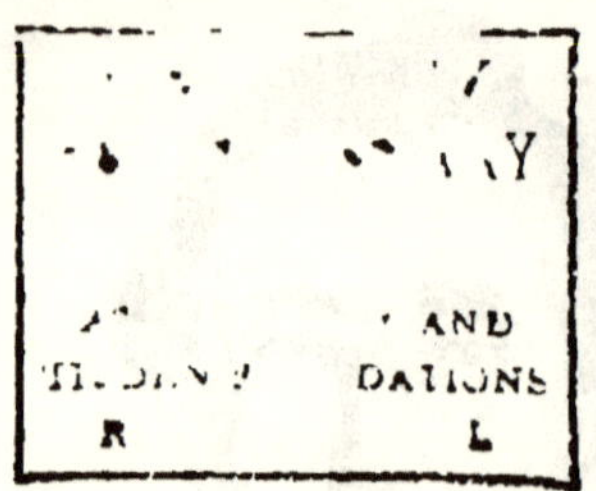

Mr. Nichols married Mrs. Orra Starkweather White, the mother of George J. and John A. S. White, on the twentieth of October, 1822. She was born in Bethel, Vt., March 17, 1796. They lived for more than fifty years on the farm where the Adams Slate Quarry is now yielding beautiful material for roofing. Their children were:

Mary Ann, b 1823; Orra E., b 1827; Olivia C., b 1829; Dudley C., b 1834; Emma, b 1841. All born in Northfield. Mrs. Nichols died in 1877.

JAMES NICHOLS, Esq.,

Was born in Putney, Vt., in 1796. He came to Northfield in 1809. He learned the carpenter and joiner's trade soon after, which he industriously pursued till compelled by the infirmities of age to retire from the more active pursuits of life.

Mr. Nichols married Annis A. Dole, of Danville, Vt., January 1, 1826, and they had two children:

George, b 1827; Annis, b 1830.

Mrs. Nichols died in 1830.

Mr. Nichols married for his second wife Harriet West, daughter of Thomas West, Esq., May 1, 1831, and they had four children:

James C., b 1832; Jane E., b 1834; John W., b 1835; Mary E., b 1837. All born in Northfield.

Mr. Nichols died in 1873; Mrs. Nichols died in 1876.

WILLIAM NICHOLS, Esq.,

Was born in Putney, Vt., in 1802. He married Roxanna Herrick, of Barre, Vt., who was born in 1803. They settled on the farm now owned by Harvey R. Keyes, and where Mrs. Nichols still resides. The house they first occupied was the *first* one erected on Main street, on the road between the two villages, and was built by Justus Burnham. Mr. Nichols acquired, through an honest industry and integrity, a handsome property, and died in 1863, lamented by a large circle of acquaintances.

Hon. GEORGE NICHOLS,

Son of James and Annis A. Nichols, was born in Northfield, April 17, 1827. He married Ellen Maria, daughter of Abijah and Maria B. Blake, of Vergennes, April 8, 1852. Mrs. Nichols was born in New Haven, April 1, 1832. To them were born Alice Margaret in 1853, and a son in 1858, both of whom died in infancy.

Dr. Nichols was educated at the common school and Newbury Seminary, fitted for College, but never entered, having determined to study medicine, and could not see the way clear pecuniarily to pursue both courses. He commenced teaching school previous to his fifteenth birthday. In 1848 he was appointed State Librarian by Governor Coolidge, and received successive annual elections till 1853. He studied medicine with Dr. S. W. Thayer, graduated at the Vermont Medical College at Woodstock in 1851, commenced business in his native town, combining with it that of Apothecary and Druggist in 1854, which latter business he still retains, and continued in the practice of his profession with eminent success till his return from the army in 1863, having served as surgeon of the Thirteenth Regiment, Vermont Volunteer Militia, in the war of the rebellion. In 1865 he was appointed Secretary of State by Governor Smith, which office he has since continuously held. In 1870 he was a member and President of the Constitutional Convention. In 1872 he was a delegate to the National Republican Convention, and made a member of the National Republican Committee, and has been a member and Secretary of the Republican State Committee since that year. In

Yours very truly.
Geo. Nichols.

1868 he was elected Director, and in 1874 President, of the Northfield National Bank. In 1872 he was chairman of the Board of Commissioners to receive subscriptions to the capital stock of the Central Vermont Railroad Company, and has been clerk of the same since its organization.

Doctor Nichols has been repeatedly honored in elections to the various municipal offices of trust and responsibility, and, what may be worthy of mention, with the exceptions of 1856-58-59-63 and 66, has been Moderator of the annual town meetings since 1854.

JOSEPH NICHOLS, Esq.,

Was a brother of Eleazer Nichols, Senior, and came from Putney, Vt., about 1805. He was a carpenter by trade, and assisted in building Judge Paine's dwelling house in Williamstown, on the turnpike. He was elected Selectman in 1807-9, and was first Lister in 1806-7-8 and 9.

Joseph and Weltha Nichols had five children.

Sally, b 1803; Leonard, b 1805; Martin, b 1808; Louisa, b 1810; Harrison, b 1812.

JASON WINCH

Was born in Framingham, Mass., September 2, 1746, and came to Northfield in 1813, and settled on the farm now owned by his grand-son, Joel Winch, Esq. He married Abigail Howe, who was born in Dorchester, Mass., and they had five children:

Asa, b 1778; Joel, b 1780; Hannah, b 1782; Abigail, b 1784; Thomas, b 1787. All born in Roxbury, Mass.

Rev. JOEL WINCH

Married Anna Kezar in 1808, and came to Northfield in 1815, living on what is now called the "Joel Winch farm." They had seven children:

Joel Jr., b 1809; Enoch, b 1812; Anna, b 1814; Elijah, b 1816; Isaac, b 1820; Benjamin P., b 1821; Mary, b 1822.

Mr. Winch was an eccentric, remarkable man. He was a preacher of the Methodist order, and when nineteen years of age joined the Conference, which at that time extended throughout New England. At the age of twenty he was ordained in Boston, June 4, 1807, by Bishop Ashbury. He was a ready speaker, full of wit and pleasantry, and sent home his arguments with great pathos and power.

Mr. Winch was a staunch Mason. In the dark days that tried men's souls, when many were going back on their principles, he remained firm and immovable, glorying the great sentiments which George Washington had honored, and which had comforted, elevated and sustained millions of our race. No place seemed dearer to him than the Lodge room; surrounded by the fraternity he was happy, and he made others so around him. Masonry was his great theme while among the brethren, and almost single handed he fought the good fight in Northfield, and lived to see the order again respected and beloved! Truly could he say to his comrades:

"A sacred burden is this life ye bear;
Look on it, lift it, bear it solemnly,
Stand up and walk beneath it steadfastly,
Fail not for sorrow, falter not for sin,
But onward, upward, till the goal ye win."

Elder Winch died in 1854.

JOEL WINCH.

ARIEL EGERTON, Esq.,

Was born in Norwich, Conn., June 8, 1789. In 1796 his father moved with his family to Brookfield, Vt. Mr. Egerton came to Northfield in the Fall of 1811. The following winter he taught school on the east hill. Of his scholars that winter only one, John Averill, Esq., is known to the writer to be living in town. The winter following he taught near Judge Paine's factory. In 1815 he built a house and store at the Center village. His store was the *first* building erected in that village for business purposes. He continued there in trade until the year 1819. In 1824 he bought from Judge Paine the grist mill on the east hill, which he carried on about five years, when the mill was abandoned. In 1829 he bought a large building at the south village, and started a chair factory, which he kept in operation about five years, and then removed from Northfield.

Mr. Egerton was among the first in this vicinity to observe the injurious effects arising from the use of liquors, and very early he became active in the cause of temperance. In the winter of 1826 he invited the people living in his neighborhood to meet at their school house and listen to some statements with regard to the use and abuse of intoxicating drinks. About forty people were present, and that was, as we believe, the first attempt in this State, aside from pulpit addresses, to present the temperance question in a public lecture. In 1828, about 20 of the citizens of the town united to form a Temperance Society. Mr. Egerton was elected its first President, and Orange Hovey, Secretary. Mr. Egerton delivered an address in the Center Meeting House, which was published in the Montpelier *Watchman* and other papers in the State.

Mr. Egerton died in Quechee, in 1859. His wife survives him, and is living with her oldest son, Hon. Charles B. Egerton, at Ironton, Ohio.

In November, 1813, Mr. Egerton married Abigail P., only daughter of Captain Abel Keyes, who was born in Putney, Vt., August 11, 1796. They had eight children:

Almira E., b 1814; Laura E., b 1816; Olive S., b 1818; Cynthia M., b 1821; Abby S., b 1823; Charles B., b 1825; John S., b 1827; Joseph K., b 1828. All born in Northfield. Four of the above are now living.

JOSEPH KEYES EGERTON, Esq.,

Lived in Quechee, Vt., until the death of his father, when he moved to Norwich, Vt., where he resided fifteen years, then came to Northfield, in March, 1877. He married Sarah F. Tyler, of Claremont, N. H., in 1856, and had two children:

Edith K., b 1858; Fred T., b 1862.

Mr. Egerton has had a number of offices conferred upon him, which he has filled with credit to himself and to his fellow citizens. He was clerk in J. C. Brooks' store, in Hartford, four years, one year in Cleaveland's, at Brookfield, and one year with Camp & Thayer, in Northfield. He was Postmaster at Quechee, Vt., from 1853 to 1861, then removed to Norwich; was Town Agent, Town Treasurer, and Justice of the Peace, joined the Odd Fellows in Northfield in 1852, joined the Masons in 1854, and was Grand Lecturer of the Grand Lodge of Vermont three years, from 1867 to 1870.

I am under great obligation to Mr. Egerton for his valuable assistance in working up the history of his ancestors, his father, and the Keyes' who built so extensively in Northfield. I am truly glad he has returned to his native town, to stay the remainder of his life, and trust he

Joseph K. Egerton.

will not only find it a good place to be born in, but a good place to be translated from.

Mr. Egerton is a merchant tailor in our Depot Village, and understands his business.

WILLIAM and TAMASIN ASHCROFT

Were from Connecticut. They had eleven children, one of them, Lois, was born in Judge Paine's grist mill: she being the second child born in town. They came to Northfield at a very early day, and Mr. Ashcroft took part in the first meetings that were held. He settled on what is now the Poor Farm, and had town offices conferred upon him. Their children were:

Daniel, b 1774: Sarah, b 1775; Abigail, b 1777; Tamasin, b 1779; John D., b 1781; Lydia, b 1783: Eliza T., b 1784: Nathan B., b 1787: Lois, b 1790: William, b 1791; Lucy, b 1794.

All but three were born in Brookline, Conn.

Rev. NATHAN BROWN ASHCROFT

Was born in Brookline, Conn., in 1787, and came to Northfield with his father, when but few inhabitants had moved into town. He was a preacher of the Methodist order, was ordained by Bishop Kendrick, as an Elder, in Bristol, R. I., September 5, 1822, and was one of the first ministers in this section. In his latter days he not only looked after the spiritual wants of the people, but attended to their physical ailments, dealing in "roots and herbs," after the Thomsonian plan.

Mr. Ashcroft married Betsey Lawrence in Plainfield,

Vt., in 1812, who was born in Freetown, Mass., March 26, 1784. They had five children:

Hester Ann R., b 1814; Nathan Sias, b 1816; John Wesley, b 1823; Infant son, b 1826; Eliza Ann, b 1828.

Mr. Ashcroft died in 1857; Mrs. Ashcroft died in 1872.

JOEL SIMONDS

Came to Northfield in 1816, and settled on the mountain where Mr. Annis used to live, and afterwards moved on to a farm in the north-east corner of the town. He married Lydia Brailey, of Hartford, Vt., and had thirteen children:

Daniel, b 1814; Polly, b 1815; Joel, b 1817; Horace, b 1819; Albert, b 1820; Clark, b 1822; Charles, b 1824; Rufus, b 1826; Seth, b 1829; John, b 1831; Lydia, b 1833; Harriet, b 1835; John, b 1837. All but two born in Northfield.

Rev. JOEL SIMONDS, Jr.,

Now resides at the Center village, and still owns the farm where his father lived. He married Olive Pitkin in 1844.

JAMES and ELETHEN PAUL

Were early settlers in Northfield, and located on the Berlin road, near the north corner. They had six children:

Lucy, b 1795; Mary, b 1798; Benjamin, b 1801; Belinda, b 1804; Daniel J., b 1807; Hosea, b 1809. All born in Northfield.

LEBBEUS BENNETT

Was born in Connecticut, in 1777. He settled on the East Hill, on what is known as the "Bennett place," and was a well-to-do-farmer. He married Elizabeth Millington, who was born in Shaftsbury, Vt., in 1777. They had seven children:

Melinda, b 1799; Ambrose, b 1801; Gamaliel, b 1805; Seymour, b 1807; Rial, b 1810; Joseph, b 1812; Lucinda, b 1819.

AMOS HOWES

Was born in Windham, Conn., in 1792. He married Melinda, daughter of Lebbeus Bennett, Esq., who was born in Bernardston, Mass., in 1799. They had the following children, of whom all are living save two, and in Northfield:

Augustus, b 1820; Harriet, b 1822; Fanny, b 1827; Lucinda, b 1830; Maria M., b 1832; Elizabeth, b 1834; Seymour, b 1837; Adelia, L., b 1840; Edward H., b 1843; Lebbeus A., b 1847. All born in Chelsea.

ISRAEL BRIGGS

Was from Williamstown, and located on the farm now owned by Royal W. Clark, on the East Hill. He married Polly Whitney, and they had seven children:

George, b 1814; Prudence, b 1816; Sarah, b 1818; Teresa, b 1820; Albern, b 1823; Warren, b 1825; Orinda, b 1828.

HOSEA KATHAN

Was born in Williamstown, 1802. He married Betsey Whitney, of Williamstown, who was born July 1, 1800. They came to Northfield in April, 1831, and settled on the East Hill, on a farm bought of Dr. Porter. Their children were:

Charles, b 1826; Alphonso, b 1828; Lydia, b 1830; Lucy, b 1832; Elijah, b 1834; Isaac, b 1838; Levi, b 1840; Grace, b 1844. All but three born in Northfield.

Mr. Kathan died in 1870; Mrs. Kathan died in 1876.

EDWARD FULLERTON

Was from Williamstown, and lived at one time on the main road to Waitsfield, about two miles from the "Factory village." He married Sophia McColloch, and they had seven children:

Horatio, b 1799; Sophia, b 1801; Calvin, b 1804; John, b 1806; Mary, b 1808; Lucius, b 1810; Harrison, b 1813. All born in Putney, Vt.

HORATIO FULLERTON

Is living at a good old age in Waitsfield, and takes delight in rehearsing, with admirable correctness, many incidents of "ye olden time," when he worked for Judge Paine, in his early manhood days. We are indebted to him for a number of anecdotes illustrating the peculiarities of Judge Paine, for whom he had great respect. Mr.

Fullerton married Sophia Jefferds, and their children were:

Mary Ann, b 1827; Henry, b 1829; Caroline M., b 1831; George H., b 1834; James K., b 1837; Calvin F., b 1842; Charles F., b 1839. All born in Northfield.

ANANIAS TUBBS

Was born in New Hampshire, and came to Northfield in 1806, from the town of Gilsum, and settled in the north-east part, in the Loomis neighborhood. He married Hannah Hill. The family consisted of three sons and six daughters, viz.:

Jeremiah, Sally, Patty, Annie, Elizabeth, William, Julia, Polly, and Solomon.

Mr. Tubbs died in 1828, aged 84 years; Mrs. Tubbs died in 1832, aged 80 years.

Ananias Tubbs was a soldier of the Revolutionary War. He enlisted under Benedict Arnold, marched under his command through the wilderness of Maine, was wounded and taken prisoner at Quebec. He left his home after enlisting, without an hour's notice, with orders to march in two days. Cold weather was coming on, his clothes were insufficient, and a pair of pants must be had. His wife, with the characteristic energy of our grandmothers of the Revolution, took her shears and went into the yard, and with her own hands cut the wool from the sheep in small patches, taking a portion from each black and white, and, with the assistance of a neighbor, carded, spun, wove, cut, and made a pair of pants before she slept, and they were ready at the time they were wanted. Not many women of the present day could have performed such a commendable service!

DAVID HEDGES

Was born on Long Island, where both his parents died before he was one year old. Most of his early life was spent in Connecticut. He was a soldier in the Revolutionary War. He married Hannah Shaw. He came to Randolph, Vt., in 1784, was one of the first settlers of that town, came to Northfield in 1794, with a family of twelve children, and his was the seventeenth family in town. The names of his children were Jeremiah, Daniel, Hannah, Phebe, Matthew, Esther, David, Stephen, Jerusha, Lewis, Richard, and Elijah, and he lived at the north corner. Stephen died at the age of twenty-six, the rest all married and settled, one in Ohio, one in western New York, and the others in Vermont, several living in this town a while, and then moved to other towns in this State. The three youngest died in Northfield.

David Hedges died in 1829, aged 94 years; Mrs. Hedges died in 1830, aged 81 years.

RICHARD HEDGES,

Son of David, was born in Randolph, Vt., in 1785, and came with his parents to Northfield in 1794. When a lad he was sent to hunt up cattle, when all was a wilderness in Dog River valley, there being no building except Stanton Richardson's log house, his father living at the time at the north corner. This was a big tramp for a boy when the country was new, and wild animals were plenty. In 1810 he married Rhoda, daughter of Joel Reed, of Williamstown, and settled on the East Hill, the first farm west of Judge Paine's grist mill, where he lived forty-three years. They had two children:

RICHARD HEDGES.

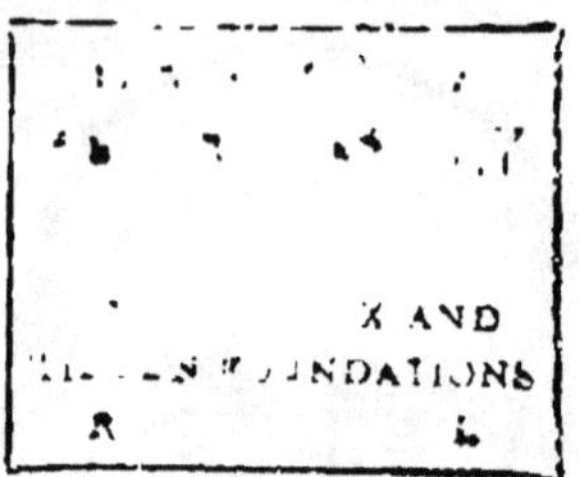

Louisa M., b 1817: Cynthia, b 1819. Mrs. Hedges died in 1819.

Mr. Hedges married for his second wife Julia, daughter of Ananias Tubbs, in 1819, who was born in Gilsum, N. H., in 1789. They had eight children:

Daniel, b 1820; Gilbert, b 1821; Rhoda, b 1823; Betsey E., b 1825; Julia, b 1827; Matthew M., b 1830; John, b 1832; Francis A., b 1835. All born in Northfield.

Mr. Hedges died in 1872, at the advanced age of 97 years, having lived in Northfield seventy-eight years: Mrs. Hedges died in 1872, aged 83 years.

THOMAS SLADE

Was from Alstead, N. H., and his name appears on the town records as an early settler. He was quite a noted *schoolmaster*. His son Thomas, the miller, who followed in the footsteps of his father, says, "He taught school in Amos Robinson district six or eight terms, boarding at home," which was where Herbert Glidden now lives. He adds, "I recollect of hearing him say that in going to and from his school he would start on the run and would keep it up until he arrived at school, or at home." He also taught school in Chelsea, and Brookfield, and was a Surveyor for many years in this town. He married Clarissa Burroughs, and had eight children:

Howard, b 1803; Lavinna, b 1805; Calista, b 1807; Clarissa, b 1809; Allen, b 1812; Thomas, Jr., b 1814; Anna, b 1818; William, b 1820. All but Howard were born in Northfield.

Mr. Slade moved to Montpelier in 1823, and died in 1829.

PARLEY TYLER

Was born in Connecticut in 1779, and soon after coming to Northfield bought of Judge Paine one hundred acres of land, on what was known afterward as Tyler Hill. He married Betsey Rood, of Brookfield, Vt., and had eight children:

Martin P., b 1804; Matilda, b 1806; Juliet, b 1809; Squire, b 1811; Daniel, b 1812; Royal, b 1815; Edward, b 1817; Jason, b 1819; Louisa, b 1822; Jason C., b 1825; John A., b 1827.

Mr. Tyler died in 1855; Mrs. Tyler died in 1849.

Daniel Tyler relates a story of the first known thief detected and convicted in Northfield, by the name of Bean. He broke into Judge Paine's factory one Sunday afternoon, and took out twenty-five rolls of cloth, and hid them under a hemlock tree top, about forty rods back of the factory. The next day, the theft having been discovered, all hands turned out to look for the stolen goods and the thief. Bean took one roll on his back and made for the East Hill, and went across Mr. Tyler's farm, then a wilderness, and left it in the woods, going to the house and asking for some breakfast. Mrs. Tyler told him he had better wait until dinner, it being then eleven o'clock, but he said that he was out surveying land, and some bread and cheese would answer.

The news soon reached the East Hill that a theft had been committed, and search was made, and not far from noon Bean returned to Tyler's house, and suspecting that he was the guilty one, Mr. Tyler asked him if he had seen any cattle in his travels, when he answered he had not. We will let Daniel tell what happened: "Father approached him, getting nearer and nearer by slow advances, when he sprung upon him and took him down, when he told me to yank off that roll of cloth upon his back, which I did very easily, as it was tied on with listing, although I was only nine years of age. Soon Bean gave up, and said he would go where we wanted he should. We fastened him with a rope and led him into the house, when he said, 'Well, mother, I have come back to dinner.' It was but a little while before all the villagers, headed by Judge Paine, Amos Robinson, and John Starkweather, had arrived, when he had a preliminary trial before Esquire Robinson. I can well remember how Starkweather's hands shook when he read the warrant as constable, it being new business to him. This was the first man convicted of stealing and sent to the State Prison from Northfield."

JOHN WRIGHT

Married for his first wife Lydia, daughter of Dr. Nathaniel Robinson, and had two children, Samuel and Weltha, and married for his second wife Mrs. Polly Richardson, daughter of Elijah Smith, Senior. They had six children:

Martin, b 1821: Mary, b 1823: John, b 1823: Fanny, b 1825: Joseph, b 1827: Lucy, b 1830. All born in Northfield.

Mr. Wright was a great Millerite, and honestly believed that the world would come to an end in 1843, the time set for the general conflagration, and was greatly disappointed when it passed without the occurrence. Whether he died of a broken heart, as William Miller did, at the non-fulfilment of his prophecy, I cannot learn. It was to him "a consummation devoutly to be wished," strange as it may appear.

Years before this, when working for Judge Paine, he undertook to proselyte the Judge to some favorite creed that he professed, by remarking, "You are getting along in years, Judge, and cannot in the nature of things live many years longer. Would it not be better for you to turn your mind to religious things, than to be engrossed so much in acquiring property, as you cannot carry your riches with you into the other world?" "Well, well," said the Judge, speaking quick and sharp, as he usually did, "Well, well, don't kill me off before my time!"

DAVID DENNY, Esq.,

Was born in Windsor, Vt., January 7, 1764, and was one of the earliest settlers in Northfield. He was a collector of taxes, and held a number of town offices. He located on the hill. near the south village, where his grandson David now resides The numerous family of Denny's in Northfield are his descendants. He married Betsey Spooner, and they had nine children:

Paul S., b 1792; Asenath, b 1794; Adolphus, b 1796; Amasa, b 1798; Sally, b 1800; Samuel, b 1803; Harriet, b 1805; Eliza, b 1807; Joseph, b 1810.

Mr. Denny died in 1821.

ADOLPHUS DENNY, Esq.,

Was born in Northfield in 1796. He lived and died at the old homestead of his father, near the south village. He married Eliza Frizzel, who was born in 1804. They had six children:

David, b 1824; Sarah, b 1827; Katherine, b 1830; George, b 1835; Mary, b 1837; Katherine, b 1839. All born in Northfield.

Mrs. Denny died in 1864.

Mr. Denny married for his second wife Mrs. Electa, widow of Colonel George K. Cobleigh.

Mr. Denny died in 1873.

JOSEPH DENNY.

Deacon SAMUEL DENNY

Was a farmer by occupation, and a respected deacon of the Congregational Church. His religious convictions were steady and enduring, and no man attended public worship with more fidelity than he did. He raised up a large family of industrious and respected children, who are all in good circumstances. He married Prudence Ellis, of Berlin, September 3, 1828, and their seven children were:

Harriet E., b 1830; Andrew E., b 1832; Addison W., b 1835; Leland H., b 1839; George B. B., b 1841; Amasa M., b 1845; Prudence J., b 1848. All born in Northfield.

Mr. Denny died in Lowell, Mass., in 1874.

JOSEPH DENNY

Was but ten years old when his father died. Being the youngest in the family, he remained at home for several years after. At the age of nineteen he left home, with just twenty-five cents to commence life for himself. He labored in Randolph one year, and then went to Berlin, where he worked upon a farm four years. About this time he commenced the tannery business at Berlin Corners, which he afterwards exchanged for the hotel there, and also bought his first farm, which occupation he always followed in connection with his other pursuits. About 1841 he entered into the mercantile business, which he continued in Berlin till 1847, when he moved his goods to Northfield Center, and filling a store there he continued in business five or six years, when he sold out and turned his attention more particularly to farming.

In 1856 Mr. Denny again formed a partnership with J. C. B. Thayer in the tailoring business, and also with George H. Crane, Esq., in general merchandise, continuing with him some three years. In the fall of 1860 he formed a partnership with his oldest son, and remained with him until he moved to Worcester, Mass., who was succeeded by the next son, the business continuing under the style of C. Denny & Co., Mr. Denny still remaining a silent partner, so that he has been interested in the mercantile business for about thirty-four years, but being a stirring, active man has preferred to give his personal attention to his out of door business.

Mr. Denny married Maria Ellis, of Berlin, and they had four children:

Edward, b 1837; Chauncy, b 1842; Homer, b 1844; Orville, b 1847. All born in Berlin.

Mr. Denny married for his second wife Mrs. Laura A. Moulton, September 7, 1859.

OLIVER COBLEIGH, Esq.,

Came to Northfield from Westminster, Vt., in 1796, when but few inhabitants had moved into it. He married Abiah Doubleday, one of the four sisters who came from that town, and were the foremost women to take up their residence in the wilderness country. They were Dinah, Ezekiel Robinson's wife, Anna, Stanton Richardson's wife, and Sally, Eliphus Shipman's wife, all extraordinary, courageous women. Mr. Cobleigh's children were:

Dinah, b 1794; George K., b 1796; Harriet, b 1804.

MARTIN COBLEIGH.

Colonel GEORGE K. COBLEIGH,

Son of Oliver, was an active, wide awake man, and held a number of town offices. He was much engaged in military affairs, and made a good officer. His residence was at the south village, where he lived many years, and died. He married Electa, daughter of Ebenezer Frizzel, and they had six children:

Caroline A., b 1826: George, b 1828: Martin, b 1830; Dennison, b 1832: Charles H., b 1837. All born in Northfield.

MARTIN COBLEIGH, Esq.,

Son of George, lives at South Northfield, and is engaged in the Sash, Door and Blind business, having good success as a workman who understood his trade. He is deservedly popular as a trial Justice, and has the confidence of his fellow townsmen. He may not be an adept at subtleties, or in the tricks of designing men, but he is well stocked with common sense, which is the best sense in the world, whether in a Justice or Judge, in a public or private way. He is one of our native born, is now in his mature manhood, and is a regular descendant of the Cobleigh's who were pioneer men in the settlement of Northfield.

Mr. Cobleigh married Clara M. Wright, and they had three children:

Fred A., b 1861 ; Addie E., b 1865 ; George H., b 1868.

JOSEPH SMITH, Jr.,

Was born in Putney, Vt., in 1775. In 1807, influenced by his brother-in-law, Captain Abel Keyes, Mr. Smith came to Northfield, bought two lots of land from David Denny, Esq., built a house near where E. K. Jones' store now stands, in the south village. On the east side of the road, opposite his house, he built a store sixteen by twenty-five feet in size, which he filled with goods, that being the first store built in the town. In 1809, not satisfied with the encouragement he had received, he sold out his real estate and goods to C. W. Houghton, of Montpelier, and the next year he returned to Putney. He had five children, only one of whom was born in Northfield.

SOLOMON DUNHAM

Lived at an early day not far from Judge Paine's grist mill, on the East Hill. Mr. Dunham was a clothier by trade, and carried on that business in that vicinity. He removed to the south village afterwards, and worked at the same trade. Mr. Dunham married Experience Smith, and they had five children:

Experience, b 1808; Mary, b 1811; Sally, b 1815; William H. H., b 1818; Albert, b 1821. All born in Northfield.

Mr. Dunham married for his third wife Harriet, daughter of David Denny, and they had two children, Franklin and George.

SAMUEL BUZZELL

Was born in 1790, and came to Northfield from New Hampshire in 1820, and settled on the East Hill. Mr. Buzzell married Jane Rollins, of New Hampshire, and they had twelve children:

Mary Eliza, b 1813; Sarah Jane, b 1814; William Rollins, b 1816; Olive, Enoch, Abigail A., Lucinda J., Samuel, Emily, Welthy, and two died in infancy.

Mr. Buzzell died in 1871, aged 81 years.

WILLIAM JENNESS

Was born December 21, 1794. He married Olive Buzzell, of Rochester, N. H., the fifteenth of February, 1819, and that year they came to Northfield, and located in the Joel Winch neighborhood. They had ten children, all of whom were born in Northfield, except the youngest, now the wife of Dr. O. O. Davis, who was born in Berlin:

Albert C., b 1820; Maria S., b 1821; Sarah, b 1823; Matilda H., b 1825; William, b 1826; Mary A., b 1828; Hermon T., b 1830; Hiram, b 1831; Samuel B., b 1833; Olive, b 1836.

ANSON ADAMS

Came to Northfield from East Roxbury, about 1816. Mr. Adams settled in the "Winch neighborhood," in the south-east part of the town. The common log house was his dwelling place, without doors or windows, using quilts in their stead. Crockery and other household goods were brought in the arms of the family, through snow banks and by marked trees, making life *real* if not *pleasant.* Little can we realize what hardships the early settlers had to endure.

Mr. Adams came originally from Connecticut to Vermont, and married Sukey Gold, sister of Deacon William Gold, and they had thirteen children :

Adaline, b 1812 : Elvira, b 1814 ; Emily, b 1816; Susan, b 1818 ; Avaline M., b 1821 : Harriet S., b 1822 ; Charlotte, b 1824 ; Ursula, b 1825 : Roswell, b 1827 ; Sophronia, b 1829 ; Anson, b 1831 : George W., b 1833 : Fanny H., b 1835. All but two born in Northfield.

SAMUEL ADAMS

Was born in Brookfield, Vt., October 11, 1796. He married Harriet Cobleigh, July 3, 1828, and immediately settled in Northfield, on the road leading from the Center to the south village. He was engaged at one time in the farming business. Mr. Adams was a sincere believer in the doctrine of the restitution of all things, and a firm and consistent Mason. He died as he had lived, and was strong in his faith to the last.

Mr. Adams' wife died in 1849. They had eight children, four of whom died in infancy, and four are now living:

John Quincy, b 1829 ; Harriet M., b 1833 ; Abbie A., b 1838 ; Laura W., b 1842. All born in Northfield.

Mr. Adams died at the home of his oldest daughter, in Revere, Mass., December 29, 1877, aged 81 years. He was brought to Northfield, and buried at the Center cemetery, with Masonic honors, having made his arrangements for the last great change, and requesting his old friend, Rev. John Gregory, to attend his last service.

NATHAN MORSE.

Hon. NATHAN MORSE

Was a resident of the south village. He was born in Fitzwilliam, N. H., and came to Northfield in 1838, from Roxbury, Vt. He held a number of offices in town, and some important ones; was elected Representative to the Legislature, and Assistant Judge in the Washington County Court. Judge Morse married for his first wife Polly, daughter of John Hutchinson, Esq., of Braintree, and had four children:

Nathan, b 1816; Polly, b 1818; Betsey, b 1820; Lucy H., b 1825. Mrs. Morse died in 1845.

Judge Morse married for his second wife Martha, daughter of Urial Abbott, of Williamstown, and they had one son: James, born in Northfield in 1847.

Judge Morse died in 1862. Mrs. Morse died in 1875.

LUCIUS EDSON

Was born in Whately, Mass., 1798. He married Matilda Ainsworth, who was born in Brookfield, Vt., in 1802, and came to Brookfield in 1799. In 1822 he moved to Northfield. He and Arba Crane bought out Solomon Dunham, who was in the cloth dressing business in Captain Jesse Averill's district, near Judge Paine's grist mill. They worked there two falls, and then Mr. Edson went to the south village, where he added wool carding to cloth dressing. It was here that our genial merchant, George H. Crane, learned to make rolls. Mr. Edson had four children:

Marshall L., b 1830; Alice J., b 1833; E. Annette, b 1836; Walter A., b 1839. All born in Northfield.

JOHN EMERSON

Was a blacksmith, and lived at an early day on the East Hill, in the Averill neighborhood. He came to Northfield from Norwich, Vt., and was a brother of Harry Emerson, the hatter, who carried on that business at the Center village.

ETHAN ALLEN.

We had an Ethan Allen in that early period of the town's history. Not the renowned hero of Ticonderoga, but a man by that name who run Judge Paine's grist mill.

JOHN BUCK

Was born in Connecticut in 1782. His father, mother, four brothers, and two sisters moved from Connecticut to Berlin on to the farm afterwards owned by Truman Foster. In 1826 he moved to Northfield, on to the farm now owned by his son Bradley. Mrs. John Buck's name before marriage was Chloe Allen, and she was supposed to have been born in Gill, Mass., in 1780. They had six children:

Chloe M., b 1810; Eliza, b 1812; Bradley, b 1814; Amanda, b 1819; Harriet N., b 1823. All born in Northfield.

ISAIAH SHAW

Came from Woodstock quite early, and settled near the south village. He married Annis Adams, and had three children :

Lavina, b 1813 ; Anna, b 1815 ; Elihu M., b 1817. All born in Northfield.

ANSEL SHAW

Was born in Bridgewater, Vt., in 1803, and came to Northfield in 1830. He married Harriet Richmond. He and his brother Alonzo live near each other, not far from Roxbury line, on the road to East Roxbury.

ALONZO SHAW

Was born in Bridgewater, Vt., in 1808, and came to Northfield in 1825. He worked for Governor Paine a number of years. He married Lucy Harrington, and had four children :

Lucy Jane, b 1838 ; Asa Alonzo, b 1840 ; Emily Almira, b 1842 ; Edward Isaiah, b 1844. All born in Northfield.

Mr. Shaw married for his second wife Charlotte Larkin, of Woodstock.

Deacon WILLIAM GOLD

Was born in Springfield, Mass., October 30, 1780. He came to Roxbury, Vt., in 1801, and settled upon one of the highest mountains in that town. He was a Deacon of the Baptist Church. Any one at this day looking the mountain land over where he located, can see under what discouraging circumstances this early settler was placed. Bruin disputed his right to the territory, and a combat ensued between them that was truly frightful. Mr. Gold one evening looked out into his cornfield, and saw a large bear helping himself to corn. Then the old rifle was loaded, and the intruder received its contents, which made him exceedingly angry, after he found he was but slightly injured. Upon being hit he fell dead, as Mr. Gold thought, or nearly so. Taking his ax to dispatch him, Mr. Gold aimed a blow at his head, when he suddenly knocked the ax out of his hands, and then commenced a struggle between them for very life. Mr. Gold closed in with his adversary Van Amburgh style, and endeavored to open his mouth wider than usual, which the bear resented, and gave his opponent some terrible wounds on his arm and hands. In the meantime a friend, who had come to stay with Mr. Gold over night saw how matters stood, caught up his ax, and with one heavy blow cut off two ribs of Bruin, which made him retreat in haste to the woods. On the next day he was tracked a considerable distance, and easily dispatched.

Mr. Gold in 1847 removed to Northfield. He married Annevera Dewey, who was born in 1780, and they had seven children:

Annevera, b 1807; William, b 1808; Sherman, b 1813; Buel, b 1815; Joseph, b 1818; Mary, b 1820; Sophia, b 1828. All born in Roxbury.

Deacon Gold died in 1859; Mrs. Gold died in 1856.

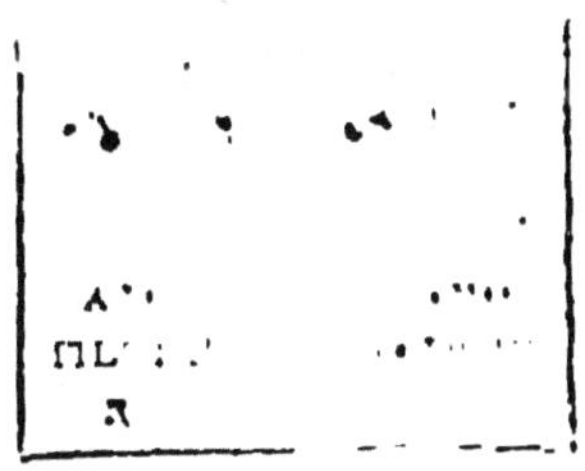

WILLIAM GOLD.

WILLIAM GOLD, Jr., Esq.,

Lives on the road to Roxbury, not far the from the Harlow bridge. He is a substantial farmer, and one of our best citizens. He was elected Justice of the Peace and Lister a number of years. He married Loretta Orcutt, of Roxbury, who was born in 1810. They had two children:

William Franklin, b 1842; Augusta Melinda, b 1846.

SHERMAN GOLD

Married Eunice Adams, who was born in 1815. For many years he carried on the sash, blind and door business at the south village. He was a sincere and conscientious man, and generally respected. For a number of years he was a member of the Universalist Church in Northfield, and acted in the capacity of Deacon. He had three children:

Caroline, b 1839; Charles S., b 1844; Abby S., b 1851. Mr. Gold died in 1873.

JOSEPH GOLD

Married Abba D. Thompson, who was born in Tunbridge, Vt., in 1817. They had three children:

Abbie D., b 1843; Albert J., b 1847; Celia J., b 1854.

JAMES LATHAM, Sr.,

With his sons, James, Ezra, and Curtis, came to Northfield from Chesterfield, N. H., at an early day. He was born in 1750. He married Susannah Brit, who was born in 1752. They had five children:

Curtis, b 1779; James, Jr., b 1780; Ezra, b 1782; Susannah, b 1784; Sylva, b 1787. All born in Hinsdale, Mass.

JAMES LATHAM, Jr.,

Settled in the Shaw neighborhood, on the road to East Roxbury. He married Polly, daughter of Amos Robinson, Esq., who was born in 1786. He lived to the advanced age of ninety-five years. They had fifteen children:

Bathany, b 1804; Leonard, b 1805; Nancy, b 1807; Patty R., b 1809; Hollis, b 1812; Arvilla, b 1813; Susanna, b 1815; Eli, b 1818; Nancy L., b 1819; Almon, b 1821; Loran, b 1823; Seth W., b 1824; Marshall, b 1827; Cynthia, b 1829; Mary A., b 1832. All born in Northfield.

EZRA LATHAM

Married Polly, daughter of Aquillo Jones, and had four children:

Ezra, Jr., b 1811; Orrin, b 1813; Harvey, b 1815; Daniel, b 1817. All born in Northfield.

CALEB WINCH,

Came from Troy, N. H., in 1826. He married Lucy Farral, and had three children:

Eliza, b 1813; William, b 1819; Caleb M., b 1822.

Deacon WILLIAM WINCH

Is an honored member of the Congregationalist Church, and owns the farm on which his father settled, on Starkweather Hill. He married Lydia Nye, and they had five children:

George W., b 1845; Caleb M., b 1847; Susan E., b 1850; John H., b 1852; Samuel W., b 1858. All born in Northfield.

CHARLES RICE

Married Sarah Frizzle. They had six children, and all but one born in Northfield:

Sarah, b 1828; Emily, b 1830; Charles, b 1832; Sophia, b 1834; Edward S., b 1837; George H., b 1840.

AMOS STARKWEATHER

Was born in Connecticut, and his first settlement in Vermont was Norwich. After residing there a few years he came to Bethel, Vt., and from there removed to Northfield in 1796. He was a farmer by occupation, and located on the farm adjoining Deacon William Winch's, known now as Starkweather Hill. He had two children:

Captain John Starkweather, and Orra Starkweather, wife of Eleazer Nichols.

Captain JOHN STARKWEATHER

Was born in Norwich, Vt., in 1790. He married Cynthia Nichols, step-daughter of Captain Abel Keyes, December 3, 1809. Nearly two years after, in September, 1811, he took the Freeman's Oath, and thereafter during his life he was almost continually in town and other public offices. He was repeatedly elected Lister, Grand Juryman, Moderator of town meetings, was a Justice of the Peace, Deputy Sheriff and High Sheriff of the county, and was elected Representative during the years 1826-7. He was also Captain of a military company two years. Several years he kept tavern at the Center village.

Captain Starkweather was a friendly, familiar man, and before forty years old, it is said, children called him "Uncle John." He was quite popular as an officer.

Captain Starkweather died in 1841.

Deacon REUBEN SMITH

Was a beloved member of the Baptist church. He came from Tunbridge, Vt., to Northfield, and settled in the south village in 1826. He married Molly Mudgett, who was born in Gilmanton, N. H., and had seven children:

Polly, Apha, William, Tabitha, Reuben, Josiah and Anna.

WILLIAM SMITH

Was from Tunbridge, in 1825. He married Sarah Hale, of Tunbridge, and had five children:

Reuben, Jackson, Sarah, Henry, and George.

We have been able to learn but little of these two families of Smiths.

WILLIAM H. SMITH

Was born in Tunbridge, Vt., in 1814. He came to Northfield not far from 1833, and worked in the factory village at the blacksmith business. He is now settled in the vicinity of Harlow Bridge, and has connected farming with blacksmithing. He married Julia Stratton, in 1835, who was born in Berlin, 1819, and their children were:

Maryette, b 1838; Vernon, b 1840; Vernon W., b 1842; Laura Ann, b 1844; Ellen F., b 1845; John C., b 1847; Ai O., b 1850; Helen J., b 1852; Herbert F., b 1854; Della A., b 1862. All born in Northfield.

THOMAS L. MAYO

Was born in Rutland, Mass., 1783, and came from Woodstock to Northfield in 1834. He married Lydia Thomas for his first wife, March 20, 1808, who was born in 1787. She died in 1814, having three children:

Henry N., b 1809; Charles P., b 1810; George C., b 1812. All born in Woodstock.

Mr. Mayo married Betsey French for his second wife who was born in 1789, and she died in 1865. They had one son: Henry N., born in Woodstock in 1815.

Mr. Mayo settled on the farm now occupied by his son George C., then owned by Dr. Rickard, near the Harlow Bridge, and died in 1854.

WILLIAM KEYES, Esq.,

Was born in Putney, Vt., in 1766. He removed to Northfield in 1799, and located on the East Hill, where he bought a farm of his brother, Abel Keyes. In 1804 he sold the hill farm, and bought a hundred acres of land near the center of the town. His house stood just back of where the Center hotel now stands, and his nearest neighbor was Stanton Richardson, on the west side of the river, and nearly half a mile distant. He sold out at the Center about 1810, and his farm was soon after divided into small parcels, and sold out for building lots. Mr. Keyes in 1816 bought the farm next south of the Stanton Richardson place, and for several years he carried on the business of brick making. His daughter, Mrs. Lucy Knapp, now living in Northfield, relates that in the year 1818 there was a great deal of sickness in town, and that Doctor Porter's bill for medical services in her father's family that year was large enough to pay for all the brick used in building his house. Mr. Keyes was one of the earliest Methodists, was quite active in organizing the church in this town, and for more than fifty-years a class leader therein.

Mr. Keyes was married in Putney in 1789, to Betsey Nichols, and they had nine children, viz.:

Polly, b 1791; Jacob, b 1793; William, Jr., b 1796; Lucy, b 1798; Sewall, b 1800; Eliza, b 1803; Abel, b 1806; Sally, b 1808; Emeline, b 1812.

Mr. Keyes died in Northfield, December 20, 1849.

Captain ABEL KEYES

Was born in Putney, Vt., September 11, 1773. In the summer of 1790, while prospecting for a new home, he came to Northfield, and in view of its great advantages in water-power, believing that it would some time become a great manufacturing town, and a center for trade, he decided to locate here. In the spring of the next year he bought of Judge Paine the mills and a hundred acres of land on the East Hill, there being the first settlement in town. He lived there about five years, and greatly improved the mills while he owned them. In 1799 he sold the farm to his brother William, and soon afterwards sold the mill property to Judge Paine. In 1801 he bought a hundred acres of land of Nathaniel Robinson, on which he built a house, kept the place about two years, and sold it. In 1804 his daughter, Mrs. A. P. Egerton, relates that her father made a journey to Putney, riding on horseback, and taking her with him on the same horse, she being then eight years old. The main object of his journey was to induce some of his relatives and neighbors to come to Northfield to live. In 1807 Captain Keyes purchased of David Denny, Esq., a saw-mill and a few acres of land in that part of the town now called South Northfield. The saw-mill he enlarged and improved, he built a grist mill, a potash, and several dwelling-houses, and in three years, mainly through his influence and labors, "Slab City," as it was for many years called, had become a lively, thriving village. His wife's brother, Joseph Smith. Jr., had a store there, and that was the first store in Northfield. In 1810 Captain Keyes sold his mills to C. W. Houghton, of Montpelier, and in 1812 he sold the rest of his property in that village, and removed to the Factory, where Judge Paine had just began to build a village. He remained there one year, living in the "Old

Abbey," a house that stood where George C. Randall's house now is, and afterwards built for Judge Paine the two houses that now stand near the bridge. In 1814 he purchased several lots of land where the Center village now is. The next year, with his son, Joseph, he built several dwelling houses, a machine shop, and a potash. In 1818 they built the Center Village Hotel, which house they kept about five years. In 1819 they built the church that was long known as the old yellow meeting-house.

In 1824 they sold all their property at the Center village, and bought the property that Captain Keyes had formerly owned at the Slab City. They rebuilt the mills and lived there three years, when they sold again and moved to the Falls, now Gouldsville, and on the site where Gould's factory now stands they built a saw and grist mill. Captain Keyes lived there till 1838, his son Joseph having sold out there some years previously. He then bought a saw mill about half a mile up the river, which he repaired, built a grist mill and a dwelling house, and lived there till 1839, when he moved to Illinois. Staying there one year, he went to Lake Mills, Wisconsin, and there died in 1848, at the age of seventy-five years. There are now standing in this town about forty buildings, erected for dwellings and for business purposes, by Captain Abel Keyes and his son Joseph. Captain Keyes was one of the most active and enterprising business men of the town during all his stay in it. He held various offices, was Lister in 1798, Captain of a military company, Justice of the Peace for many years, Selectman in 1824 and 1825, and represented the town in the Legislature the same years. Captain Keyes was in many respects a most remarkable man. Possessed of robust health, ceaseless activity, and untiring energy, he could do everything but persevere and wait. As a farmer he could prepare his land, could plant and hoe, but he could not wait for the corn to ripen; in preparing to build, the noise and bustle of framing, raising, and enclosing the

Faithfully yours

Joseph Keyes

building were just to his taste, and he could plan for and direct a multitude of men, but the quiet work of finishing the structure must be left to more patient workers. To such an extent was this restlessness carried that it became a common saying among his townsmen that "Captain Abel always moves just before harvest." He possessed strong religious convictions, and in their defence and support was always ready to make any sacrifice. Quick and excitable, intense in feeling, and prompt in action, to his friends he was most loyal, tender, and helpful, and, notwithstanding, his quick temper and blunt speech, he had no enemies. Industrious, frugal and honest, his success in life was limited only by his habit of leaving to others the pleasant task of reaping the reward of his labors.

Captain Keyes married Mrs. Esther Nichols in 1793. She had a daughter Cynthia by a former husband, in 1791. They had two children:

Joseph, b 1794; Abigail P., b 1796. Both born in Putney, Vt.

Captain JOSEPH KEYES

Was born in Putney, Vt., November 20, 1795, and came to Northfield with his father in 1796. He married Zeruah Eggleston in 1816, and they had two children:

Simon Smith, b 1817; Cynthia, b 1819.

Mr. Keyes married for his second wife Olive Williams, January 18, 1821. She was born in Chelsea, Vt., July 16, 1800. They had five children:

Abel, b 1822; Catharine W., b 1825; Elisha W., b 1828; Oliver A., b 1831; Emily O., b 1843.

Mr. Keyes died at Menasha, Wis., September 17, 1874.

In early life Captain Keyes became a mill-wright by trade, and followed that business both in Vermont and Wisconsin, in which later State he was very successful in establishing mills. His was a temperament that could not remain inactive, and it is said he and his father, Abel Keyes, erected buildings in all the four villages in Northfield. His power was immense, and he became quite an extensive operator of various kinds of machinery in this, his native State. He was an inventor of several pieces of machinery, for which he obtained patents.

Many of our citizens can remember that he built a machine shop at the Center village, on the east side of the common, that was run by steam, the first motive power by steam in Northfield, and which was a great curiosity at that early day. On its sides were painted the words "Machine Shop." The building now stands near the old Town House, having been converted into a dwelling.

We take a few extracts from the "Wisconsin Journal" relative to the sterling character of Mr. Keyes. "As the crisis which came upon the country in 1837 was approaching, Mr. Keyes, finding it difficult to proceed with his extensive business, made disposition of it in 1836, and in the spring of that year, with but little left but his head and hands, backed up by the most indomitable courage and energy, and a powerful constitution, he struck out to seek his fortune in a new country, and landed in Milwaukee in June, 1836. Wisconsin at that time was an inviting field for men of his type. It needed intelligent, enterprising and hard working men to develop its immense resources. Mr. Keyes being one of that class, found a cordial welcome to the Territory by the few bold spirits who had preceded him, and an ample scope of country in which to operate. * * * * *

"In 1837 Mr. Keyes and his family removed to Lake Mills, being the first white settlers in that town. He proceeded at once to the erection of a grist and saw mill, that proved of vast advantage to the settlement of a new country, and very soon he laid out the village of Lake Mills, being its original founder. Here, in accordance with his public spirit and liberality, he erected the first school house in the town, and employed the first teacher, being a Miss Catlin, of Cottage Grove, in this county, all with his individual means. Such an act, of itself, is a proud monument to his name and fame, and proves that his life has not been a failure." * * * *

"For over fifty years Mr. Keyes was an active and prominent Free Mason. It is an order that he loved with his whole heart, and was one of its most honored and respected members. * * * * *

"Their golden wedding was duly celebrated in 1871, surrounded by children, grand children, and great-grand-children. Fifty-three years of happy married life is seldom vouchsafed to mortals in this world. The offspring of this marriage have been Mr. Abel Keyes, now of Menasha, Hon. E. W. Keyes, Postmaster of Madison, Oliver Keyes, now of Hudson, Mrs. George Hyer, deceased, and Mrs. H. D. Fisher, of Menasha. Their children and children's children have grown up around them in considerable numbers, whose prattling noise has been the sweetest music to the old pioneers for several years. Truly, this happy couple has fully realized the golden period of life! and while the burdens have been severe, they have been vastly over-balanced by the sweets that have been so liberally mixed with adversity.

Mrs. Olive Williams, relict of Captain Joseph Keyes, departed this life at Menasha, on the 18th of February, 1878, in the 78th year of her age. * * * "And in all positions in life she acted well her part, as a wife, mother and friend. She was honored for her many virtues, and died without leaving an enemy behind her in this world. She has done her work faithfully; lived to a ripe old age, and gone to her reward in the confidence of realizing a happy future."

Hon. ELISHA W. KEYES.

The subject of this sketch is a son of Joseph Keyes, and was born in Northfield, Vt., January 23, 1828. With his father's family he left Northfield, May 2, 1837, for Milwaukee, Wis., and removed thence after a short stay to Lake Mills, in Jefferson county. In early life he exhibited many of those traits of character which have since made him a man of marked influence in the affairs of the Badger State. At school he was first in his classes, in sports and games; following in the wake of his father and grandfather, he led the van. Entering upon the study of the law while yet quite young, he was admitted to the Bar in Madison at the age of twenty-three. He soon acquired an extensive and lucrative practice, which occupied his whole time and absorbed his entire energies until he was elected District Attorney of Dane county in 1858. This office he filled with great acceptability for two years. In 1861 he was appointed Postmaster of the city of Madison, which office he has ever since and now holds. He was Mayor of Madison in 1865 and '66. His zeal as a Republican brought him into extended notice throughout the State, and in 1867 he was elected Chairman of the Republican State Central Committee. For ten years he conducted the affairs of the Republican party of the State with such strength and power of organization as to earn for him the now widely known title of "The Bismark" of western politics. In 1872 and 1876 he was a delegate to and Chairman of the Wisconsin Delegation in the National Republican Conventions of those years. His fame as a politician is now greatly extended, and as "Boss Keyes, of Wisconsin," he is familiarly known in every State in the Union. In 1877 he declined a re-election as Chairman of the State Republican Committee, and at once resumed an active practice of law. He is one of the Regents of the State University of Wisconsin.

Elisha W. Keyes

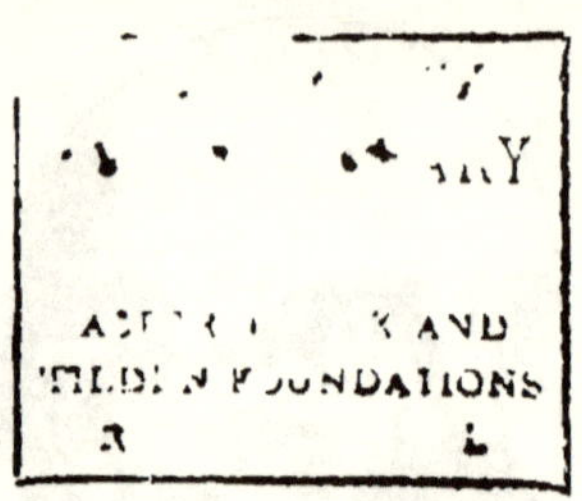

The future of men in political life is proverbially uncertain, but it is believed that Mr. Keyes might during the past ten years have secured any position he desired within the gift of the people of his State.

In person Mr. Keyes is of a stout, compact build, has a strong constitution and good health, and bids fair to live many years; being possessed of a resistless energy, that delights in constant and exacting activity, he may wear out, but will never rust. He is esteemed a good hater, a firm friend, and one whom men at large instinctively recognize as a leader.

Mr. Keyes married Caroline Stevens, May 13, 1854, and they had four children:

Joseph S., b 1854; Elisha W., b 1858; Katie, b 1860; Carrie, b 1865. All born in Madison, Wis.

Mrs. Keyes died July 1, 1865.

Mr. Keyes married for his second wife Louise Shotes, December 4, 1866, and they had one child:

Louis R., born in Madison, Wis., in 1868.

Rev. NATHANIEL KING

Was born in Hampstead, N. H., April 4, 1767. He married Lydia Noyes, of Bow, N. H., who was born August 22, 1778. He first settled at Tunbridge, where he remained until 1838, and then removed to Northfield. He resided in this town fourteen years, preaching for the Free Will Baptist denomination eight years. Their children were:

Dilly, b 1795; Lydia, b 1797; Hannah, b 1799; Hatty, b 1801; Abigail, b 1803; Nathaniel, b 1805; Eliza H., b 1807; Sally H., b 1809; Philip, b 1811; Nancy F., b 1813; Daniel P., b 1815; Harvey, b 1818; Aaron N., b 1820.

Mr. King died in 1852; Mrs. King died in 1869.

EBENEZER FRIZZLE

Was born in Weathersfield, Conn., January 10, 1766, and came to Northfield in the year 1823. He kept tavern at the Center village awhile, and run the tannery near the Center. He married Azubah Hayward, who was born March 12, 1771, and they had nine children:

Caleb, b 1795; James, b 1797; Erastus, b 1801; Eliza, b 1804; Electa, b 1805; Azuba, b 1807; Sarah, b 1808; Ebenezer, b 1811; Harriet, b 1817. All born in Randolph, Vt.

Mrs. Frizzle died in 1847; Mr. Frizzle died in 1849.

HIRAM HENRY

Was born in Alstead, N. H., January 14, 1804, and when he first came to Northfield settled on the West Hill, in the Loren Fuller neighborhood; afterwards he bought the Colonel Robinson farm on the East Hill, where his son John now lives, and where he died in 1851. He married Polly Bean, of Gilmanton, N. H., who was born January 8, 1805. They had five children:

Jane A., b 1828; Johnson H., b 1829; John, b 1833; Mary, b 1844; Martha, b 1846. All born in Northfield.

Francis Davis Henry was born in Brookfield, Vt., in 1815. He married Emily Adams, who was born in Roxbury, in 1816. They had three children:

Francis T., b 1839; Emily Augusta, b 1842; Helen M., b 1844.

Alvah Henry was born in Alstead, N. H., in 1799, and was killed June 28, 1831, by the fall of a tree.

WILLIAM BLOOD

Was from Pepperell, Mass. He married Susannah Cummings, and settled in the south east part of Northfield, in what is called the Moffat neighborhood. They had five children:

Daniel, b 1804; Mary, b 1806; Joel, b 1807; Sophia, b 1809; William, b 1810. All born in Northfield.

EDMOND SHIPMAN

Married Betsey Nichols, and they had the numerous family of thirteen children. He was a blacksmith by trade, and worked at the Center village. His children's names were:

Orrin, b 1822; Jane, b 1824; Julia, b 1825; John, b 1828; Elisha, b 1830; Catherine, b 1832; Harriet, b 1834; George, b 1836; Henry, b 1838; Mary, b 1840; Ann, b 1842; Olive, b 1844; Caroline, b 1846. All born in Northfield.

Rev. HOSEA CLARK

Was a preacher of the Methodist Episcopal Church, and enjoyed the reputation of being a sincere and devoted man. He was elected Justice of the Peace, and had a way of administering the law in a forcible manner, sometimes to the discomfiture of the legal profession. He was not afraid of expressing his opinion on any subject that came before him for consideration.

Mr. Clark married Mrs. John Richardson, and they had two children:

Lucia Ann, b 1839; Stephen Alonzo, b 1842. Both born in Northfield.

ELIJAH BURNHAM, Esq.,

Was born in Brookfield in 1795. He removed to Williamstown, and from there to Northfield, in 1819. He married Maria Simons, of Williamstown, who was born in 1795, and they had thirteen children. They lived in a log house five years, near where John A. Tyler now resides, after which they lived on the Ezra Dean farm, kept tavern at the Falls village, where John Fisk formerly did, and finally settled on the Waitsfield road, near the Depot village. Mr. Burnham was a prominent man in the early days of Northfield, was Selectman ten years, Justice of the Peace, Lister, and held other offices a number of years. He was a skillful veterinarian, and was frequently sent for in different parts of the town to relieve the animal creation of their ailments. He died in Northfield, March, 1873. Mrs. Burnham still lives with a daughter in Williamstown, at the advanced age of eighty-four years. The children were:

Laura, b 1817; an infant, b 1818; Mary, b 1819; Aaron M., b 1820; Marshall D., b 1823; Philanda, b 1825; Philura, b 1827; Sophronia, b 1828; Dennison S., b 1830; Joshua J., b 1831; Emily, b 1833; Ellen, b 1836; George M., b 1840.

JOEL BROWN

Was born in Old Deerfield, Mass., in 1799, and came to Vermont with his father, who settled in Williamstown, and when the Indians returned from the burning of Royalton they took him, with others, and carried them to Montreal, Canada, and lodged them in jail, but through the indomitable courage and perseverance of one Steel, who was also a captive, and others, they liberated themselves and picked their way back to their homes. When quite a lad Joel was frequently sent to Royalton to mill, by means of marked trees, and often heard the howling of wolves and catamounts, they being quite numerous at that early day.

Mr. Brown at the age of twenty-one came to Northfield, and CUT THE FIRST TREE in what is now the Center village, very near the old machine shop, where he subsequently lived. But few buildings were then erected on Dog River. Stanton Richardson's log house, where the late John H. Richardson lived, was the only one accessible, and here Mr. Brown boarded, crossing the river on a tree that had fallen over it. Mr. Brown built a shanty very near the old town house, to shelter himself in rainy days. It was his intention of making a permanent home at the Center, but his intended being in poor health, and her friends objecting to her coming into this new country, caused him to return to Brookfield, and he did not return until 1828, when he located on what has been known as the Deacon Denny farm, on the road from the Center to Roxbury.

Mr. Brown was an industrious, busy man when enjoying good health, and did considerable teaming to Burlington, bringing back flour and other staple goods, which he disposed of. He married Anna Edson, of Brookfield, in 1801, and had two children:

An infant son, died young; Rebecca, b 1803.

Mr. Brown married for his second wife Dorcas Nichols, in 1807, and they had eight children:

Daniel, b 1809: Anna, b 1811; Isaac W., b 1813; Susan, b 1814; Eliza, b 1817; Ruth, b 1821; Joel, Jr., b 1825; D. Amanda, b 1831. All but one born in Brookfield.

Mrs. Brown died in Northfield in 1863; Mr. Brown died in Northfield in 1869.

ISAAC W. BROWN, Esq.,

Was a prominent man at the Center village. He bought out his father in the hotel business at that place in 1837, and for a number of years carried it on, being a wide-awake, industrious, and obliging landlord. In 1855 he moved to the Depot village, and built some eight buildings there, among them the *first* Odd Fellows Hall, on Central Street, where General Jackman now resides. He was elected Selectman, Lister, Constable, and Deputy and High Sheriff, serving in some capacity as an officer for thirty-four years. He was a Director in the Wells River Railroad in 1872, and was an agent for the Central Vermont Railroad.

Mr. Brown married Sylva Elvira Partridge in 1835, who died in 1863, and they had two children:

Jane, b 1836; George W., b 1841.

Mr. Brown married Janette Taylor, who died in 1865, for his second wife. He moved to Montpelier in 1866, and married Mrs. Carrie W. Camp for his third wife, in 1868, who died in 1873. He moved to Boston, and married Mrs. Sarah A. Warren for his fourth wife, in 1874.

Mr. Brown died in Northfield, August 10, 1875.

CLIFTON CLAGGETT.

Dr. CLIFTON CLAGGETT

Was born in Merrimack, N. H., in 1808, and came to Northfield in 1832. He located in the Center village, and has had quite an extensive practice, being a very good physician. He married Catherine, daughter of Harry Emerson, and they had two sons:

Charles C., b 1840; William C., b 1850. Both born in Northfield.

HARRY EMERSON

Was born in Norwich, Vt., in 1781. He came to Northfield in 1821, when about forty years of age, and located in the Center village. He was a hatter by trade. He married Dorcas Demmon, and had nine children:

Rueben, b 1802; Henry C., b 1805; Emily C., b 1808; Catherine, b 1811; Mary, b 1814; Sarah, b 1816; Fanny, b 1818; Jane, b 1824; George E., b 1834. All but two born in Norwich, Vt.

ALBIJENCE AINSWORTH, Esq.,

Was a merchant in the Center village, in the store on the corner adjoining the brick dwelling of Colonel Oliver Averill. He built the brick house in that village where Elijah Winch lives. His father kept the well-known "Ainsworth Tavern," on the hill road to Cleaveland village. Mr. Ainsworth married Emily, daughter of Rev. Mr. Lyman, of Brookfield, and they had two children:

Mary J., b 1825; Annette, b 1827. Both born in Northfield.

STANTON RICHARDSON, Esq.,

Was born in Haddam, Conn., in 1755, and came from Westminster, Vt., to Northfield, about 1785. He was a prominent man in those early days, and held a number of town offices, being the first Selectman chosen, and finally settled on the farm near the Depot village where his descendant, John H. Richardson, lived and died. He married Anna Doubleday, who was born in Westminster, in 1760, and they had eleven children:

Nathaniel, b 1781: Sarah, b 1783; Samuel, b 1786; Ezra T., b 1789; John, b 1791; Anna, b 1795; Sarah, b 1795; Sylvanus, b 1797; Horace, b 1800; Prudence, b 1801; Chauncey, b 1802. All but two born in Northfield.

The wife of Stanton Richardson was a noble, couragous woman. She undertook on one occasion a journey to Westminster, Vt., a distance of more than one hundred miles from Northfield, on horseback, with a small child in her arms, carrying her eatables in a pair of saddle bags, and she completed her journey without injury to herself, child, or beast! Think of that, gentle reader, of a woman's going so long a distance, when the country was new, through woods, and when wild beasts were plenty, waiting to spring upon travelers without a moment's warning! Such heroism is worthy of mention in the town records!

Bears were numerous in that early day, and Mr. Richardson having caught one with a pair of cubs, he tamed the young ones, and they became an interesting couple, making themselves at times familiar without invitation. The family lived in a log house with an old fashioned chimney, inside of which you could sit, and, looking up, see stars in the evening. One night, when Mrs. Richardson had retired with Ezra T., an infant, one of the young

Bruins crawled on to the roof and came down the chimney, and, wonderful to relate, worked his way into the bed, nestling down between Mrs. Richardson and her babe. The child remonstrated, when the mother, seeing the kind of company she had received unasked, took the bear by the nape of his neck and tumbled him on to the floor! This is no *fiction*, but a *reality!*

On one Thanksgiving day Mrs. Richardson made a party, and invited all the people in Williamstown and Northfield to be present. They came, and had a jolly good time. They had for dinner boiled victuals, roast pig, beans, and baked Indian pudding. For extension tables they took the doors off their wooden hinges, and used them. No doubt they had, even in the wilderness, a "feast of reason, and a flow of soul."

Mr. Richardson was a generous hearted man, and made arrangements for the first burying ground, near the center of the town, on what has been called "Richardson meadow," now owned by Mr. Gallup. The following is a copy of a lease recorded on the town's book:

"To All People to Whom these Presents Shall Come,

Greeting:

Know ye that I, Stanton Richardson, of Northfield, in the County of Orange, (now Washington,) and State of Vermont, for and in consideration of the inhabitants fencing, and keeping fenced, do lease, let, and confirm unto them, a certain tract or parcel of land bounded as follows, viz.: * * * * * each way to be for the use of said town for to bury their dead, this lease including the within privileges thereto belonging, to them, the said inhabitants of Northfield, and their heirs and assigns, for their own use, benefit, and behoof, as long as *wood grows and water runs.*

N. B.—Be it always remembered that the said Richardson, nor any other person claiming the right of soil, are not to improve the above named premises to the damage of the graves therein contained.

Signed, sealed, and delivered in presence of

ELIJAH SMITH,
NATHAN ROGERS.

Northfield, 1811.

JOHN RICHARDSON,

Son of Stanton, lived and died on the farm of his father, near the Depot village. He was a prominent farmer, and many depended on him for assistance. He married Huldah, daughter of Daniel Worthington, and died of consumption. They had seven children:

Sarah S., b 1823; George M., b 1824; John Harris, b 1826; Marshall H., b 1827; George S., b 1829; Mary J., b 1831; Daniel W., b 1833. All born in Northfield.

Mr. Richardson died in 1834.

The first son of John Richardson was drowned in Dog River, opposite the house, when a little boy about three years old, and the father took the precaution to build a yard fence, so that his little ones might not leave without notice, but even this fatherly care did not prevent another son, George S., from meeting with the same sad fate, for he was drowned in a wash tub by creeping to it, and pulling himself up by it, lost his balance and fell in.

NATHANIEL RICHARDSON, Esq.,

Was a son of Stanton, and was a millwright. He held offices in town, and was an industrious man. Previous to his going to Canada, he lived where Lucius Edson subsequently lived. After returning from Canada he built the two story brick house beyond the Center village, where Israel Avery now resides, after which he built a house and saw-mill about half way to Roxbury. He married Nabby Bosworth, of Berlin, and had seven children:

Nathaniel B., b 1811; Abigail, b 1814; Caroline M., b 1816; Sarah Ann, b 1819; Melissa, b 1821; Alonzo, b

NATHANIEL RICHARDSON.

1827 : Adelia, b 1829. All but the two first were born in Canada.

Mr. Richardson died at the age of 76 years ; Mrs. Richardson died at the age of 86 years.

SAMUEL RICHARDSON

Was born in Haddam, Conn., in 1742. He was a shoemaker by trade, and his first settlement in Northfield, which was very early, was on what has been known as the Wales place, and he afterwards lived near Hosea Kathan's.

"Uncle Sam Richardson," as he was called, was a great story teller. While hammering out soles for the understandings of his customers, he would frequently indulge in telling marvelous stories, and was not always careful to see how they would come out ; and he was a devout man.

It is related on a time, when Judge Paine had loaned his trusty old horse to a woman who worked for him, to go to the south village to do a little trading, the Judge requested her to stop at Mr. Richardson's and do an errand. On her return he asked her the reason of her tardiness, and was informed that when she arrived there she heard the old gentleman praying, and not wishing to disturb him she waited until he got through. This had detained her some little time. On hearing the explanation, the Judge said, "Well, what did the old horse say about it?" Her reply came quick, "He did not say anything about it, for he had never heard one before."

Samuel Richardson married for his first wife Clarissa Wanbelton, and they had two children :

Hannah, b 1764 ; Jonathan, b 1767.

It was this son of Mr. Richardson who was the owner of the dog that Thompson in his Gazetteer refers to, that the river was named after. It was a favorite dog, that he brought from Connecticut, and while out hunting the dog attacked a large Moose, and was drowned, in what is known as the Moose hole in the river. It was in the Spring of the year, and the Moose broke through the ice, and the dog being close to him, both went under, and were drowned. The Moose hole was a deep place in the bend of the river, near where Joseph Gould resided at the Falls Village, and is known by all fishermen acquainted with Dog River.

Jonathan Richardson was a noted hunter, and killed ten wolves in one day. His sister Hannah married a Mr. Jefferds, and after the wedding went to Williamstown, riding behind her husband, dressed in white, through marked trees, and could hear the howling of wild animals on all sides as they rode along.

Samuel Richardson married for his second wife Jerusha Royce, and they had eight children:

Stanton, Lemuel B., Clarissa, Prudence, Arael, Amisa, Martha, Jerusha.

Mr. Richardson died in 1832, aged 90 years.

Mrs. Richardson died in 1843, aged 85 years.

JOHN L. BUCK, Esq.,

Was born at Reading, Windsor County, Vt., January 1st, 1862, and continued to live there until he was twenty years old. He then attended Cavendish Academy for a time and afterwards studied in the same town with Hon. Reuben Washburn for about one year.

In 1823 he went to Montpelier into the law office of Hon. Jeduthan Loomis, and afterwards studied in the office of Hon. Samuel Prentiss, and was admitted to the bar at the September Term of the County Court, at Montpelier, in 1825, and in October of the same year he took

JOHN L. BUCK.

up his residence in Northfield, at the Center village, and remained there in the practice of law until April 1851, when he removed to Lockport, N. Y., where he has ever since resided.

Mr. Buck married Mary Ann Hildreth, November 29, 1826. She died at Lockport, November 6, 1864.

There were born to them three children: John H., with whom he now resides; Mary D., who died at Lockport in 1852, and is buried there, and George B., who died at Northfield in 1841, and is buried in the old cemetery at the Center village.

Esquire Buck, as he used to be called, was not the first lawyer who lived in Northfield. When he went there he found one Simon Smith, who had been admitted to the bar at the same time he had, but Smith remained but a few months, and left. For many years after he was the only lawyer in town. He saw its growth and prosperity, and aided much in the culture and improvement of its inhabitants. He was a man generally esteemed by his fellow townsmen, and is remembered to-day as a good worthy citizen.

He was elected Representative to the Legislature, was Assistant Clerk, and State's Attorney, and filled many town offices with credit, and he was Justice of the Peace nearly all the time he lived in Northfield.

He recalls, among others, the *story said* to have been told by Samuel Richardson, that he was mowing on the meadow one day in July, a very hot day, when he heard hounds barking on the hill west of them, and soon a splendid deer came down chased by the hounds and plunged into the river, disappeared under the ice, and was never seen again.

The story is the same one so often told, and many are now living who heard it in their boyhood days.

JOHN HILDRETH BUCK, Esq.,

Son of John L. Buck, was born in Northfield, November 22, 1827, and grew to his majority among the Green Mountains. He graduated from the University of Vermont in the class of 1850, and returned to Northfield, where he remained in the office of his father until February, 1851, when he removed to Lockport, N. Y., his present home. His father having removed there the following spring, he studied law with him, and in February, 1854, he was admitted to the bar of the Supreme Court of the State of New York. On the twenty-fourth of August, 1854, he married Harriet M. Fletcher, daughter of the Hon. Paris Fletcher, of Bridport, Vt. In 1874 he was elected Mayor of his adopted city, and served one term, declining a renomination.

Mr. Buck is proud of his adopted city, but never allows any one in his presence to say *one word* in disparagement of the climate and people of his native State.

JOHN WEST, Esq.,

Was a substantial citizen of Northfield, and built the brick house on the farm now owned by Daniel Guild. He married Nancy Adams, and had one child, named Asahel Gray, born in Northfield in 1826, and who now resides in Morristown, Vt.

Mr. West died in Morristown in 1871, and Mrs. West died in 1878.

HARVEY R. KEYES

Came from Putney to Randolph, and from there to Northfield, in 1838. He married Emeline Keyes for his first wife, and they had one child, viz.:

Sarah Jane, born in Northfield, in 1841.

Mr. Keyes married Mrs. Laura Tilson for his second wife, who was the daughter of Eleazer Nichols, Senior. She died April 1, 1877.

Mr. Keyes married Mrs. Caroline Goodno for his third wife, in 1878.

HARVEY W. CARPENTER, Esq.,

Was born in Sharon, Vt., February 22, 1790, and in 1814 he settled in Moretown, Vt., and lived there until 1832, when he moved to Montpelier, and resided there until his removal to Northfield, in March, 1836, where he resided until his death, August 29, 1849. He was married three times.

First, to Hannah Shurtleff, September 12, 1816, by whom he had one child, William S. Carpenter, born March 31, 1818. She died at Moretown, April 16, 1818.

Second, to Jane Campbell, July 11, 1822, by whom he had four children:

Cornelius J., b 1824; Cornelia J., b 1824; Cornelius N., b 1826; Cordelia E., b 1828.

Mr. Carpenter's second wife was born in Windham, N. H., May 31, 1796, and was drowned at Moretown in what is known as the great freshet July 26 and 27, 1830. His third wife, by whom he had one child, Charles Henry, born August 7, 1842, survived him nearly ten years, dying at Northfield, February 24, 1859.

Of his children three are now living, to wit: Cornelia J., married to E. Y. Farrar, and residing in Chicago, Ill.; Cornelius N., married and residing in Broadhead, Green County, Wis., and Cordelia E., married to Ammi Burnham, and residing in the city of Milwaukee, Wis. Cornelius J. died July 31, 1825; Charles H., his youngest child, died in infancy, at Northfield; William S. Carpenter, his oldest son, died in Chicago in 1855, at which place he was practicing medicine at the time of his death.

Dr. BENJAMIN PORTER

Was born in Old Volentown, Conn., in 1788. He lived with his father, who was a Congregational clergyman, and settled in Plainfield, N. H., until he was twelve years of age. Benjamin attended the Academy at Meriden, and afterwards taught school, and studied for the medical profession, graduating at Dartmouth. Northfield was his first settlement as a physician. On his first visit here, as he was passing along by where the Episcopal Church now stands, he saw Judge Paine and John Green sowing wheat on newly cleared land, and he took the liberty to inquire of the Judge if this town would be a good place for a physician to locate. The reply was it would, if a man had a strong constitution, and was willing to work hard for poor pay.

The Doctor settled on the East Hill in 1816, boarding three years with Captain Jesse Averill. From there he moved to the "Post farm," near by, where he remained four years, and from there he went to the Center village, and built the two story brick house where he lived and died. He married Sophia Fullerton, and they had four children:

Elizabeth, b 1823; Edward, b 1826; Edwin, b 1826; Benjamin F., b 1833. All born in Northfield.

BENJAMIN PORTER.

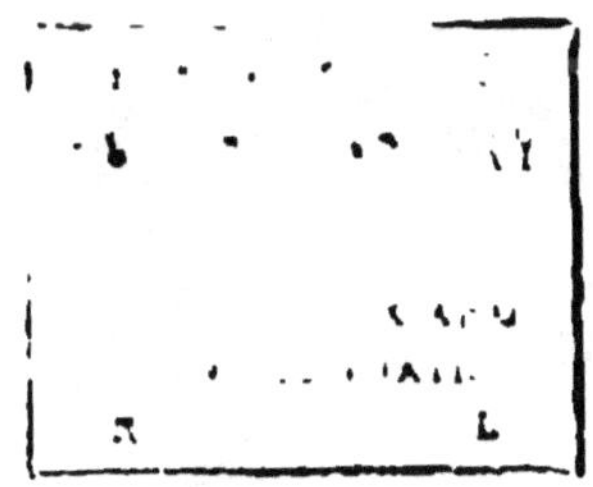

Edwin Porter.

Dr. Porter had quite an extensive practice, being the first physician in town, save Nathaniel Robinson and Jeptha White, and was considered a very good practitioner, especially in fevers. He died February 21, 1876.

Dr. EDWIN PORTER

Is the only practicing physician here, born in Northfield. He went to a district school until he was twelve years old, then went to a select school kept by Rev. Calvin Granger some two or three years, from there he went to the Academy at Randolph Center, studying some eighteen months, and then went to Meriden, N. H., about the same length of time. In Montpelier he finished his studies for College, and entered the University at Burlington in 1846, and graduated in 1850. During his College course he taught school winters.

After the Doctor graduated he commenced studying medicine with his father, was a private student of Professor Peaslee of Dartmouth, and attended three courses of Lectures there, graduating in the Medical Department in 1853 at Hanover, N. H.

In 1854 the Doctor commenced the drug business in connection with his practice, in company with George Tucker, but at the end of one year the company dissolved, the Doctor carrying on the business ever since.

Dr. Porter has been considered a reliable physician, and is a very good surgeon His practice has been large and generally successful. He married Carrie S., daughter of Hon. Heman Carpenter, in 1867.

JOHN GREEN

Went to live with Judge Paine when a lad, and worked for him many years. He was an industrious citizen, and took a great interest in the prosperity of Northfield. He married Isabella, daughter of Justus Burnham, and had nine children:

Charles Paine, Lucy, William, infant, Maria, William second, Lydia, Huldah, and Charles second.

Mr. Green died in 1874, aged 78 years.

ROSWELL DEWEY, Esq.,

Was born in Royalton, Vt., in 1801, and came to Northfield March 9, 1828. His first settlement was near Harlow Bridge. In 1842 he moved into the Center village, and in 1843 he built the house where he now resides. He enjoys very good health, and is enabled to carry on his little farm, cutting his own hay, raising his own corn and potatoes, and having time to read the newspapers, keeping up with the times in politics and matters generally.

Mr. Dewey has been a Surveyor, a Constable, a Justice of the Peace, and held the office of Postmaster six years. He was an excellent teacher of sacred music, and followed that vocation thirty years. He married for his first wife Polly S. Whitney, of Tunbridge, and they had three children:

George, b 1829; Roswell, Jr., b 1833; Mary, b 1841. All born in Northfield.

Mr. Dewey married for his second wife Caroline Reed, of Williamstown, and they had two children:

Eunice W., b 1854; Alice, b 1861. Both born in Northfield.

EDMUND POPE.

JOHN BRALEY

Came to Roxbury from Hartford, Vt., and located on the Moffitt farm. Afterwards he settled in the south-east part of Northfield, where A. J. Braley subsequently lived. He married Mary Gibson, and they had seven children:

Roxanna, b 1809; Daniel, b 1813; Persis, b 1815; Hepsibah, b 1816; Mary, b 1820; Jane, b 1823; Andrew J., b 1828. All born in Roxbury save one.

LEMUEL POPE

Was born in Rochester, Mass., in 1791, and settled in the "Shaw neighborhood," on the road to East Roxbury, in 1850. He was a farmer and shoemaker by trade, and a worthy Christian man. He married Rebecca Shaw, and they had four children:

Edmund, b 1810; Lewis, b 1812; William T., b 1826; Louisa, b 1829. All but one born in Brookfield.

EDMUND POPE, Esq.,

Was born in Northfield September 24, 1810. He went to Brookfield with his father in 1812, and remained there until 1850, when they moved to East Roxbury, and Mr. Pope purchased the large farm once owned by Isaiah Shaw, Esq., some three hundred and fifty acres.

In 1858, when taking down a barn on his place, Mr. Pope was thrown down, by its falling on him, and crushed in a fearful manner, so that his life was considered very critical. For six weeks he was not able to lie down, and when the Dr. came to re-set his bones he exclaimed, "You might as well try to set a dead man's bones." But a kind Providence had ordained that his life of usefulness should continue longer, and though he is not free from the aches and pains that flesh is heir to, he has so recovered that he is enabled to attend to his ordinary business as correctly as ever.

Mr. Pope has been quite successful in settling estates, and such has been his popularity in that direction that he has administered on some sixteen, and invariably given good satisfaction. He never was an office seeker, but office very often sought him, and conferred her honors upon him. While living in Roxbury he represented the town three years in the Legislature, was Selectman nine years, and was elected to other offices.

Mr. Pope moved to Northfield in 1867, and since his residence here he has represented the town two years in the Legislature. This town being his birth-place, and feeling an interest in her public, religious, and educational movements, he has contributed liberally to them. Here has been his post office address for twenty-eight years, here has been his place of religious worship, and here doubtless he will spend the remainder of his days, respected by the whole community.

Mr. Pope married Roxana Braley, of Northfield, and they had four children:

Abby S., b 1835; Persis B., b 1837; *Edmund Jr., b 1840; Mary L., b 1848. All born in Brookfield.

Mrs. Pope died January 4, 1859.

Mr. Pope married for his second wife Emily S. Gale, of Barre, and they had one child:

Abbie Emily, born in Roxbury, in 1865.

---

*This was a promising young man, who laid down his life for his country. He enlisted in 1861, was taken prisoner at Wilson's Raid, June 19, 1864, and died the following December, on board of a transport going from Charlestown to Annapolis, on his way home.

SAMUEL KEITH.

his profession. From early manhood he has ever been active in all progressive movements—anti-slavery, temperance, education and the church. For most of the time for thirty-nine years he has been a Sabbath school Superintendent, an office he now holds. His success as a Superintendent is attributable to his deep love of children. It is a common remark, "all the children love Dr. Keith."

With all the Doctor's love for his new home, he says he desires to return to Northfield to spend the eve of his life with his family, and rest in Elmwood Cemetery.

Dr. Keith married Millicent Benson, of Norwich, Vt., June 17, 1847. They had three children:

Gertrude A.; Dellie May; and Millicent. The two youngest died in early childhood. Gertrude A. has been a teacher of reputation in the public schools of Iowa.

LUTHER J. WARNER

Was born in Williamstown, Vt., in 1805, and came from Braintree to Northfield in 1834 He located near the south-west line of the town, on the road to West Roxbury. He was a farmer, a blacksmith, and a mason, following all these occupations as his services were desired. He married Charlotte Flint, of Braintree, who was born in 1806, and they had five sons,

Ashael M.; James P.; Elera P.: Henry C.: Ludo.

JOEL PARKER

Was from Pepperell, Mass.—was born in 1803. He lived where his son Fred now does, and married Eliza Crawford, having four children, all born in Northfield:

George, Fred, Eliza, George.

JOHN P. DAVIS, Esq.,

Has been in the mercantile business at the Center village since 1850. He was born in Barnard, Vt., in 1819. He has been quite successful in his calling, and has the confidence of his townsmen, having been elected to a number of offices. He married for his first wife Calista Gale, of Barre. For his second wife he married Phebe L., daughter of the Hon. John L. Marsh, of Clarendon, Vt. They have one child: Charles M., b 1861.

SAMUEL DOLE

Came from Bedford, N. H. He married Mary Sargent, of Danville, Vt., and they had nine children; all but one born in Northfield:

Christopher, b 1815; Jane, b 1816; Mary, b 1818; Cynthia, b 1820; Harriet, b 1824; Samuel, b 1826; George, b 1828; Jason, b 1831; French, b 1834.

Mr. Samuel Dole finally settled on what has been known for many years as the "Dole Hill," where Christopher, Samuel and George now reside.

SAMUEL WHITTEN

Was an early settler in Northfield, and at one time owned all the land at the Center Village, before it was cleared. He was a farmer and a Baptist peacher. He had nine children, named Samuel; Woodbury; Joseph; Mercy; Rebecca; Clarissa; Caroline; and Julia.

Mr. Whitten moved to Malone, N. Y., where he died.

ISAAC P. JENKS

Was from Lyme, N. H. He settled in the Center Village, Northfield, in 1832, adjoining the Universalist Church, and lived there many years. He built the stone building on Main street, Depot Village, where he now resides, taking the material from his quarry just over Dog River, on Water Street.

Mr. Jenks married Cordelia Hurlburt, of Hanover, N. H., and their children were:

Betsey, b 1829; Thomas, b 1834; Newton, b 1838.

DAVID M. LANE, Esq.,

Was born in Hampton, N. H., March 29, 1793, and came to Northfield, from Strafford, Vt., in 1820. He was a prominent surveyor, and followed this profession a number of years with success. At that early day, the country being new, and property changing, his services as a surveyor were greatly needed, and the writer has frequently heard Mr. Lane mentioned as a very worthy, promising business man. But he was cut down in the full vigor of his manhood, dying at the early age of thirty-seven years.

Mr. Lane built the first brick building in town, viz: the old brick school house at the Center, making the brick himself, and burning the lime, and doing most of the carpenter work with his own hands.

He bought of Judge Paine one hundred acres of timber land, where J. M. Dana now lives, a little way east of the Depot Village. He afterwards, with his brother Joshua, bought out Eleazer and Dyer Loomis, on the mountain, and was a very active, industrious man, beloved by the community. He held some offices of trust in town.

Mr. Lane married Elvira Ladd, of Strafford, and they had four children, all born in Northfield:

Cordelia, b 1823; Caroline, b 1825; Jenette, b 1826; Louisa, b 1831.

JOSHUA LANE, Esq.,

Was born in Chichester, N. H., November 17, 1798, and moved into Northfield, from Strafford, Vt., in 1821. He was one of the most enterprising citizens of that early day. His first move in building was on what is known as the Patterson farm, used lately for Slate purposes, and without specifying, bought and erected dwellings in a number of places, living in the winter in a house he built at the Center. Among his largest purchases, with his brother David he bought out the farm on the mountain, and in all it is thought he cleared with his help around him some three hundred acres of timber land.

Mr. Lane finally settled in West Berlin, and the place known to this day as "Lanesville" was named after him. He was a devoted Mason. To him Masonry was his beginning, middle and end of the highest enjoyment, and never was he so happy as when he met with his brethren in their stated gatherings. He loved the institution for its intrinsic worth, and dying was buried with its honors, according to a long standing request.

Mr Lane married Catherine G. Tarr, and they had one child:

Moses Lane, C. E., who was born in Northfield, November 16, 1823.

Mr. Lane died in 1877, seventy-nine years of age.

MOSES LANE.

JOSIAH LANE

Was born in Chichester, N. H., March 25, 1804, and came from Strafford to Northfield in 1825. He is a brother of Moses, David and Joshua.

Mr. Lane married Alpa Chamberlin, who was born in Strafford in 1807, and had six children, all born in Northfield:

Betsey Ann, b 1827; Joseph A., b 1828; Lucia E., b 1833; Marcia H., b 1836; Charles L., b 1843; Frances, b 1854.

MOSES LANE

Was born in Chichester, N. H., August 14, 1808, and came from Strafford to Northfield, in 1832, and settled on his brother David's place, after his decease. He afterward bought of Rev. Calvin Granger the "red house" on Main street, the second house built on said street. He now resides not far from his first purchase in the village, with land sufficient to keep him busy, and is a very kind and obliging man. In fact, if any favor is asked for, if in his power "Uncle Moses," as his neighbors call him, is ever ready and willing to grant it.

Mr. Lane married Mary, daughter of Daniel Worthington, Esq., May 2, 1833, in Northfield, by Rev. Elisha Scott. She was born September 26, 1808. "Aunt Mary" is indeed a helpmeet to her husband, and in all the ups and downs of life, like Mary of old, she is willing to do her part.

MOSES LANE, C. E.,

Son of Joshua Lane, was born in Northfield, November 16, 1823. He graduated at the University of Vermont in 1845.

Through the courtesy of Gov. Paine he was appointed Assistant Engineer in one of the parties organized in August, 1845, for the location and construction of the Vermont Central Railroad. He was employed as a Civil Engineer, on this and other railroads in New England, until the close of the year 1849, when he left the State, and engaged as Principal of an academy in Springfield, Erie County, N. Y., which position he held three years. After this he was engaged for a short time as Resident Engineer on the construction of the Albany and Susquehanna railroad at Albany, N. Y.

In 1856 he was appointed to the position of principal Assistant Engineer for the construction of the Brooklyn water works.

Mr. Lane has been constantly employed for the past twenty-two years as a hydraulic engineer. He was employed thirteen years on the water works of Brooklyn, six as principal assistant and seven as Chief Engineer. He had charge of the construction of the Milwaukee water works, as chief engineer, where he was employed seven years. He has also been connected with other important public works, as chief or consulting engineer.

Mr. Lane married the daughter of the late Dr. Varney Ingalls, of Erie County, N. Y., in 1851, and has four children. He now resides in Milwaukee, Wis.

MOSES LANE, C. E.

ALVIN BRALEY.

Hon. BENJAMIN FRANKLIN GOSS

Was born in Peacham, Vt., October 28, 1806. At the age of nineteen he came to Northfield from Montpelier, where he had been a clerk for Roger Hubbard, and was employed as a clerk in the Center village a while, and then became a partner of Governor Paine, who run the *first* store in the then Factory village. Here he occupied a very responsible position, having the entire charge of a large store, and also acted as paymaster of the hands employed by Governor Paine in his factory, and other enterprises at that time requiring the disbursement of a large amount of money. While here he built the two story house near the foot of Main street, where John A. Kent now resides, it being the fourth house built on that street.

Mr. Goss married Nancy Hutchins, of Waterbury, in 1833, she living but two or three years after marriage. In 1839 he married for his second wife Mrs. Mary Jane Moore, and they had four children, two of whom died, and two are now living in Vergennes, Vt. From Northfield he moved to Waterbury, living there eighteen years, and from there to Brandon, Vt., where he was general manager of the Brandon Iron and Car Wheel Company. His last settlement was in Vergennes, where he died in 1877.

Hon. ALVIN BRALEY

Was born in Hartford, Vt., November 26, 1807. He married Lucy Hutchinson, of Braintree, Vt., who was born February 1, 1806. They had four children:

George, b 1832; George second, b 1835; Charles, b 1842; Lucy, b 1847. All born in Roxbury.

Mrs. Braley died in 1870.

Mr. Braley married for his second wife Mary M. Blanchard, May 7, 1871.

Mr. Braley died in 1875.

In Mr. Braley we had a substantial farmer, who by industry and economy amassed a good fortune. He owned and carried on for a number of years a productive farm in East Roxbury, and had the esteem and confidence of his townsmen. He was elected Representative, Assistant Judge for Washington County, and other minor offices while living in Roxbury, and after his removal to Northfield was elected Bank Director, Justice of the Peace, Village Trustee, and was interested in manufactures. In 1868 he was elected President of the National Bank, which office he acceptably filled until his death. His demise was a loss to our town, for he was not only able but willing to assist in the establishment of such institutions as promised to build up Northfield.

BENJAMIN FISK, JOHN FISK, NATHANIEL FISK, AND DAVID FISK

Were brothers, all stalwart men, and of whom it might be said in scripture language, "and there were giants in those days." They all came from Williamstown, and had the following families:

Benjamin Fisk was a store keeper in the South Village about 1816; he married Hannah Herrick, and they had seven children; all born in Williamstown and Northfield;

Delphine, b 1812; Philander, b 1814; Caroline, b 1815; Dennison, b 1817; Sophia, b 1819; Rosina, b 1822; John D., b 1826.

John Fisk was born in Williamstown, Vt., in 1783. He kept tavern in the Falls Village about 1825, and it was quite a noted place for *trainings* that abounded in

Yours Truly
Geo. M. Fisk

those days, affording recreation for the people. He married Betsey Martin, who was born November 16, 1784; and they had thirteen children, all born in Williamstown and Northfield:

Olive, b 1808; Betsey, b 1808; Siloma, b 1810; John, b 1811; Lydia M., b 1813; Melindia, b 1815; Eunice, b 1816; Azro J., b 1818; Sarah, b 1829; Lucinda, b 1822; Maria L., b 1823; Mary, b 1826; Hannah, b 1828.

NATHANIEL FISK was born in Williamstown, and moved to Northfield in 1819, and lived here until he died in 1861, aged eighty seven years. He married Mehitable Bates, who died in 1826. They had eight children, among them being Willoughby, Patty, Jonathan, Daniel, Curtis, and Newhall. We can learn but little reliable history of this family.

DAVID FISK, the father of George M. Fisk, Esq., was born in Williamstown. He married Sarah Reed, who was born May 25, 1791, and they had seven children:

Sarah Ann, b 1818; David R., b 1820; Harvey R., b 1823; Ann Eliza, b 1825; George M., b 1830; Fanny C., b 1833; Van Loren M., b 1838.

Mr. Fisk died in 1864; Mrs. Fisk died in 1865.

GEORGE M. FISK, Esq.,

Was born in Wolcott, Vt., June 7, 1830. When one year old the family went to Williamstown, and there he learned the blacksmith's trade of his father. When twelve years of age the family came to Northfield, and George, desirous of getting a good education, attended a select school in Berlin a few terms, and also the Northfield Academy. He studied law with the Hon. Heman Carpenter, and was admitted to the Bar of Washington County at the March Term of 1854, the Supreme Court in 1856, and the United States Court in 1874. In that year, 1854, he went to Prof. John W. Fowler's law school in Poughkeepsie, N. Y. In 1863 he represented the town in the Legislature.

Mr. Fisk was a Delegate to the National Democratic Convention that met in St. Louis in 1876.

In 1864 he built the two factories in the Depot village now run by Mr. Howarth, and put in the machinery now in use, had a large interest in the lumber business at Granville, Vt., sold the Union Slate Quarry. and other quarries of slate in town, is now President of the Northfield Savings Bank, and has the confidence of an excellent Board of Trustees.

Mr. Fisk as a lawyer has traits of character that make him quite popular with the masses. He is bold, shrewd, and demonstrative, and, being well read, and forcible as a debater, is very successful for his clients.

Mr. Fisk married Jane E., daughter of James Nichols, in 1856.

DANIEL WORTHINGTON

Was born in 1775. He came to Northfield from Williamstown, and located on the Garfield place in 1818. Afterwards he went to the Falls village, and bought the saw mill of Freedom Edson and built a house, when that village was comparatively new, there being but one or two log houses on the east side of the river. *Under-brush* and *huckleberry bushes* covered the land that is now spread over with buildings. He married Polly Fisk, February 27, 1800, who was born May 12, 1780, and they had eleven children:

Huldah, b 1801; Elijah. b 1803; Sophia, b 1805; Lyman, b 1807; Mary, b 1808; Rhoda, b 1811; Daniel, b 1813; David, b 1815; Theodore S., b 1817; Elias, b 1819; Francis, b 1822. All born in Williamstown.

Mrs. Worthington died April 30, 1851.

Mr. Worthington died July 4, 1866.

DAVID R. TILDEN

Was born in Williamstown, Vt., in 1800. His first residence in Northfield was where William Gold now lives. He married Mary Newcomb, and they had one son:

Ai N., born in Williamstown, in 1826.

Mr. Tilden married for his second wife Mrs. Nancy (Wales) Nutter, and they had five children:

Heber, b 1829; David R., b 1832; Mary N., b 1834; Olive, b 1837; Charles B., b 1839. All but one born in Northfield.

Mr. Tilden married for his third wife Martha Ann Morris, and had two children, Mary Ann and Bradford. He died in Plattsburgh, N. Y., March 15, 1847.

Mr. Tilden was a *humorous* man. He liked a good joke, and knew how to *give* and *take* one. He was quite fond of Chronicle writing, and he wrote and published in the Montpelier Watchman a chapter on the war made upon Governor Paine, and the friends of the projected railroad route through Northfield. Barre and Montpelier were very indignant to think that the Governor should insist in locating it in what they called "the outskirts of population," and so Mr. Tilden characterized the opposition in the following admirable style, creating at the time great amusement and satisfaction. We think it worthy a place in the history of Northfield, and so insert it for the benefit of the coming generations:

CHRONICLES, CHAPTER I.

1. Now it came to pass in the days of John, the ruler, that the wise men of the Province gathered themselves together at the Metropolis, to consult for the good of the people.

2. Then there arose certain men who said, let us make a great thoroughfare for the good of all this people, and they said it shall be so.

3. Let it commence at the great waters on the West, and

passing up the stream whose name is a sweet flavor unto many, thence down the valley of the river of pleasant waters, even to the borders of this Province.

4. And John departed to his people, and William ruled in his stead.

5. Now the people of the West, even the outskirts of population, arose and said, let us find cunning men, well skilled in the art of finding such thoroughfares, and say unto them, search through all our borders, that if such thoroughfare can be built we in our poverty would enjoy the benefit.

6. And the cunning men said, the way is to be found, even on your side of the Province; haste ye and procure the means.

7. Now there will be wanting much gold and precious stones.

8. Then there arose one Charles, the son of Elijah, a man high in reputation as a ruler of the people, and he said, Gather ye together all the gold and silver in your store. I will interest the great and mighty men of other Provinces in your behalf.

9. And it was even so. The men of other Provinces brought gold and silver, and said, We are ready to assist you in this great work.

10. Now the chief men of this Province gathered themselves together and said, Let us be governed by seven of the chief men among us, wise men and honorable; so they appointed seven—Charles, Samuel, Robert, Jacob, Daniel, John, and James.

11. Now when the appointment was being made there arose one Thomas, the usurer, and said, Are you attached to local interest? And they said, We are not; with care and wisdom will we carry out this design.

12. Then there arose in the East of the Province one George, a dealer in fine linen, who said, we also would be heard, for we have found a way, even by the mineral waters and the pass of rocks.

13. And the wise men said, We will see it.

14. So they appointed men of skill and cunning to search out that land and bring them word again.

15. And the chief of these men said, Their way is more difficult than the far off valley of the Province of the West.

16. And the seven wise men said, Let the way be made on the West, if your saying be true; but search ye again with all care, that ye be not deceived.

17. Then the men of the East were very wroth, and anger filled their hearts.

18. Now Thomas, the usurer, arose and called to his scribe, saying, Indite ye the words that I shall speak to you, that this people may hear and not be deceived. If this way be not located by the way of the East of this Province, then keep your gold and sil-

ver in your store, that the way of the by-lanes be not benefited by it. We are the great men of this Province, and not attached to local or other interests. We know that the way by the East is the right way. Does it not pass by the habitations of the rich? Is it not the way I have chosen?

19. And the people of the East listened to his sayings, and published through all their land that there be called a Convention of great indignation against the seven wise men, and against the men of skill and cunning, that they be deceivers of the people.

20. And the people of the East gathered themselves together at the Metropolis of the Province, even in the Tabernacle of the Most High.

21. Now Julius, the son of Simeon, called the convention to order, and they chose John, the keeper of the bag, to preside, and Fernand and George to be scribes.

22. Then arose Thomas, the usurer, saying, He that created the Heavens and spake the earth into existence clearly pointed out the way for this great thoroughfare. As one who knoweth and keepeth His sayings, we would say to the seven wise men, Be not blinded, but obey His will. Are we not inhabitants of this great Metropolis, the seat of the law makers? We gave the charter existence. Was it not created even for their accommodation? We who furnished the gold and the silver, have we not said, Ours is the right way? Build ye thereon, put no affront on the knowledge of this people, if the way cost more. Acknowledge our judgment, and let the way be for our accommodation. Listen therefore to our sayings. We will not cease from our efforts till ye remove this thoroughfare and give it to us. If ye deceive and fail us, we will put our trust in God for final success.

23. Then ar. se Jonathan, surnamed the Miller, not a grinder of corn, but a great officer of the Greeks, Charles, the dealer in wares for the people, Oramel and Hezekiah, expounders of the law, and Wooster, a cunning worker of brass and iron, with great swelling words of Thomas, and the people of the convention said Amen.

24. Now arose Wooster, the worker of brass, and said the acts of the wise men are a paltry attempt on the rights of this Metropolis, and merit our ridicule and contempt.

25. And Oramel said, Let twenty be appointed to effect a location by the way of this great Metropolis.

26. Thereupon John, the keeper of the bag, appointed Thomas, the usurer, and nineteen other mighty men of valor, and said, Let me also join myself to your number.

27. Now Julius, the son of Simeon, said, Let our doings be published throughout this land, that all may hear of our wisdom.

28. Then spoke Jackson, an expounder of the law, Let the sayings of this convention of great indignation be copied by the scribes, and sent to the seven wise men, that they may learn wisdom from us, and build this great thoroughfare even as we have directed, lest a worse evil befall them.

29. Ye men of the West be of good cheer. Await the decision of him whose right it is to judge. A bruised reed shall he not break, and the smoking flax shall he not quench. His decision shall send forth judgment unto victory. D. R. T.

Northfield, January, 1846.

Col. CHARLES H. JOYCE,

The present Member of Congress from the First District of Vermont, came to Northfield in 1850, and commenced reading law at the Center, with John L. Buck, Esq.; read with him one year; then with F. V. Randall, Esq., at Northfield Falls, one year; then with F. F. Merrill, Esq., at Montpelier, one year, when he was admitted to the bar of Washington County, at the September term, 1852.

In 1853 Mr. Joyce entered into co-partnership in the practice of law at Northfield with C. N. Carpenter, Esq., and subsequently with F. V. Randall. In 1853 he was appointed State Librarian. In December, 1855, he opened a law office in Northfield. In 1856 he was elected State's Attorney, and was re-elected to the same office in 1857.

As soon as Mr. Joyce was elected State's Attorney his practice of law began to increase, so that in March, 1861, he had a fine docket, and did a good business. When President Lincoln issued his call for seventy-five thousand men he was at Montpelier, attending a term of court. He immediately returned home to Northfield, and with the aid of some others raised a company of men which they tried to get into the 1st Regiment, commanded by General Phelps. He did not succeed in this, but Governor

Truly Yours
Charles H. Joyce

Fairbanks tendered him the position of Major in the 2d Regiment, which he accepted, and on the 7th of June, 1862, he was promoted to the rank of Lieutenant-Colonel of his regiment. He remained in the service until January, 1863, when he was compelled to resign his position, on account of poor health.

After returning from the army, and partially recovering his health, he located in Rutland, resuming the practice of law in company with C. C. Dewey, Esq. The partnership continued until the spring of 1866, when it was dissolved, and he carried on business on his own account. In 1869 he was elected to the House of Representatives from Rutland—and again in 1870 71. The last two years he was elected Speaker, conducting that responsible office in a manner that pleased all parties, and made him decidedly popular.

Mr. Joyce took a lively interest in the campaign of 1868, stumping his own State, and making many speeches both in New York and New Hampshire. In 1874 he was nominated as the successor of Hon. C. W. Willard, and elected to the Forty-fourth Congress, and re-elected in 1876 and also 1878. In the campaign of 1876 he made speeches in Vermont, New Hampshire, New York, Connecticut and Indiana, for Hayes and Wheeler.

Mr. Joyce, during the time he has been Congress, has made the following speeches: In the Forty fourth Congress he made the first eulogy on the death of Henry Wilson; speech on the currency, in favor of honest money; a speech on the presentation of the statue of Ethan Allen, to be placed in Memorial Hall in the National Capital; next a speech on the Centennial Exposition to be held at Philadelphia in 1876; also a speech in confirmation of certain land claims in the Territory of New Mexico; also a speech on the counting of the electoral vote of Louisiana; also one on counting the electoral vote of Vermont.

In the Forty-fifth Congress Mr. Joyce made the following speeches: One on the contested election case of Patterson against Belford, from Colorado; one in the contested election case of Acklen against Darrell, of Louisiana; a speech on the "Resumption act, and the remonetization of silver"; a speech on a proposed amendment to the Constitution of the United States, relating to the election of President and Vice-President, and also relating to the Civil Service of the government; a speech on the Mexican Pension Bill, against restoring to the pension-roll the names of those which had been stricken off for participation in the rebellion; also a speech on the Tariff.

In addition to all this, the Colonel has delivered speeches and orations on nearly every Fourth of July and on nearly every "Decoration Day" since the war. His magnetic power and forcible way of stating his arguments makes him popular with the masses, and we predict for him a still more brilliant future! We give an extract from his late speech in Congress on the Tariff, the peroration of which is truly eloquent:

In addition to this, we have cut down the forests, and opened up the prairies; we have lightened the burdens of the toiling, struggling millions, and filled the world with our inventions. We have built school-houses in every valley and upon every hill-side; we have erected churches in every village; we have touched the banks of creek and river with the magic wand of our mighty progress, and behold villages and cities have at once sprung up, filled with a brave, intelligent and industrious people, and echoing the rattle of machinery and the hum of honest industry. Amid the fiery flames of civil war we have cemented anew the bond of our Federal Union with untold treasures and the blood of a million brave men; we have broken down the red Moloch of war between nations and erected upon its ruins the throne of justice and the golden scepter of peaceful arbitration; we have tunneled the Ocean with wires, annihilated space and time, and filled the world with wonder and knowledge; we have ascended on high, plucked the lightning from the clouds, chained it to the chariot wheels of our progress, and made it the servant of genius and science; we have dived into the bowels of the earth, unlocked the secrets of nature, and compelled them to minister to our comfort, our knowledge, our progress; we have crystalized the great principles of liberty, justice and equality, and burned them into the organic law of the Republic; we possess the only free government in the world, and enjoy more real happiness than any other nation on earth. Such is the history of our country under the benignant influence of a protective tariff.

We stand to-day "upon the dividing line between the centuries, looking back through one hundred years, with all their grand achievements, and forward to the illimitable future, with all its magnificent possibilities."

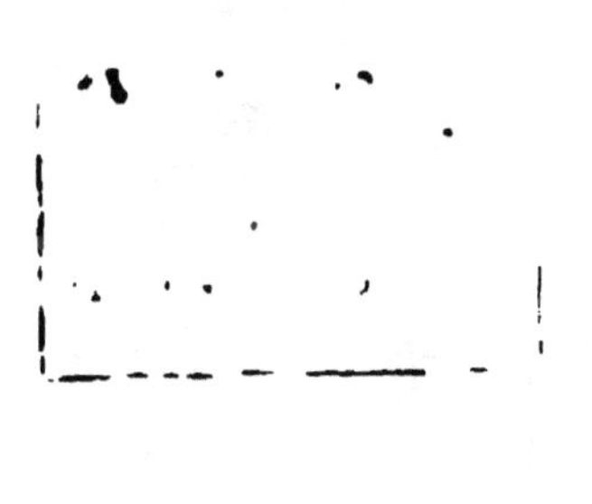

Yours Truly
John Gregory

Mr. Joyce married Rowena M. Randall, and they had three children:

Inez R., b 1854; Grace R., b 1864; Charlie R., b 1868.

Rev. JOHN GREGORY

Was born in Norwalk, Conn., November 18, 1810. He went to New York State when quite young, and served an apprenticeship of seven years at fancy painting, in the city of Albany. When 21 years of age he commenced studying for the ministry in the Universalist denomination. He was ordained in Salisbury, Herkimer county, N. Y., where he made his first settlement, in 1832. After two years labor in this town he removed to Burlington, Vt., where he preached one year; from there he went to Woburn, Mass., and preached two years, and after a year's labor in Vermont, went to Charleston, S. C., where he edited the "Southern Evangelist," and supplied the pulpit of the Universalist church in that city one year. From Charleston, the climate not agreeing with him, he returned to Vermont, and preached in Montpelier, Berlin, Williamstown and Northfield one year, when he received a call to settle in Quincy, Mass., where he remained three years.

In 1842 Mr. Gregory was elected Representative to the General Court from Quincy, and from there went to Fall River, Mass., where he preached two years, and then came back to Vermont, and preached three years in Williston.

In 1850 he came to Northfield and settled on a farm on the West Hill, thinking with St. Paul it was no disgrace for a minister to labor with his hands, and engaged in stock raising. For 25 years he was connected with the Vermont State Agricultural Society; claims to have been one of the originators of that society, was Director of it during that time, and President of it two years, and some years had as great a variety of choice animals at the Fair as any other man. He was prominent in the raising of Morgan horses, French Merino sheep, Hereford, Devon, Ayrshire and Shorthorn Durham cattle, paying $400 for one French Merino sheep that was raised in the vicinity of Paris, all of which were brought to Northfield to improve the stock of farmers. He assisted in establishing the very successful "Dog River Valley" Association, and served as President of it three years, having during that time Fairs that were not excelled by any in the State.

For the last quarter of a century he has preached as opportunity presented in the "region round about" Northfield. In 1850 he was elected Representative to the Legislature from Northfield, and also the following year. In 1856 he was elected Senator from Washington county, and re-elected in 1857. He received the appointment of Assistant Assessor in the Revenue Department under Abraham Lincoln; was re-appointed by Andrew Johnson, and continued in the service ten and one-half years.

Mr. Gregory desires to put on record his fidelity to the two great *reforms* that have agitated the country during the last forty years, "*Human Freedom*" and "*Temperance*." November 8th, 1844, the following vote was passed and published in the Boston "Trumpet": "UNIVERSALISTS ON SLAVERY. At the recent annual meeting of the Old Colony Association at New Bedford, Mass., the following resolution, offered by the Rev. John Gregory, of Fall River, was adopted:

Resolved, That as Slavery has been voted by this body to be "in everlasting hostility to the true spirit of Jesus Christ," we here pledge ourselves to discountenance this evil in all possible ways and forms; and will agitate the question in our several societies, and endeavor to diffuse abroad an honest moral sentiment on the subject.

While in the Senate Mr. Gregory delivered a speech on "Suffering Kansas," that was instrumental in a vote being passed directing the Governor to appropriate $20-000 for the relief of the people in Kansas, should he as-

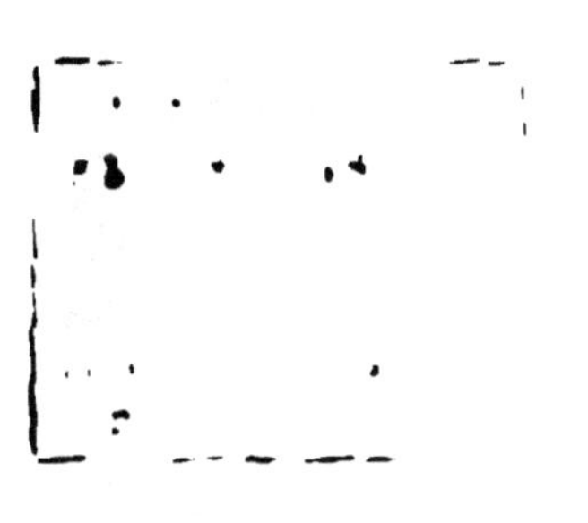

As Ever

O. D. Edgerton

certain they were in a suffering condition. He has delivered a large number of addresses in Massachusetts and Vermont on those reforms, and *always without compensation.*

Mr. Gregory resides in Northfield (Depot Village), on Main street, in the only brick house in that part of the town, it being the *third* house built on that street.

ORVIS DARWIN EDGERTON, Esq.,

Was born in Potsdam, St. Lawrence county, N. Y., August 15, 1821, and was the second of a family of seven children. His father, James Harvey Edgerton, was among the early settlers of that county, from Brookfield, in this State. The minority of Mr. Edgerton was passed very little different from that of many others—going to a district school, working on a farm, and at mechanical business with his father, teaching school, etc., with a few terms at the St. Lawrence academy.

In the spring of 1843 he went to Ohio, which was then considered "far West." For three years from the spring of 1846 he was with F. & T. R. Taylor, building a fork factory at Brasher Falls, N. Y., putting in the machinery, and making and selling forks and hoes.

In January, 1849, he was married to Roxana Sophia Taylor, daughter of the senior member of the firm.

The next spring he purchased a stock of goods, consisting of drugs and medicines, groceries, dry goods, etc., and for several years was engaged in mercantile business with others, and in outside operations of butter, cattle, horses, etc.

In the spring of 1856 he sold out to his partners, and for ten years kept an office as Justice of the Peace, and business naturally connected with the office; held several town offices; was Postmaster during President Fillmore's administration, and was four years Justice of the Sessions, or Assistant Judge for the county.

In August, 1856, Mr. and Mrs. Edgerton's first and only child was born, Charles Darwin Edgerton, who is now in his senior year in Dartmouth College.

In 1866 he sold his entire interest in Brasher, and removed to Northfield, where he formed a partnership with his brother, C. A. Edgerton, in the mercantile business, and has since resided. Mr. Edgerton has a literary taste, possesses scholarly attainments, was an early advocate for free schools, and since his residence has identified himself with all interests having in view the public welfare. He has been village and town Treasurer, two years one of the Selectmen of the town, and four years one the Trustees of the Savings Bank, all of which positions he has filled with credit and fidelity. As a business man he has been successful; is honest and industrious, caring for others as for himself, and by example and precept studying to improve the morals of the community. He is a respected member of the Congregational church, and, while he is not bigoted in his religious views, consistently adheres to his profession of faith, and ornaments it by a well ordered and consistent Christian character.

CHARLES A. EDGERTON, Esq.,

Was born in Potsdam, St. Lawrence County, N. Y., July 21, 1825. He is a son of James H. Edgerton, who was born in Meredith, Conn., September 27, 1796, and emigrated to Brookfield, Vt., when he was ten years old. Mr. Edgerton came to Northfield in the Spring of 1847, and worked at the mechanical business several years. In 1855 the Union Store Division, No. 678, was organized, and he was appointed agent, and managed it until it closed in 1857. In the Spring of 1858 he commenced

Yours truly
C. A. Edgerton

mercantile business in Union Block, with S. H. King, the style of the firm being Edgerton & King, doing a good business in a general way until the summer of 1860, when they dissolved, Mr. King taking a store in the new block east of the Universalist Church, and Mr. Edgerton kept the store in Union Block until 1866, when he formed a partnership with his brother, O. D. Edgerton, who moved to Northfield from Brasher Falls, N. Y., the firm being known as Edgerton Brothers, who continue to do business at the present time.

Mr. Edgerton was elected Town Clerk in the Spring of 1865, and continued to hold the office till 1875, when he declined to serve longer, on account of his large business. He was for several years Treasurer of the Vermont Manufacturing Company, and in December, 1871, was appointed Superintendent, and continued to discharge the duties of Treasurer and Superintendent till the company's shops were burned, December 14, 1876. He has been a Director of the Northfield National Bank since January 13, 1874, and Vice President since January 9, 1877. He has been a Director in the Graded and High School since its present organization, in 1873, and is a reliable, worthy man.

Mr. Edgerton married Harriet A. Newcomb, daughter of Charles and Fanny Newcomb, of Waitsfield, March 7, 1852, and they had two children:

Charles A., Jr., b 1856; Cora E., b 1857. Both born in Northfield.

HALSEY R. BROWN

Was born in Burke, Vt., in 1834. He remained at home until he was twenty-one years of age, teaching school winters from the age of fifteen, when he went to Beloit, Wis., and went into a hotel as clerk, where he stayed one year, and then returned to Burke, where he was engaged in merchandise eleven years. He then turned his attention to farming two seasons, during which time he was elected Representative for the years 1866-7, and, as a compliment to him, he received all the votes cast save one. He was also chosen to fill a number of offices in town.

Mr. Brown came to Northfield in 1868, and formed a copartnership with Rufus Young, Esq., and was with him three years in the Paine Block, in the grocery and dry goods business, after which he went into company with Andrew Denny, Esq.: who are now carrying on an extensive business of store keeping, tannery, milling, and are in the lumber trade, and they may be said to be one of our most prosperous firms in Northfield. Mr. Brown became connected with the Methodist Church in this town in 1869, has been one of its stewards eight years, and since the demise of Joseph Gould, Esq., has been Superintendent of the Sunday school. Before leaving Burke, he was without exception selected to conduct funerals, and is employed frequently in the same business in Northfield.

Mr. Brown married Zilpha Smith, of Burke, in 1856, who was born in 1835, and they have had three children :

Nancy Elva, b 1860, and died November 29, 1863; Flora S., b 1862: Mabel Anna, b 1866. All born in Burke.

RICHARD MARTYN

Came to Northfield from Williamstown, in 1813, and worked for Judge Paine in his factory some five years. He married Polly Gilman, of Williamstown, and had four children:

Lester, b 1809: Mary, b 1810; Eveline S., b 1818; Michael R., b 1820.

LESTER MARTYN

Is now living at the Depot village, and retains his recollection of the early history of Northfield to a good degree. He taught school when a young man, was of industrious habits, and well liked as a citizen and neighbor. He remembers hearing the report of the big guns at Plattsburgh, on the eleventh of September, 1814. News came that volunteers were wanted, as the British were out in great force, threatening to lay waste the country, and a number of men from Northfield, like Cincinnatus of old, left their business at home and hastened to Burlington, where they were to cross the Lake, but before they arrived information was received that a battle had occurred, and had gone in favor of the Americans, and they returned to their homes rejoicing.

Mr. Martyn married Mrs. Mary Flint, of Williamstown, and they had one child: Emma O., b 1846.

James R. Martyn was an adopted son of Lester, and gave his life for his country. He was born in Williamstown in 1840, enlisted in 1861 in Company J., fifth Vermont Volunteers, and was mortally wounded in the battle of the Wilderness. He came home to Northfield, lived near seven months, and died in 1864.

JOHN H. BLODGETT

Married Lucinda Royce, and worked for Judge Paine in his factory until it was burnt, a period of five years. They had two children, as follows:

Orlando F., b 1832; Cordelia E., b 1838.

Mrs. Blodgett died in 1877.

Deacon NATHANIEL JONES

Was from Claremont, N. H., and built the two-story house on Water street now owned by John Willey. He was a prominent Justice of the Peace, and a man of good abilities. He had seven children:

Roys, b 1810; George, b 1812: Elisha, b 1815; Henry, b 1817; Cynthia, b 1820; Nathaniel, b 1824; Orena, 1827.

JAMES W. JOHNSON, Esq.,

Was from Cornish, N. H., and settled on the farm now owned by French Dole, 1827. He married Lydia Haven, and had five children, all born in Northfield:

William M., b 1828; Louisa E., b 1830; Elisha S., b 1832; James N., b 1833; Caroline L., b 1842.

JAMES N. JOHNSON, Esq.,

Was born in Northfield, September 4, 1833. A light-complexioned, girlish-looking boy, he developed scholarly tastes when quite young, and a fondness for politics and public speaking. His advantages for an education were limited to a few terms of district school in winter, and about a year at Northfield Academy, in 1851–52. He taught school with good success for a few years, studied law with F. V. Randall, at Northfield, and was admitted to the bar of Washington county in the fall of 1854. In 1856 he went to Chicago, Ill., and into the law and collection business with Cornell & Jameson, where he re-

Yours truly
Jas. N. Johnson

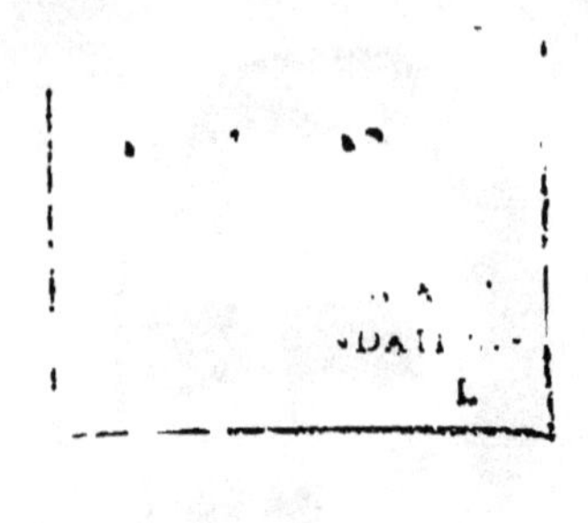

P. D. Bradford.

mained, with the exception of a few months, till the fall of 1860. He then returned to Northfield, on account of failing health and that of his wife, and has since resided here, practicing his profession with a good degree of success. As a practicing lawyer Mr. Johnson has the reputation of being well read and a forcible pleader, characteristics that make a man successful, and in time will lay the foundation for great influence before the courts.

In 1858 Mr. Johnson married Eloisa, eldest daughter of Luther Burnham, Esq., and they have one son:

Luther, b 1869.

Hon. PHILANDER D. BRADFORD

Was born in Randolph, Vt., April 11, 1811.

His father, John Bradford, was a native of Kingston, Mass., born December 26, 1765. In early life he removed to Alstead, N. H., where he married Miss Lucy Brooks, January 9, 1799. Subsequently he came to Randolph, where he resided until his death, which occurred November 19, 1814. Four years later, upon the death of Mrs. Lucy Brooks Bradford, Philander D., the youngest of six children, went to Alstead, N. H., to live with relatives of his mother. At the age of fifteen he returned to Randolph, and entered the Orange County Grammar School, where he received his education preparatory to the study of the medical profession. At twenty he commenced the study of medicine with his brother, Dr. Austin Bradford, and at the age of twenty-three graduated the Woodstock Medical School, then a branch of Middlebury College, and in 1850 received the degree of A. from the University of Vermont. He practiced his profession in Braintree, Randolph and Bethel, until 1854, when he removed to Northfield, where he has since resided, having proved a very skillful practitioner.

In 1853 and 1854 Dr. Bradford was elected to the State

Legislature by the Free-soil party of Randolph, and was a prominent member of that party when in its infancy. And when others forsook their free principles and joined those who elected Robinson and Kidder, Governor and Lieutenant-Governor, Dr. Bradford remained true to his convictions, and labored zealously for the cause of human freedom. In 1854 he was elected Commissioner of Insane, and re-elected in 1855. In 1857 he was elected Professor of Physiology and Pathology in Castleton Medical College, and continued with the same until its suspension in 1862. In December, 1862, he was commissioned by Governor Holbrook, Surgeon of the 5th Regiment Vermont Volunteers, but was compelled by ill-health to resign his commission in March following. In 1862 and 1863 he was elected a member of the Vermont Senate, also President of the Vermont Medical Society in 1863. In 1860 he was elected Grand Master of the Grand Lodge, I. O. O. F., of Vermont, and in 1861 was at the head of the Grand Division of the Sons of Temperance of Vermont. He was elected Trustee, also Professor of Physiology, in Norwich University in 1867; and was a member of the Right Worthy Grand Lodge of the United States, Independent Order of Odd Fellows, in 1875-76. He early threw the weight of his influence into the scale of temperance—is a worthy "Good Templar," and foremost in everything that promises blessings on our race. He is a capital presiding officer, and by his good humor and happy adaptation to circumstances makes even a crowded assembly orderly and attentive. Dr. Bradford was married to Miss Susan H. Edson, daughter of John Edson, M. D., of Randolph, in 1835, by whom he had one daughter, Miss Ellen E., now the wife of George W. Soper, Esq., of Northfield, who is a very efficient Postal Agent in the service of our government, over the Central Vermont railroad.

Mrs. Susan H. Bradford died October 15, 1865, and in May, 1867, the Doctor married Mrs. O. W. Moore, widow of the late Hiram Moore, Esq., of Sharon, Vt.

Truly Yours
J. H. Orcutt

To Dr. Bradford are we indebted for bringing forward and pressing to a vote the publication of this history of Northfield.

Hon. JASPER H. ORCUTT,

The seventh son of Samuel M. and Mary B. Orcutt, was born in Roxbury, Vt., February 25, 1821. He lived at home, with the exception of two seasons, when he taught school, until 1846, when he went to Manchester, N. H., and remained there six months, when he returned to Vermont, and moved to Northfield, March 19, 1849. From 1848 to 1858 he was most of the time in the employ of the Vermont Central railroad, engaged in the construction of buildings and other mechanical work.

In 1858 Mr. Orcutt entered into the mercantile business with Freeman Page, in the building now occupied by Chauncey Denny and Stebbins & Richmond. In 1864 he bought out Mr. Page, and carried on the business for about one year alone; then went into trade with A. E. Denny, and continued with him four years, during which time they built the store where Denny & Brown are in business. In 1870 he sold out his interest with Mr. Denny and bought an interest in the Paine Factory property, and from that time has been engaged in manufacturing slate, lumber and strawboard, is now interested in the Adams Slate and Tile company, and is Clerk and Superintendent of the same.

Mr. Orcutt was village Trustee several years, Deputy Sheriff six years, Constable and Collector of taxes two years, High Sheriff of Washington county two years, Representative in the Legislature two years, county Senator three years, has held offices of Selectman, town Auditor, Justice of the Peace, Enrolling officer during the Rebellion, is one of the Trustees of the Northfield Savings

Bank, appointed Postmaster under President Grant's administration in 1869, re-appointed in 1874, and appointed by President Hayes in 1877.

Mr. Orcutt is one of the most prominent business men in Northfield, and engages in the reforms that come up for consideration with a commendable zeal. He is the friend of education, and has contributed of his means to the support of all good institutions that promise to elevate and bless our race. He was chairman of the building committee of the Graded School Academy. He is a fine specimen of a self-made man, and makes business lively around him.

Mr. Orcutt married Mary Jones Ainsworth. May 27, 1848.

Mrs. Orcutt died August, 1871.

Mr. Orcutt married Mary Elizabeth Williams, April 17, 1873, and they had two children:

Carlos Jasper, b 1874; Mary Charlotte, b 1875.

The mother of Mr. Orcutt is living in Northfield, with her sons, and is the oldest inhabitant, being in her 96th year.

Hon. HEMAN CARPENTER

Was born in Middlesex, Vt., July 10, 1811, was fitted for College at the Washington County Grammar School at Montpelier, Vt., studied law with the Hon. William Upham, and was admitted to the bar at the November Term of the Washington County Court, A. D. 1836, and came to the "Factory Village," Northfield, the first of December following, and commenced the practice of law. He was admitted to the Supreme Court of Vermont two years after, and to the District Court of the United States in 1842.

Mr. Carpenter was State Librarian four years, from 1832 till 1837, and removed the State Library from the

Respectfully,

H. Carpenter.

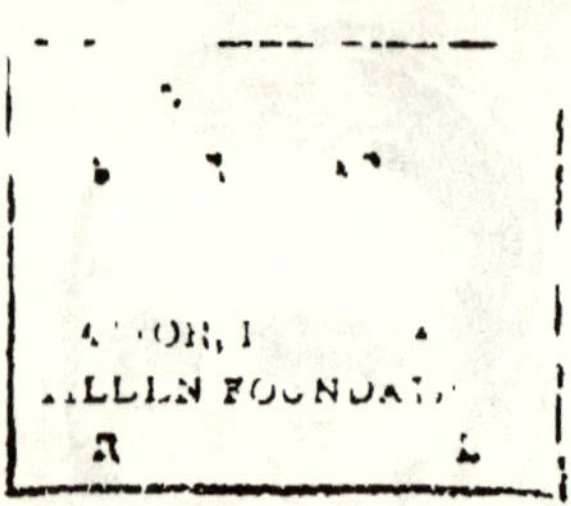

"old State House" to the new, numbering and cataloguing all the books therein. He held the office of Superintendent of Schools, and devoted from ten to twenty-five days in examining teachers and visiting schools each year, giving his services to the town, and held other minor offices. He was elected to the Legislature for the years 1847-48, and introduced the "Homestead Bill" for the first time, and pursued that measure until it was enacted into a law. He was made Judge of Probate for the years 1849-50, appointed on Governor Eaton's staff in 1847, with the rank of Colonel, was Selectman for the years 1852-53, was appointed Receiver of the South Royalton Bank in 1857, was State's Attorney for Washington County for the years 1865-66, was Trustee for the United States deposit money for the years 1851-52, and was elected to the State Senate for the years 1870 72.

Mr. Carpenter procured the charter for the "Northfield Academy" in 1846, raised the subscription for building it, paying more than any other man except Governor Paine, was Secretary, Treasurer and Trustee of the institution, was one of the Executive Committee from its organization down to April 18, 1868, when he resigned all of said offices, having completed the education of his children at said school.

Mr. Carpenter was a prominent man in the denomination to which he belonged, was President of Goddard Seminary from 1868 to 1876, when, by reason of poor health, he resigned that office, having paid liberally and generously for its establishment, and on resigning the office of President he received from the Trustees a very complimentary resolution.

Mr. Carpenter was foremost in establishing the graded school in Northfield, gave liberally towards Norwich University, and educated his children in a manner creditable to himself and advantageous to them, so that he ranks among the first as an educator in this community, and in 1860 the University of Vermont conferred upon him the Honorary Degree of Master of Arts.

Mr. Carpenter became a voter in 1832, and identified himself with the "National Republican" party, and has remained faithful to its principles ever since. He has attended forty-five State Conventions of his party, forty of which he attended in thirty-nine successive years. He was a delegate from Vermont to the Republican Convention at Philadelphia in 1856, which nominated John C. Fremont. He attended the two National Conventions which nominated General Grant. He was the Marshal for Washington County at the "Log Cabin" Convention at Burlington in 1840, and President of the State Convention at Rutland in 1870 which nominated General P. T. Washburn for Governor. Being a positive man, he was never in doubt as to his support of men or measures.

Mr. Carpenter taught school in the Center Village in the winters of 1833 and 1834, being hired by Mr. Dryer by reason of ability to govern a turbulent school that had been very disorderly for a few winters, and the scholars were brought into good subjection and discipline by him, so that for many years the school felt the influence of his teaching and government.

Mr. Carpenter has been a firm believer in the final restoration of all human intelligence to holiness and happiness in God's own good time. He has been a delegate, Vice President and President of the Universalist State Convention for many years, and in 1877 it passed the following resolution :

Resolved, That the thanks of this Convention be tendered to the Hon. Heman Carpenter for the able and efficient manner in which he has executed the office of President of this Convention for several years past, and for the urbanity and good spirit he has manifested toward all the members of that Convention.

When Mr. Carpenter came to Northfield, there were but fourteen houses in the "Factory Village." He has borne his part manfully in all the positions he has filled by the suffrages of his fellow citizens : and in his profession has enjoyed the respect of his associates and the members of the Court, and the community where he has lived so long, bearing always his share of the burdens.

JOHN MOSELEY.

Mr. Carpenter married Harriet S. Gilchrist, of Chelsea, Vt., February 14 1838, who was born in Goffstown, N H., December 24, 1816. They had four children:

George Nathaniel, b 1840; Caroline Sophronia, b 1841; Jason Heman, b 1843; Abigail Fidelia, b 1849.

Mrs. Carpenter died June 21, 1865.

Mr. Carpenter married his present wife, Mrs. Betsey S. Edgerton, October 16, 1866, at Burlington, Vt. She was born in Berlin, July 20, 1822, and was the widow of John H. Edgerton, and daughter of Solomon Nye.

JOHN MOSELEY

Was born in Montpelier, Vt., June 1st, 1801. He came from Bethel to Northfield, and settled on the farm now owned by Deacon William Winch, in 1833. He moved to the Center Village in the spring of 1849. He was a farmer by occupation, and one of that kind of men who are well liked, not having an enemy in the world.

Mr. Moseley married Lydia C. Knight, of Oakham, Mass., Sept. 19th, 1812, and they had the following children:

Harriet A., b 1833; Lois Ellen, b 1837; John Luther, b 1840; Ada Annette, b 1852. All born in Northfield.

Mrs. Moseley died in 1853.

Mr. Moseley married for his second wife Sarah Child, of Charlestown, Mass., in 1854, and for his third wife Mrs. Eliza Dean, of Pittsfield, Vt., in 1857. Mr. Moseley died Feb. 19th, 1871.

JAMES CARY BARREL THAYER

Was born in Braintree, Vt., August 10, 1824. He was the fourth son of Dr. Samuel W. Thayer and Ruth Packard, his wife. When about five years of age his father moved to Thetford, Vt., and commenced the practice of medicine. Here Mr. Thayer spent his boyhood days, and got a common school education. When he had nearly reached his sixteenth year (April, 1840,) he went to Woodstock, and entered into the employment of Dunbar & Munger, as clerk. He remained with them but a short time, when he came to Northfield, and became clerk for George B. Pierce.

With the exception of a few months in 1848, Mr. Thayer has been a resident of this town since he first entered it, in 1840. Those few months were spent in the employ of Erastus Hubbard, of Montpelier. When he returned to Northfield he become clerk for H. H. Camp, and soon entered into partnership with him, and continued one year, when they dissolved, and Mr. Thayer went into the clothing business, which he has since followed without change.

When the Northfield Savings Bank commenced operations, in 1869, Mr. Thayer was elected Treasurer, and has been continued in the office ever since. During the last four or five years, as the operations of the Bank have become more extended, by far the greater portion of his time and attention has been bestowed upon its unblemished reputation and financial soundness, which testifies to his honorable character and business ability. In fact this Bank owes its great prosperity to the steady, persistent efforts of Mr. Thayer, and well may he feel proud of its high standing in our community.

Mr. Thayer has never been a very ardent politician, although he has always manifested considerable interest

J. C. B. Thayer

LEANDER FOSTER.

in politics. He was a staunch Whig as far back as 1840. He went to Burlington with Governor Paine's Log Cabin, and was a Republican until the campaign of 1872, when he switched off the track and went for Greeley, since which time he may be considered rather shaky, though bearing to the Republican side. He often says that he never run for office but once, and then he was beaten by an overwhelming majority.

In religion Mr. Thayer is an ardent Episcopalian, and honors his profession by a well ordered life.

January 7, 1850, he married Martha Jane Pratt, daughter of John A. Pratt, of Woodstock. They had four children:

John A., b 1850; Ellen M., b 1855; Alice C., b 1856; Harry B., b 1858. All born in Northfield.

Mrs. Thayer died May 12, 1869.

Mr. Thayer married for his second wife Mrs. Lucretia M. Gregory, widow of the Hon. John B. Hutchinson, of West Randolph, June 27, 1871.

LEANDER FOSTER, Esq.,

Was born in Keene, N. H., February 25, 1803. He passed the year of 1818 with the Enfield Shakers, for whom he ever entertained the highest regard, and came to Berlin in 1819. In January, 1825, he married Abigail Drew, of Strafford, who became the mother of two children: Josephine Maria, born in 1832, now Mrs. Hayes, and Sarah Minnette, born in 1834, now Mrs. Bennett.

In 1837 Mr. Foster removed to Northfield Falls, where he lived till 1853, when, having purchased the planing mill property at the Depot village, he removed to his late residence on Union Street, and there resided until Mrs. Foster died, August 12, 1872, and until his death, which occurred while visiting some friends in Royalton, December 5, 1873.

Mr. Foster added to the growth of our village by building and other business pursuits.

In the first subscription for raising money for building the Academy, in 1847, Mr. Foster's name appears as contributing twenty-five dollars toward the project, and he was appointed one of the Trustees, and took an active interest in its growth and prosperity.

In politics he was originally a Whig, but ever after its organization he voted with the Republican party. He was ever a firm friend of the temperance movement, a leading member of several organizations devoted to its interests, always doing what he could, as Gerritt Smith remarked concerning his own efforts, "to keep the people sober."

On being asked by an intimate friend what his religious views were, he replied, good naturedly, "I have no very definite creed of my own, but one thing has occurred to me in reference to that of other people. It has seemed to me that when the great day comes, and the attempt is made to separate the sheep from the goats, it will require a good many pens, for I should think there would be a good many who wouldn't be quite mean enough to damn, nor quite good enough to save."

Mr. Foster as a man was prized the highest where known the best, a man of stern integrity, his word being everywhere considered as good as his bond; in his family he was a kind and faithful husband, an indulgent and affectionate father, as a neighbor upright and obliging, as a friend genial, confiding, and true.

REUBEN M. McINTOSH

Was born in Bethel, Vt., in 1823. He was brought up a farmer, but when he became of age he learned the Daguerrean business, and practiced in and about his native town. In 1853 he moved to Northfield, and worked in

Rev. Mr. McIntosh.

the first Daguerrean saloon that was ever established in this place. From that time to within a few years he worked at making pictures in the Daguerrean, Ambrotype, and Photograph process with marked success. Latterly he has made a specialty of taking stereoscopic views, and among the noted places that he has visited for that purpose we would mention the Ausable Chasm, Mount Mansfield, and Black River Falls in Cavendish, taking a great variety of scenes that commend themselves to all the lovers of this wonderful art. His pictures are of a high order, and possess the charm of being clear and distinct, reminding one of those taken in Switzerland, where the air is ambient, and the sky clear and beautiful.

Mr. McIntosh married Perces L. Wheeler, of Pittsford, Vt., and they had two children:

Abbie L., b 1860; Hattie B., b 1871.

ROSWELL CARPENTER

Came to Northfield when the country was very new, not far from 1787, and had many *trials* and *hardships* in those early days. He was from Charlestown, N. H., and married Louisa Larkins, of Rockingham, Vt. They had five children:

Elvira, b 1798; Louisa, b 1800; Roswell, b 1805; Ursula, b 1815. All born in Northfield.

Mr. Carpenter, it is said, was a *good dancer*. So Colonel George Cobleigh and Adolphus Denny, Esq., loved to "trip the light fantastic toe in the mazy dance," and took great delight in attending parties, driving away dull care. Probably there was no scientific *violining* in those days, but a good deal of *fiddling*, and they could sing:

Hoot away despair,
Never yield to sorrow,
The blackest day will wear
A sunny face to-morrow.

ROSWELL CARPENTER, JR.,

Married for his first wife Prudence Royce, and for his second Philura Kinsman, who was born in 1813. Their children were:

Caroline, b 1835; Mary Sophia, b 1837; Marshall, b 1839; Darwin, b 1841; George C., b 1843; Ellen, b 1846; Julia A., b 1849; Frank N., b 1857. All but the last three born in Northfield.

JAMES PIKE

Was born in Mount Vernon, N. H., in 1789. He moved to Barre in 1815, and from there to Northfield in 1835. He and his son built the house and barn where Heman Carpenter now resides, in 1833, and worked at the blacksmith business at the north end of the bridge, beyond the hotel in Depot village. He was a hard working, industrious man.

Mr. Pike married Rhoda Jones, of Mount Vernon, N. H., and they had seven children:

James Pike, Jr., Rhoda, Mary, Sophia, Martha, William, and Charles.

Mr. Pike died in 1877.

Dr. MATTHEW McCLEARN

Was born in 1829, in the Province of Nova Scotia, town of Wellington, and came to Boston in 1857. He commenced the practice of medicine in Northfield in 1855, and continues to this day his residence on State Avenue, but his principal office is at 206 Tremont Street, Boston.

The Dr. is an Analytical Physician, and successor to J. Clawson Kelley and J. Wesley Kelley, with whom he graduated in 1855. He came to Northfield for his health, and finding the mountain air healing to his lungs, so that his weight was increased twelve pounds in three months,

M. McClean.

PHOTO ENG. CO. N.Y.

he concluded, by the solicitation of friends, to take up his residence here. The Dr. is one of the charter members of the Vermont State Eclectic Medical Society, was its Treasurer twenty-seven years, its President one year, and is also a member of the National Eclectic Medical Association.

Dr. McClearn married Ruth S. Ripley, of Plimpton, Mass., in 1856, and they had four children:

Charles W., b 1858; Mary F., b 1861; Helen A., b 1863; Olive S., b 1869.

FRANK PLUMLEY, Esq.,

Was born in Eden, Lamoille County, Vt., December 17, 1844. He was reared on a farm, and had no other advantages than farming boys generally have: had what education District schools and Academies afforded. For several years he taught school in Districts and Academies, both east and west, with good success. In 1866 he entered the law office of Powers & Gleed, at Morrisville. In 1867 he entered the Law Department of Michigan University, and also pursued a selected course of the Literary Department of said University.

In 1869 Mr. Plumley was admitted to practice law at the May Term of the Lamoille County Court, and in June following came to Northfield, and entered the law office of Hon. Heman Carpenter. In January, 1870, the firm of Carpenter & Plumley was formed, which was dissolved by limitation in 1876. Since then he has been in practice by himself until December last, when he became the senior partner of the firm of Plumley & Johnson.

Mr. Plumley is a young man of good promise, is an off-hand speaker, and whether before the courts or in the large assembly pleading the cause of right and temperance, he is forcible and interesting. But few young men are his equals in debate, and his way of stating his subjects are peculiarly his own. He goes at his work with an ardor that is refreshing, and strikes out right and left, disregarding in any particular manner the rules of elocution and rhetoric. Still he has influence before the courts, and is a growing man.

In 1871 Mr. Plumley married Lamina L. Fletcher, of Eden, Vt., then Preceptress of Northfield Graded School, and they have now two children, Charles Albert and Theodora May.

DAVID PARTRIDGE

Was born in Guilford, Vt., February 14, 1792. He married Sophia Moore, who was born in Putney, Vt., July 6, 1792. They were married July 2, 1812, and came to Northfield in 1828. Mr. Partridge was a shoemaker by trade, and built his shop in what was then the Factory village, in 1835, and his house near the railroad track, now owned by George Randall, in two or three years after. They had the following children:

Sophia Eleuthen, b 1813; David Anson, b 1815; Sylvia Elvira, b 1816; Clarissa Lurena, b 1819; Susannah Corintha, b 1821; Mercy Janette, b 1822; Philitta Philena, b 1825; Mary Zaphica, b 1828; Eliza Submit, b 1845; David Anson, b 1847; Jasper Clark, b 1850. All born in Putney, save the first.

Mr. Partridge married for his second wife Eliza G. Smith.

Mr. Partridge died in 1866, aged 73 years.

Mrs. Partridge died in 1842, aged 50 years.

SIMON EGGLESTON

Was born in Middletown, N. Y., July 23, 1793. He moved into Northfield from Danville in 1822. He married Sally F. C. Dole, of Danville, who was born July 19, 1804. They had six children:

Zernah, b 1823; Laura, b 1826; Charles, b 1827; Judith, b 1829; Mary E., b 1831; Emily E., b 1835. All born in Northfield.

Mr. Eggleston worked for Judge Paine in his factory twenty-one years, and for the Governor sixteen years, making thirty-seven years in all. He was a boss spinner much of the time, but during his last years he was a sorter of wool, and a more faithful man to his employers perhaps never lived.

ALMON WEATHERBEE

Moved from Moretown to Northfield in 1845. He married Betsey Brigham, from Acworth, N. H., December 30, 1833, and had three children:

Mary M., b 1836; Angeline A., b 1839; Lydia M., b 1844.

Mr. Weatherbee worked for Governor Paine in his factory before it was *burnt*, and afterwards in his grist mill. He bought the land and built the house where his family now lives of Governor Paine, the *first land* used for that purpose on that hill. He was killed on the eleventh of December, 1867, in the terrible railroad disaster at Harlow Bridge. He was a quiet, good, and industrious citizen, and his sad death was deeply lamented by his fellow townsmen.

JOSIAH B. and CLARISSA STRONG

Had two children: Isaiah L., b 1812; Nancy, b 1814. Both born in Northfield.

WALTER BOWMAN

Was born in Springfield, N. H., in 1798, and his wife, Abigail C. Calef, was born in East Plainfield, N. H., in 1803. They came to Northfield in 1835, and first lived on a farm east of Depot village, then known as "Joshua Lane's" farm. Their children were:

Sarah P., b 1826; Alonzo, b 1828; Lucy Ann, b 1831; Druzilla C., b 1833; Sylvester, b 1836; Abbie M., b 1841.

SILAS SHELDON

Was born in Dorset, Vt., January 25, 1794, and came to Northfield in 1816. He married Sarah Richardson, January 25, 1818, for his first wife, and Anna Richardson for his second, December 30, 1821, twin daughters of Stanton and Anna Richardson. The first wife died December 1, 1818, leaving twins—Silas Harmon and Samuel Richardson—when *five* days old. The second wife had:

Chauncey D., b 1825; Martin B., b 1831; Chauncey G., b 1835. All born in Northfield.

ERASTUS DEWEY

Came from Tunbridge, Vt., in 1842, and settled on the West Hill. He was born in Hanover, N. H., in 1808. He married Eunice Moxley, of Tunbridge, for his first wife, and had three children:

Mary J., b 1836; Laura A., b 1839; Emily M., b 1840.

Mr. Dewey married for his second wife Mrs. Elizabeth Poor, March 6, 1878.

CALVIN CADY.

Deacon CALVIN CADY

Was born in Pomfret, Conn., in 1786. He located in Berlin, Vt., and worked for Porter Perrin for twelve dollars a month in haying, he agreeing to do all the pitching both ways, and he and the hands would work until eight o'clock at night, and then milk the cows, eat bread and milk, and go to bed. He lived at one time at Lanesville, and attended a saw mill. It is said one night he was standing on the carriage of the mill that ran out over the end of the mill, and, falling partially asleep, he stepped off and fell some twenty feet, where it was all rocks below; but there happened to be a slab which stood one end against the mill and the other on the rock, and he struck that on his back, and bounded off on to his feet, and was not hurt.

In 1828 Mr. Cady removed to Northfield, and there, by working hard and keeping Judge Paine's boarding house, he succeeded in getting into comfortable circumstances. He took a great interest in his children as long as he lived, and made it a point to get them together as often as he could, especially on Thanksgivings.

Mr. Cady was one of the Deacons of the Congregational Church in Northfield, and had the esteem and confidence of his church and townsmen. He married Betsey Merrill, May 18, 1809, who was born in 1785. They had nine children:

Almira, b 1810; Abigail, b 1812; Calvin, Jr., b 1813; George, b 1815; Eliza, b 1816; Laura, b 1818; Luther, b 1821; Lyman, b 1823; Mary A., b 1826. All born in Berlin.

Mr. Cady died in 1867; Mrs. Cady died in 1858.

Rev. WILLIAM S. HAZEN

Was born in Hartford, Vt., August 18, 1836. His parents were the Rev. Austin and Lucia (Washburn) Hazen. When one year and a half old the family moved to Berlin, and here William's boyhood days were passed. He fitted for College at Washington County Grammar School, at Montpelier, and Royalton Academy; was graduated at the University of Vermont in 1858, taught in Thetford Academy two years, one year as Principal, and was graduated at Andover Theological Seminary in 1863.

Mr. Hazen commenced preaching in Northfield for the Congregational Church and Society in September, 1863. In October, 1864, he was ordained their pastor, and has continued as such to the present day. As a preacher he is decidedly popular with his people, and when during the past year Manchester tried to induce him to remove there, the affection of his Church was so strong in his favor that he remained with them. He is also respected by other societies, and preaches many "occasional sermons" outside of his parish.

In secular matters Mr. Hazen has taken a lively interest. He was Town Superintendent two years, was Graded School Director seven years, five of the time President of the Board; for eleven years he has been a Director of the Vermont Domestic Missionary Society, and holds other offices of less importance. His allegiance to the reforms that are elevating the people, his readiness to speak with "no uncertain sound" in favor of temperance and human freedom, show him to be a true man, and worthy of the high station he now occupies by his own unaided strength and perseverance. But few, if any, young men in Vermont have been as highly esteemed, and remained as long as he has in his first settlement.

Mr. Hazen married Martha A., daughter of William S.

Wm. B. Hazen.

and Martha A. Merrill, of Providence, R. I., September 20, 1866. They had two children:

William M., b 1873; Martha A., b 1874.

Mrs. Hazen died in 1874.

NOAH CARLTON

Was born in Barre, Vt., in 1801. He worked in the old factory a number of years for Governor Paine; was his boss weaver. He was a strong temperance man, and showed his fidelity to its principles by his every-day life. He married Betsey Nichols, of Barre, April 9, 1829, and they had two children:

Warren, b 1830; Elizabeth, b 1834. Both born in Northfield.

Mrs. Carlton died in 1842.

Mr. Carlton married for his second wife Eliza Cady, daughter of Deacon Cady, September 15, 1843, and they had two children:

Joseph, b 1846; Noah W., b 1849. Both born in Barre.

Mr. Carlton died in 1869.

WILLIAM ALLEN

Is now living on the old homestead, and is one of the oldest inhabitants born in Northfield. He married Esther E. Libby in 1835, who was born in Strafford, Vt., in 1814, and they had eight children:

Harrison P., b 1836; Nancy, b 1838; John L., b 1840; Edna, b 1842; Emily E., b 1844; Mariettea C., b 1848; John W., b 1849; Amanda L., b 1852. All born in Northfield.

ITHAMAR ALLEN, Jr.,

Was born in 1778, and came to Northfield from Gill, Mass., with his father, at a very early day, and they settled near the north corner. Ithamar, Jr., married Nancy, daughter of Aquillo Jones, and moved to the Falls village, and located on the farm now owned by his son William, where his father lived and died. At that time the whole valley north of our Depot village was all a wilderness, and Aquillo bought this farm, together with the Burnham place, for almost a song, and gave the former land to his daughter Nancy. They had the following children:

Elijah, b 1803; William, b 1805; Charles, b 1808; Sally, b 1811: Chloe, b 1812; Amanda, b 1814; Edna, b 1816; Warren, b 1819; Adaline, b 1825. All born in Northfield.

Mr. Allen died in 1861, aged 83 years.

ABIJAH HOWE, Esq.,

Was born in Middleton, Mass., in 1788. He married Martha Bridgman, who was born in Hanover, N. H., in 1789. He came to Northfield in 1834, and settled on the farm formerly owned by Eleazer and Dyer Loomis, east of the Depot village, where Walter Bowman now lives. Mr. Howe was educated at Dartmouth College, and completed his college course in 1810. They had seven children:

Theoda, b 1813; Asa, b 1816; Martha A., b 1819; Sophia D., b 1821; Hannah S., b 1823; Isaac B., b 1827; Miraett, b 1830.

Mr. Howe died in 1872, aged 83 years.

Mrs. Howe died in 1865, aged 76 years.

ABIJAH HOWE.

J. B. Howe

ISAAC B. HOWE, Esq.,

Came to Northfield, with his father, when about seven years old, where his boyhood days were passed on a farm. At the age of eighteen he commenced teaching school, but abandoned this in two years for civil engineering on the Vermont Central railroad. He was employed on that road and the Vermont and Canada about twelve years, having charge of the civil engineering and road repairs.

Mr. Howe is now a resident of Clinton, Iowa, and has acquired a name for skill, energy, and honesty of purpose that the best might feel proud of. He may be called a self-made man. Beginning life with only the good moral precepts and example of his father and mother for capital, and with no influential friends or influence to assist him, he was forced by necessity to be self reliant. * * * * * Endowed with genuine Yankee inventive genius, he at various times made valuable improvements now in general use on railways, although but few of them have been secured by letters patent. He also introduced several novel and useful improvements in the construction of the City Water Works while President of the Clinton Water Works Company.

In the spring of 1861 Mr. Howe went to Iowa, to take the position of Chief Engineer and Assistant Superintendent of the railway from Clinton to Council Bluffs. The next season he was appointed Superintendent of the three hundred and fifty miles of railroad across the State, from Clinton to the Missouri River at Omaha, which position he held until the summer of 1872, when ill-health obliged him to withdraw from active railway service.

For several years Mr. Howe has been extensively engaged in operating stone and marble quarries in Iowa and Illinois, and with his Banking business keeps him in constant employment. He is one of those kind of men who prefer to "wear rather than rust out."

Mr. Howe was elected Representative of Northfield during the years 1857-58, and received other marks of appreciation during his citizenship among us. That his love for the town of his adoption is as strong as ever, we publish an extract from a letter he sent us in reference to this history, which shows his loyalty to "good old Northfield," as he calls her:

"I think it the duty of all towns to preserve their early history. Northfield has no time to lose before doing this, for time is obliterating the landmarks, and the names of the first settlers are rapidly being transferred from business signs to cemetery marbles!

"What can now be authenticated as facts may soon be classed as unreliable traditions. Secure them while the evidence remains.

"This proposed history will not only be of great interest to us who are now here, but it will have a greater interest to those who are to succeed us. My little "Hawkeye" son delights in hearing me tell of what I did when I was a little boy, and I derive pleasure from the recital, as the dream-like memories of the olden time almost bring back the perfume of the wild flowers and fruits I gathered when a little bare-footed boy, forty years ago! Your history of Northfield would be to me what *my* early history is to my children.

It is almost seventeen years since I left Vermont, but my interest in the State and in good old Northfield remains as strong as ever, and it gratifies me to know that I am not yet quite forgotten, but may still claim citizenship in your hearts, if not in your elections."

MONUMENT OF ISAAC B. HOWE, ESQ.

The family monument is what is termed a "canopy," or portico monument, and is of the Doric order of architecture. The base is seven feet, and the height twelve feet from the surface of the ground to the top of the pediments.

Between the square pillars which support the entablature is an octagonal urn nearly six feet high, on the polished panels of which are cut the inscriptions for the several members of the family. The burial place of each person is designated by the name carved on the face of the curbing enclosing the lots. All of the material is of Vermont granite.

The urn was executed by J. S. Collins, of Barre, all other work by Jones Trow, of Berlin, original designs by Isaac B. Howe, stereoscopic view taken by R. M. McIntosh, engraved by Photo Engraving Company, New York.

ABIJAH HOWE
I.B.HOWE

JUSTUS BURNHAM, Esq.,

Came from Hardwick, Mass., to Northfield quite early, and worked at the carpenter trade, building, in connection with John Green, the first house on Main street, where Mrs. William Nichols resides. He had ten children:

Betsey, b 1790; Anna, b 1792; Hannah, b 1796; Assa, b 1798; Isabella, b 1800; Arbijah, b 1802; Rhoda, b 1804; David, b 1805; Lydia, b 1806; Violet, b 1809.

LUTHER S. BURNHAM, Esq.,

Was born in Brookfield, Vt., February 18, 1797. He came from Orange, Vt., to Northfield in 1840. He settled on the well-known farm at the Falls village, known as the "Burnham farm." and was a prominent man, industrious and well liked by his townsmen, respected and beloved. He married Lucy Nelson, who was born in Orange, June 15, 1798, and they had six children:

James H., b 1821; Harris, b 1823; David N., b 1825; Elosia, b 1827; Lucy Ann, b 1831; Helen M., b 1841. All but one born in Orange.

Rev. JAMES HARVEY BURNHAM

At an early age evinced a remarkable aptitude for study, and especially a strong desire for Theology. As he grew up he expressed a wish to enter the ministry of the Universalist denomination. His whole soul seemed bent in that direction. His parents did not much favor the idea, but at last consented, and Harvey spent several years in self-education. He attended school at Newbury Seminary a few terms, and taught school with very good success, and after awhile commenced preaching to the societies in Irasburgh, Barton, and Coventry, Vt. His sermons, like his uniform manly bearing, were noted for clearness, candor, and marked conscientiousness, rather than for lively imagination, love of sensation, or effort for present popularity.

Not far from this time he married Ann P. Alexander, of Northfield, and settled as a Universalist minister in Troy, Vt. Here his health failed him, and he returned to this town, and engaged in trade at the Center village. His wife's health began to decline, and she died of consumption in 1848. After her death Mr. Burnham resumed preaching again, and settled in Sacrappa, Me. In 1850 he married for his second wife Mary A. Barnard, of Southbridge, Mass., became a partner of the Rev. Eli Ballou, at Montpelier, in the book business and in the publishing of the "Christian Repository," where he remained till the time of his death, which occurred September 11, 1853. He died in the full prime of his manhood, of consumption, a loss indeed to his relatives and the denomination of which he was a worthy member.

MARVIN SIMONS, Esq.,

Was born in Williamstown, June 28, 1804. His wife, Olive Fisk, was also born in Williamstown, December 11, 1806, and they were married in Northfield by Rev. L. Holbach, March 24, 1829. Mr. Simons moved to Northfield in March, 1829, and died December 19, 1870, aged sixty-six years.

Mr. Simons was one of the oldest and best citizens of

MARVIN SIMONS.

the town. He had resided here forty years, and shared largely in the honors and responsibilities of its local affairs. He was Justice of the Peace for nineteen years, and a Selectman twelve years in succession, and during his life held many positions involving large pecuniary trusts. He never sought preferment, but his fellow citizens, without distinction of party, relying on his good judgment and unquestioned integrity, kept him in service as an officer of the town or a manager of individual interests.

He was a devoted husband and father, and a kind and generous neighbor, and his death was deeply lamented by the whole community. His children were:

Marcellus M., b 1831; Lycurges L., b 1833; Darrion A., b 1837; Cordelia J., b 1839; Olive M., b 1841; Alma A., b 1845; Willie G., b 1848. All born in Northfield.

FREEDOM EDSON

Married Phebe Shipman, April 28, 1808. At one time he owned all the land in the Falls village, and lived on the farm known as the "Burnham farm." He had ten children:

Daniel, b 1809; Martin T., b 1810; Betsey, b 1812; Eli, b 1812; Sally, b 1816; Sophia, b 1817; Marietta, b 1819; Sylvester, b 1820; Cynthia M., b 1823; Caroline E., b 1825.

WILLIAM R. TUCKER

Was born in Norwich, Vt., in 1812. He came to Northfield in 1835. He and his father bought out Joshua Lane, who owned the farm where Hopson Barker now resides, in the 250 acres of land that they purchased of Judge Paine. At one time they owned 650 acres of land in

Northfield. Mr. Tucker married Theode, daughter of Abijah Howe, and they had two children:

Malvera C., b 1838; Jane, b 1843.

In 1847 Mr. Tucker married Armena Simons for his second wife.

JAMES GOULD, Esq.,

Was born in Amesbury, Mass, July 20, 1803. Of his early childhood we know but little, except that, his parents being in indigent circumstances, the children were obliged to depend mostly upon their own exertions for maintenance and education, as soon as old enough to do so. When about twelve years old James found employment in the family of an honest, noble hearted Quaker family, where the simple "Quaker habits" of his entire life seemed to have been formed.

Mr. Gould married Rebecca Morrill, November 10, 1831, who was born in Salem, Mass., August 1, 1806. They had four children:

Mary E., b 1832; Harriet B., b 1833; Hannah R., b 1836; James P., b 1841.

In or about the year 1835 Mr. Gould came to Northfield, and, in company with Walter Little, established a Potato Starch factory at Falls village, which they successfully operated for a few years, until it was destroyed by fire. He then engaged in woolen manufacturing, a part of the time with Erastus Palmer, extending and enlarging as increasing business and capital warranted, until failing health forced him to withdraw from active business, when he disposed of his entire manufacturing interest to his brother Joseph. After this, for a few years, much of his time was passed with his children in Wisconsin and Iowa, until 1867, when he permanently removed to Wisconsin, and in company with his son engaged in the

JAMES GOULD.

lumber business, and the manufacture of sash, blinds, doors, etc., at Oshkosh.

Under the pressure of active business his health again failed, when he withdrew from the firm, and removed to Janesville, where he died May 18, 1877, of nervous prostration and disease of the heart.

A simple record of the every day life of James Gould would be a higher and more eulogistic tribute to his merit than any a biographer could write.

Cautious, shrewd, and methodical in business, but more anxious to do justice to others than to exact the same in return; foremost in all worthy public enterprises, yet never seeking to make himself conspicuous, and accepting public offices only when forced upon him: modest and diffident, tender-hearted as a child, his highest ambition seemed to be to do good and make others happy.

Generous and sympathetic almost to a fault, and with child-like confidence in the honor and integrity of his fellow men, the objects of his benevolence were always numerous, if not always grateful or entirely worthy.

Never boasting of his good deeds, or unnecessarily referring to them, even in the privacy of his own family, many of them become known to others only through accident, and doubtless many others are yet known only to the recording angel!

Stranger or neighbor, no matter who or where, if only suffering and needing assistance, ever found him ready with comforting words, sympathising heart and a generous hand to give relief.

Never speaking harshly or unkindly to or about any person, he always tried to excuse rather than magnify the faults of others, and, so far as the writer is aware, *he never had an enemy!* Seldom can this much be truthfully said at the close of a long and eventful life of even the best of men! And yet Mr. Gould was frank and free in the expression of his opinion upon any subject, and fearless in performing what he considered to be his duty.

His love for and devotion to his family seemed unlimited, and no sacrifice was too great which would add to the comfort or enjoyment of his wife and children.

Although not a member of any church, he usually attended the services of the Congregational society. Following the example and obeying the precepts of the humble Nazarine, his daily life, rather than his public professions of faith, demonstrated his sincerity, piety and belief in the doctrine of the Christian religion.

His interest in and his attachment for his old friends and associates seemed remarkably strong, and his love for Vermont was like that of a child for a parent. In compliance with his expressed wishes, and the provision made in his will, his form was brought back for burial in our cemetery, and his last long resting place is marked with a shaft of Granite from the green hills of the State he loved so dearly.

JOSEPH GOULD, Esq.,

Was born in Amesbury, Mass., Feb. 6, 1809. He married Hannah W. Green, who was born in Pittsfield, N. H., June 16, 1812. They were married in Amesbury, Oct. 11, 1835, and moved to Northfield in March, 1836. Their children were:

Joseph W., b 1836; Hannah C., b 1842.

Mrs. Gould died Feb. 5, 1852.

Mr. Gould married for his second wife Melissa, daughter of Nathaniel Richardson, April 15, 1853. They had one child, named Alice M., born in Northfield, 1854.

Mr. Gould died Jan. 13, 1876.

Joseph Gould was a resident of Northfield about 40 years, residing first at Gouldsville, (the Falls Village, named after him), then at the Center Village, then again at Gouldsville, where he closed his eventful and successfull career. In 1857 he purchased the Woolen Factory at Gouldsville, which was consumed by fire January 31,

JOSEPH GOULD.

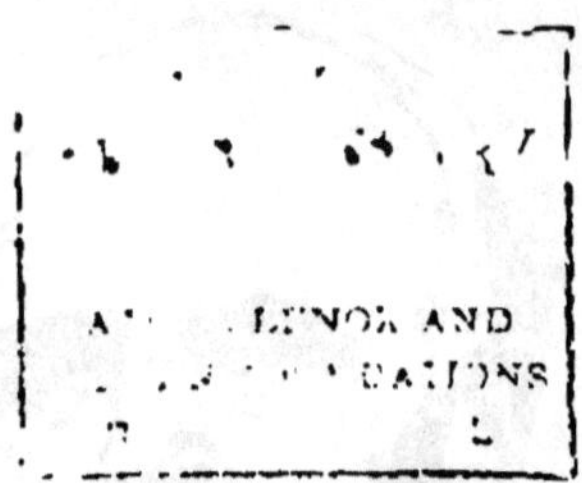

WALTER LITTLE.

1873. On the 23d of June following he commenced to re build on the old site, and in March, 1857, put in operation a first-class mill. For twelve years previous to his death his son Joseph W. had been in partnership with him in the manufacturing business, on whom now rests the whole responsibility of the large concern.

Mr. Gould united with the Methodist Episcopal Church in Northfield, February 1, 1863, and was a prominent and worthy member until his death, and to which he sustained a greater part of the time an official relation. He was a leading member, and to which he gave of his substance liberally. The Pipe Organ, in the Methodist Church at Northfield stands as a monument of his *beneficence.*

WALTER LITTLE, Esq.,

Was born in Haverhill, Mass., in 1797. In 1813 he was drafted as a soldier and stationed at Portsmouth, and after his discharge he worked in the factory at Salisbury, Mass. He came to Vermont in 1820, and worked for Judge Paine in his factory, and remained there three years. In 1823 he went back to Salisbury, and remained there, working at his trade, until 1830, when he returned to Northfield, and brought his carding machinery with him, and set it up at the Falls village. James Gould, with eight horses, moved him from Salisbury, and bought out Joseph Keyes' half interest in the grist, saw and cloth mills which they were running. Mr. Little and Joseph Keyes commenced the first building for a mill in 1824, at the Falls; James Gould going into partnership with Mr. Little in 1831. In 1832 Messrs. Little & Co. built the starch mill. In 1837 they dissolved partnership, Mr. Gould taking the custom mill, and Mr. Little the starch mill. In 1847 Mr. Little went to Barre, remaining two years, when he went to North Montpelier and engaged in woolen manufacturing, acquiring a good property, and dying there in 1859.

Mr. Little married Jerusha, daughter of Samuel Richardson, September 30, 1824, and they had three children:

Hazen A., b 1827; Sarah H., b 1832; Walter S., b 1842.

Mr. Little was a successful business man, and Northfield is indebted to him for starting manufactures at the Falls Village. By his spirit of enterprise and perseverance he gave employment to many laboring men and women, and with his genial good nature he contributed much to the enjoyment of those around him. He liked a good joke and a good story, and knew when to make business pleasant and agreeable.

Mr. Little was a warm-hearted, true and zealous Mason. He was a co-laborer with Joel Winch, Senior, Elijah Smith, Jr., Jesse Averill, and Dr. B. Porter and others, when it cost something to be a Mason. His life was ornamented by an earnest, industrious and well-ordered daily walk, and his death was lamented by all who had enjoyed his confidence. He was, in short, a good man, and a worthy citizen.

DANIEL HAVENS DEWEY

Was the oldest son of Israel Dewey, and was born in Berlin, Vt., in 1801, and came from there to Northfield in 1826. He married Evaline Stow, of Brookfield, Vt., November 14, 1827, who was born in Woodstock, Vt., in 1807. They had five children:

Laura, b 1819; Laura E., b 1832; William H., b 1840; Mary E., b 1841; Lucy P., b 1844.

Mr. Dewey, while in Northfield, worked at the cabinet making business at the Center village, and had the first *horse power*, which attracted much attention. From here he removed to Canton, Ill., but there being no opening for that business he went into the Scale business, and manufactured successfully scales of his own invention.

West Part of Northfield.

A number of inhabitants settled at an early day on what is called the "West Hill," on land belonging to the town of Waitsfield, but in 1822 four tier of lots were by an act of the Legislature annexed to Northfield.

WILLIAM COCHRAN

Made a beginning there in 1798, four years after the town was organized. He came from Hanover, N. H., and located on land now owned by Elliot C. Fish, Esq. He married Polly Graves, and had eight children, among them Stephen, who was the first child born in that part of the town. His children were:

William G., b 1785; Lyman, b 1787; Weltha, b 1790; Stephen, b 1801; Washington, b 1803; Edmund, b 1805; Polly, b 1807; James, b 1810.

STEPHEN COCHRAN, Esq.,

Resides at the Center village, is a tailor by trade, and is a man highly respected. He married for his first wife Nicoletta Graves, and for his second Sabrina Bridges, and from the last marriage had six children:

George B., b 1842; William G., b 1844; Edmund W., b 1847; Mary E., b 1848; Emogene, b 1851; James N., b 1853. All born in Northfield.

Deacon DANIEL PARKER

Came from Jaffrey, N. H., in 1799, a year later than Mr. Cochran, and located on the West Hill, on the farm now the property of Henry Jones. He was a religious man, and took an interest in spiritual affairs. He married Jennia Cochran, of Petersboro, N. H., and had five children. Among these children that lived to grow up was one who became a writer of considerable notoriety, named Daniel.

After a thorough preparation, Daniel, Jr. entered the University of Vermont, and graduated with high honors, it being said he was the best scholar that attended college. He then returned to West Northfield, and turned his attention to farming with his father. From there he went to Northfield Falls, and afterward, being ordained as a minister of the Congregational order, he removed to Craftsbury, Vt., where he preached some three or four years, and then came back to South Northfield, where he lived on the Kathan farm. From there he went to Brookfield, and published a book called "The Constitutional Instructor," designed for colleges and common schools. It was while canvassing for this work that he visited Glover, Vt., and while at the house of Rev. Levi H. Stone died.

Mr. Parker was quite a poet, and among his writings we find some sterling pieces showing the ability of the man, sent us by his son from Texas, who is a physician of considerable note. We select a short piece that has produced much mirth, entitled

THE DYE TUB.

A PARODY.

How bright is the picture of childish emotion,
  When memory paints what I used to enjoy—
The frolic and fun, and each curious notion,
  And all the droll capers I cut when a boy!

The wide spreading fire-place, and pile of wood by it,
  The pot hook, and candle-stick, hung on a wire,
The porridge pot, kettle, and frying pan nigh it,
  And e'en the old dye-tub that stood by the fire;
That old wooden dye-tub, the wooden hooped dye-tub,
  The blue begrimmed dye-tub that stood by the fire.

That blue begrimmed vessel I love to distraction,
  For often, when weary with toil or with strife,
I found it the source of the most satisfaction
  I ever enjoyed in the whole of my life.
How directly I steered to it with legs that were aching,
  And quick to the lid I began to aspire,
And gave to my shins a delectable baking,
  Perched on the old dye-tub that stood by the fire,
  The old wooden dye-tub, etc.

How proud on the smoothly worn lid was my station,
  As gaily my juvenile stories I told!
Not the throne of a monarch could tempt emigration,
  Tho' covered with velvet and spangled with gold!
And now far removed from the seat of Jack Horner,
  Recollection awakens a quenchless desire,
As backward it points to the old chimney corner,
  And sighs for the dye-tub that stands by the fire,
  That old wooden dye-tub, etc.

NORTHFIELD, 1838.

NORTHFIELD HILLS.

BY REV. DANIEL PARKER.

When with a heart with care oppressed,
Wandering I seek a place of rest,
    In which to find repose,
Where I in friendship's bowers reclined,
    Enjoying rural bliss, may find
Oblivion for my woes.
From fancy's visionary flight,
O'er distant woods and rills,
Pleased with the well-known scenes I light
On Northfield's rural hills.

Imagination loves to climb,
And backward sail the streams of time
To scenes of by-past years;
While I in mind those scenes renew,
And all my early youth review,
How lovely it appears!
Care was a stranger in my breast,
And every restless strife;
No bliss I knew but I possessed,
And happy was my life.

Ambition had not touched my heart,
Nor disappointments bitter smart
Had spoiled my childish joy;
I saw the stately towering trees,
I felt the soft and fragrant breeze,
A wild romantic boy;
I heard the robins early song,
I heard the warbling rills,—
With vast delight I roamed along
O'er Northfield's rural hills.

And e'en when cheerless winter frowned,
And snows white vail o'erspread the ground,
And when I heard afar
O'er the high hills and through the vales,
With clangrous roar the sweeping gales,
Arrayed in brumal war,
Safe in the dear paternal cot,
And by the fireside warm,
I in contentment with my lot,
Enjoyed the howling storms.

And when the sun began to rise,
And mount along the northern skies,
Dissolving winter's chain,
The softened snow, by night congealed,
Made solid footing o'er the field,
High hills and lowly plains,
Then swelled my breast with boundless glee,
And light in heart and heels
I rioted in liberty,
On Northfield's rural hills.

Then onward led in fairy dance,
The vernal genii advance,
To clothe the earth in green;

Mild zephyr's whispered in the trees,
Young flowers perfumed the fluttering breeze,
And decked the woodland's scene
Then I beheld with raptured eye
(Not thinking they could fail)
The beauty of the brightening sky,
And glory of the vale.

But now, alas, those joys are fled,
And like the leaf of autumn dead,
While I at a distance roam,
And no dear friends my presence greet,
But only stranger forms I meet,
Far from my much loved home;
Yet, O! may they of whom my mind
The fond idea fills,
Of Heaven the choicest blessings find,
On Northfield's rural hills.

RANDOLPH, 1823.

SAMUEL FISK

Was born in April 13, 1795. He married Keziah, daughter of Thomas Averill, September 7, 1820. The same year he settled on Dog River, on the farm now owned by Stephen Cochran. In March 7, 1831, he moved to the West Hill, on the farm where his son Elliot C. now resides. He was a good substantial farmer, and was well liked. They had four children:

Levina A., b 1821; Eveline M., b 1827; Elliott C., b 1832; Elizabeth A., b 1836. All born in Northfield.

Mr. Fisk died July 21, 1848.

Mrs. Fisk still lives with her son, Elliott C., and had a "surprise" the past year, on her eightieth birthday, the children and grand children and friends being largely represented.

TITUS RICE

Was born in Rockingham, Vt., August 2, 1798. He lives on the old homestead on the West Hill. His father moved into Northfield in 1810, when Titus was twelve years old. He married Louisa Jones, who was born in Charlestown, N. H., May 1, 1801. He has been a hard working, industrious man, and although crippled with rheumatism, he attended our last town meeting, and took quite an interest in town affairs. His children were:

Mary H., b 1827; Eliza A., b 1829; Ellen J., b 1834; Edgar A., b 1836; Betsey S., b 1838; Benjamin, b 1838; Marcus M., b 1840; Franklin L., b 1843; Francis L., b 1843. All born in Northfield.

SILAS RICE, Jr.,

Came on to the West Hill from Acworth, N. H., quite early, and pitched his tent where William Newton now lives. Not long after the father of Silas and Titus came into this part of the town, when Silas, Jr., sold out to Harry Ainsworth, and moved back to New Hampshire.

SAMUEL DUNSMORE

Was from Charlestown, N. H. He settled on the West Hill, a little north of Captain Knapp. He married Anna Powers, and they had nine children:

William, b 1815; Mary Ann, b 1817; Jane, b 1820; Samuel, b 1824; Hiram, b 1826; Sarah Ann, b 1829; Fanny, b 1831; Willard, b 1834; Edwin, b 1835. All born in Northfield.

HENRY KNAPP.

Captain HENRY KNAPP

Was born in Claremont, N. H., November, 1787. He came to Northfield in 1808, being then twenty-one years old, and, in connection with Harry Jones and Silas Rice, Jr., young men of about his age, commenced clearing land round about what is now known as the four corners on the West Hill, where Mr. Knapp finally settled, and by industry and perseverance made for himself a good home. These young men built a shanty, using hemlock boughs for their bedding, and getting their bread baked at Deacon Parker's, spent a few summers in clearing land, while in the fall of the year, when old winter gave signs of his approach, they would like birds migrate South as far as Claremont, their native town, to return when spring should again put in her appearance to gladden the earth. It was a happy day for Mr. Knapp when he succeeded in clearing an acre of land, and getting it well sown with rye, because it was his, and the result of his labors.

At that day there being no stores in Northfield, and all through this valley was a wilderness, they were obliged to go to Waitsfield to get their potatoes and other commodities, if peradventure a horse could be procured; if not, then these hardy pioneers had to go without, or foot it, and make pack horses of themselves.

Years after, when Mr. Knapp had prospered and field crops had accumulated so that it required more room to preserve them, he conceived the idea of building a *large barn,* and so after getting the timber together and preparing it by the old rule, the question was how to raise it, for the inhabitants were few and greatly scattered; but at the end of three days hard labor from all that could be induced to lend a helping hand from the towns of Northfield, Waitsfield, and Roxbury, the barn was raised, and stands to-day upon the old foundation, a monument of the enterprise and perseverance of this worthy old settler.

Mr. Knapp, living on the main road from West Roxbury to what is called the "north neighborhood" in Northfield, frequently had the new comers who were locating farms call on him, and to his credit he always had his "latch string out," and assisted to his ability these people, who became substantial citizens of our growing and prosperous town.

Mr. Knapp married Lucy, the daughter of William Keyes, in 1818, who was born in Northfield in 1798. She is now living in the Depot village, with her children, enjoying very good health for one of her age. They had four children:

Alvira Keyes, b 1819; Sophia, b 1820; George H., b 1827; Abel K., b 1832. All born in Northfield.

Mr. Knapp died September 7, 1859.

George Henry died of bad treatment in Libby Prison, Richmond, Va., in 1864, he having enlisted in the Union army from Minnesota, and was taken prisoner by the rebels.

PAUL RICHMOND

Was from Barnard, Vt. He settled on the West Hill in 1834. He married Fanny Udall, of Hartford, Vt., October 24, 1795. They had twelve children, all born in Barnard, Vt.

Mercy, b 1796; Paul C., b 1798; Fanny W., b 1800; Sophia, b 1801; Samuel U., b 1803; Almira, b 1805; Armenia, b 1807; Dolly, b 1808; Ebenezer, b 1811; Julia, b 1812; Alexander B., b 1816; Susy M., 1818.

Mr. Richmond died in 1846.

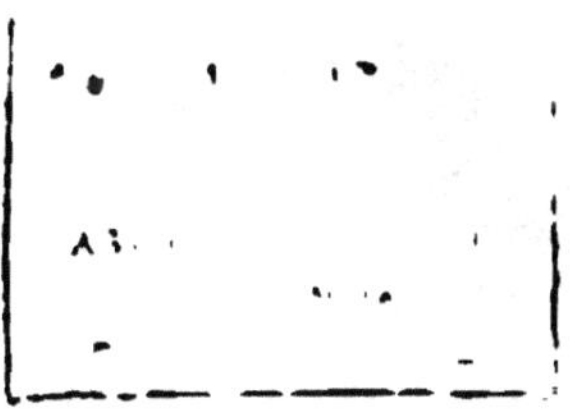

SAMUEL U. RICHMOND.

SAMUEL U. RICHMOND, Esq.,

Was born in 1803, and came to Northfield with his father in 1823. He was a prominent man in the Methodist church, in which he was a devout member, and did a great deal for his religious cause, was a leader in the Democratic party, and remained unto the end a firm advocate of his professed principles. Mr. Richmond was a benevolent man, kind to all classes of people, and no man was ever turned away hungry from his door. He was prompt, industrious and well regulated, and his word was as good as his bond. When struggling to sustain those dependent upon him, and his father had a large family with poor health, he would frequently work for what would now be called very small wages, and one winter he worked all through it with his oxen for seventy-five cents a day.

Mr. Richmond moved to the Depot Village in 1867, and died very suddenly April 24, 1873.

He married Sophia, daughter of Capt. Henry Knapp, and had five children, all born in Northfield:

Samuel A., b 1843; Henry C., b 1845; Carlos S., b 1847; Lucy S., b 1851; George H., b 1856.

DAVID HADLEY

Was born in Sandwich, N. H., in 1778. His wife, Hannah Hadley, was born in Ware, N. H., in 1780. They were married in 1803, and came to Northfield in 1804.

Mr. Hadley died in 1811, aged 33 years.

Mrs. Hadley married for her second husband John Brown, in 1816, and lived to the good old age of 91 years and nine months.

David W. Hadley says of his parents, "they suffered all the privations of a wilderness country, having to go to Brookfield for their stores, and for the doctor, guided by *marked trees*. I have heard mother say she has rode over a road where the underbrush cut served for highways, five miles to a neighbor's on horseback on a man's saddle, carrying a child in her arms." They had three children:

Lydia, b 1805; David W., b 1808; Emeline, b 1810.

JOHN PLASTRIDGE

Was born in Cornish, N. H., June 16, 1780. He was married to Mary A. Blodgett, in 1808, and moved to Waterbury, Vt., March 30, 1810. They had the following children:

Chester, b 1809; Mary A., b 1812; Jason, b 1815, who was killed instantly by falling from a building in Detroit, Mich., at the age of thirty years; Caroline, b 1817.

Mrs. Plastridge died in Waterbury, in 1817.

John Plastridge married for his second wife Martha, daughter of Amos Robinson, in 1818, who was born in 1791. They have the following children:

Charles, b 1819, died December 14, 1855. He was killed by the cars in Concord, N. H. He left a wife and seven children:

Jeannett, b 1820; Amos, b 1822; John, b 1824; Asa, b 1827; Amasa, b 1829; Martha, b 1831; George, b 1832; Julia, b 1833, died September 21, 1870; Martin, b 1836. All born in Waterbury.

Mr. Plastridge moved to Northfield in 1838. He died December, 1850, aged seventy years.

Mrs. Plastridge died of cancer in 1877, aged eighty-six years.

DAVID W. HADLEY.

Hon. DAVID W. HADLEY

Resides on the same place where his father located. At the age of sixteen, on the death of his father, he took charge of the farm and family, and managed it in a successful manner. He represented Northfield in the Legislature during the years 1843, '45, '56 and '70. He was elected Selectman for the years 1836, '40, '41, '42, '43, '44, '45, '46, '55, '56, '58, '59, '63, '64, '70, '71, '72, '74 and '75. He was made Assistant Judge for Washington county in 1850 and '51, and has held minor offices in town. He is deservedly a popular man, and has a fine record. Judge Hadley has the honor of owning the lot that, by actual calculation by General Jackman, is not only the center of Northfield, but the center of Vermont. It is lot 9, range 5, and originally belonged to Peres Gallup.

Judge Hadley married Louisa Brown, of Williston, Vt., and they have eight children:

Helen M., b 1837; Louisa J., b 1839; Jane E., b 1841; Lucina A., b 1843; Caroline A., b 1845; Mary E., b 1847; George W., b 1849; Flora L., b 1851.

IRA HOLTON

Was born in Dummerston, Vt., in 1796, and came to Northfield from Putney, in 1825. He married Mary Houghton, of Putney, who was born in 1798, and had the following children, all but one living in Northfield:

Ira Alanson, b 1824; Mary Elizabeth, b 1827; Harriet Newell, b 1830; Mary Louisa, b 1831; William Henry, b 1840.

N. W. GILBERT, D. D. S.

Norman W. Gilbert, a native of Morristown, Vt., was born in 1830, married to Sarah Atwell, of Waterbury, in 1854, studied Dentistry in Lowell, Mass., and in 1858 settled in Northfield. In the spring of '67 they removed to Montpelier, and six years later to Boston, where in January, 1877, Mrs. Gilbert, a very estimable woman, closed her earthly career, and was, by her own request, brought to Northfield for burial. Shortly after that event the Doctor, having sold his interest in his Boston office to his partner, returned to Northfield, and is still among us. Dr. Gilbert is a graduate of the Boston Dental College, stands high in his profession in that city as well as in his native State: and is also distinguished for his literary ability. We select from his poetical writings the following tribute to John G. Whittier, on the occasion of his seventieth birthday, which was so largely celebrated in December, 1877, by Boston publishers and contemporary poets:

Dear Quaker bard, did I possess the power
  Of minstrelsy which has so long been thine,
My grateful muse would spend a happy hour
  In weaving garlands which she might entwine
  Around thy brow—or lay upon the shrine
Of gifted poesy. Could strong desire
  To emulate thy pen inspire mine,
My harp would fain salute thy magic lyre.

My honored friend, thy locks are growing gray,
  And thou, in years at least, art growing old.
As we commemorate thy natal day,
  Thy life approaches to the sunset gold;
  Its guileless story will at length be told,
And fondly cherished in the hearts of men,
  And thy familiar name must be enrolled
In realms beyond the reach of mortal ken;

A life of beauty drawing to a close—
  Though yet apparently but in its prime—
More beauteous still while looking towards repose,
  As I have seen in mellow autumn time,
  The loveliest days of our sweet northern clime—
The peaceful days, superlatively fair—
  Of nature's music heard the sweetest chime,
Though borne in silence on the balmy air.

And while thou sittest in the genial sun
  Of life's fair afternoon, I trust and pray
Its fast approaching evening may be one
  Whose last bright, long and fondly lingering ray
  May reach so nearly to the opening day
Of that celestial home beyond the strand,
  Thy soul may nearly shun the darkening way,
Which all must pass to reach the heavenly land

And when at last the mystic veil is rent,
  That loosely hangs and separates between
The then and now, and angel bands are sent
  To guide thy feet beneath the silvery sheen
  Of heaven's brightness, joyous and serene,
In God's own kingdom, may we hope that then
  The poet's magic wand will still be seen,
And thy celestial harp be tuned again.

GURDON RANDALL

Was born in Scotland, Conn., in 1795, and when 8 years old came to Northfield with his father, who settled in what was called "Connecticut Corner." Mr. Randall was a carpenter and joiner, and followed that vocation as long as he lived. He married Laura S. Warner, of Putney, Vt., who was born in 1803, and they had nine children:

Gurdon Paine, b 1821; Francis Voltaire, b 1824; Laura T., b 1825; Jean J. R., b 1828; Minerva, b 1831; Rouena M., b 1834; Edward H., b 1837; Citizen Frances Voltaire, b 1839; Charles Rush, b 1842.

ALLEN BALCH

Moved into town in 1829, and settled on the West Hill, one-half mile north of the four corners, where John Plastridge lives. He was born in Old Topsfield, Mass., in 1791, and when he came to Vermont he came from Charlestown, N. H.

He started out in the month of March, for his new home, and great were his trials in moving his family and effects, having nothing better than a yoke of oxen attached to a common sled. Getting as far as Springfield, Vt., he found the snow so deep that he made an arrangement with a stage driver to take his family to Northfield; but this he failed to do, for Mr. Balch found them a few days after at Mr. Sampson's, in Roxbury, the driver not being able to go any further with his team. Journeying along up through the west part of the town, they stopped over night at Captain Henry Knapp's. The women on the next morning had to wade through the snow to get to their log house home. Such were the *trials* and *hardships* our fathers and mothers had to experience when Northfield was new.

He married Hepsebuah Dodge, of New Boston, N. H., and had nine children:

William D., b 1813; Maragaret D., b 1815; Sarah, b 1818; Betsey, b 1821; John A., b 1823; Almeda, b 1828; Ezra D., b 1830; Zilpha, b 1832; Angeline, b 1837.

WILLIAM PARKER

Was born in Alstead, N. H., and came to Northfield in 1822. He married Susan Churchill, and they located in what has been called the "Parker neighborhood."

ALLEN BALCH.

ADIN SMITH

Was born in Monkton, Vt., in 1791, and came from Roxbury, Vt., to Northfield, and settled on the West Hill in 1835. He married Lydia Waterman, who was born in Brookfield, Vt., in 1792, and had nine children, all but one born in Roxbury:

Alvin F., b 1815; Elvira E., b 1817; John W., b 1819; Levi, b 1821; Danforth A., b 1825; Fanny B., b 1827; Gilbert O., b 1830; Mary L., b 1831; Wm. M., b 1834.

"Uncle Adin" and "Aunt Lydia" made the greatest sacrifice of any of our citizens, in consenting that four of their sons, Levi, Danforth, John and Gilbert, might enlist to assist in putting down the Rebellion, all of whom gave their lives to this end, except John, who returned. Levi died at Bell Plains, Va., March 11, 1863, of small-pox. Adin D. was killed at the battle of the Wilderness, May 6, 1864. Gilbert O. died at Washington, D. C., February 2, 1864, with small-pox.

Mr. Smith died October 18, 1873. Mrs. Smith died April 12, 1874.

LEWIS C. HASSAM, Esq.,

Was born in Williamstown, Vt., October 30, 1799. He married Mary Royce, of Williamstown, and they settled in Northfield, on the road leading to Waitsfield, about a mile from the Depot Village, about 1821. They had ten children:

George Paine, b 1820; Lewis, C. Jr., b 1822; Sophia S., b 1823; John M., b 1824; Nelson, b 1825; Laura, b 1827; Jane, b 1830; Sarah, b 1832; Martha, b 1834; Caroline, b 1836.

Mr. Hassam died in Northfield, February 15, 1865.

WILLIAM A. GALLUP, Esq.,

Was born in Hartland, Vt., May 26, 1795. He came to Northfield in 1817, and began the clearing known as the Hosea Kathan farm, boarding with David Denny and Isaiah Shaw. After a time, growing homesick, he went back to his native town. He was quite a military man, and received a commission as Lieutenant of Light Artillery, from Gov. C. P. Van Ness, in 1825.

Mr. Gallup married Betsey Dodge, of Hamilton, Mass., who was born July 4, 1785. In 1828 he came back to Northfield to stay, settling in the north-west part of the town, where his son, Jonathan C. Gallup, until lately resided. They had three children:

J. C., b 1824; Wm. W., b 1827; Roderick O., b 1830.

Mrs. Gallup died March 9, 1859.

Mr. Gallup was a very industrious good citizen. He died April 23, 1868.

J. C. GALLUP, Esq.,

Was born in Hartland, Vt., in 1824, and came to Northfield, with his father. He was very successful as a farmer, and possessed one of the largest tracts of land in Northfield. At the time he sold his West Hill farm it contained 930 acres. He moved from it into the depot village in 1866, and bought the fine residence formerly owned by Perley Belknap, commanding one of the best views of the village, where he now resides.

Mr. Gallup has held several offices in town, and is an industrious citizen. As a Lister he is well

WILLIAM A. GALLUP.

J. C. Gallup.

qualified, and was elected to that office in 1864–5–6, and in 1874–8. He is interested in his town's welfare, and labors for its prosperity; was Director and President of the Chair Manufacturing Co.; is Director in the Northfield National Bank.

Mr. Gallup married Laura A. Braley, who was born in Brookfield in 1833, and they have had three children:

Adaline, b 1854; George, b 1858; Charley, b 1866.

SEWALL DAVIS

Was born in Charlestown, N. H., in 1791. On coming to Northfield they settled in the West part of the town. Their children were:

Howard, b 1817; Louisa, b 1821; William, b 1822; Hannah, b 1825.

A remarkable circumstance occurred in the olden time with Mr. Davis' Bible, at the burning of Charlestown. While all the other books in the book-case were burned, even those that laid on the Bible, the "Good Book" was preserved from destruction, although one cover was somewhat charred.

JONATHAN BRIGGS

Was from Putney, Vt., about 1817. He settled finally, after living a while in the Center village, on the farm on the West Hill where his son Harvey Briggs now resides. He was a Constable in Northfield a few years, and gave the land where the yellow meeting house stood, on condition that it should revert back to his heirs should it not be used for such a purpose, which was done accordingly after its removal. Mr. Briggs married Betsey Clark, and they had four children:

Silas Clark, b 1801; Edmond L., b 1803; Asa S., b 1805; Hiram L., b 1810.

Mr. Briggs married for his second wife Betsey, daughter of Dr. Nathaniel Robinson, and they had seven children:

Lucy, b 1816; Betsey, b 1818; Charles R., b 1821; Esther, b 1823; Martha M., b 1825; Harvey N., b 1828; Caroline N., b 1832.

WILLIAM WALES

Was born in Dorchester, Mass., March 21, 1767. His wife, Mary May, was born in Jamaica Plain, Roxbury, Mass., January 15, 1772. He moved from said place to Weathersfield, Vt., where he lived ten years, and from there to Northfield, and located on the farm where William Gold now lives. They had ten children:

Mary May, b 1795; William, b 1796; Olive May, b 1799; Nancy, b 1801; Lemuel, b 1803; Abigail, b 1805; Benjamin M., b 1808; Abigail, b 1810; Aaron K., b 1813; Catherine, b 1815.

Mr. Wales died at the age of 82 years; Mrs. Wales died at the age of 95 years.

HARRY AINSWORTH

Was from Claremont, N. H., and settled near the four corners on the North Hill, in the Knapp neighborhood, in 1818. He married Fanny Jones, of same place, and they had five children; all living in Northfield.

Fanny Maria, b 1821; Catherine M., b 1822; Mary Jones, b 1824; Sarah R., b 1826; Annette A., b 1834;

Mr. Ainsworth came to Center Village in 1849, and died in 1857; aged sixty-two years.

ISAAC KINSMAN

Was born in Williamstown, May 18, 1768. He married Matilda Knapp, who was born March 17, 1789. He settled on the West Hill, and built the house now owned by Mr. Hill. He was a strong anti-slavery man, and in days that tried men's souls he was not *ashamed* nor *afraid* to declare his sentiments. Every advancement made to overthrow the giant wrong he hailed with joy, and had he lived to have seen slavery abolished it would have given him unspeakable satisfaction. He was married July 9, 1806, and had eight children:

Nelson, b 1808; Philura, b 1813; Bilpha, b 1815; Mary, b 1818; Lucy A., b 1820; Diantha, b 1824; Armea, b 1826; Samantha, b 1827.

All but one born in Northfield.

JOHN LEONARD

Was born in Framingham, Mass., April 8, 1778. He came from Massachusetts to Walden, Vt., from there to Berlin, and then to Northfield, September 9, 1825. He settled on the West Hill, beyond the Four Corners, on the road to Waitsfield. His wife, Eliza Lougee, was born in Gilmanton, N. H., August 1, 1789. They were married in Walden, March 11, 1811. They had the following children:

Chauncey B., b 1812; Eliza Ann, b 1815; Adaline S., b 1818; Oliver G., b 1821; Jonas A., 1822; Fanny N., b 1827; Mary A., b 1829.

Mr. Leonard died in Northfield, August 5, 1860, and Mrs. Leonard died in Berlin, March, 12, 1873; both of them were interred in Elmwood cemetery.

STEPHEN THRESHER

Was born in Connecticut in 1788. He came to Northfield in 1831, and settled on the West Hill, on the farm now owned and occupied by Jonathan Edwards. He had, like many other early settlers, his trials in clearing up and preparing a home, but a brave heart and willing hands made him successful. His third son, then twelve years old, who has gained some notoriety as a school teacher, and rejoices in the cognomen of "Freeman," had his trials too, for it was his lot to follow an ox team on its way into Northfield, driving a cow and a young calf and some other stock, going the last four miles all alone after dark, through a wilderness interspersed with an occasional clearing, with no other road to guide him through a region he was totally unacquainted with but a foot-path.

Mr. Thresher married Sally Smith, of Randolph, Vt., who was born January 11, 1790, and they had ten children:

Lewis B., b 1809; Lyman, b 1811; Mary M., b 1814; Emeline, b 1816; Freeman, b 1819; Betsey, b 1821; Infant, b 1823; Cephas, b 1825; Fidelia, b 1827; Wilbur, b 1830.

Mr. Thresher died in 1857.

Mrs. Thresher died in 1878.

JOSEPH WILLIAMS

Settled early on what has been known as the Ira Williams farm, and had five children:

Phebe, b 1806; George, b 1807; Sally, b 1809; Ira, b 1812; Oliver, b 1814.

All born in Northfield.

Lyman Houghton was born in Putney, Vt., in 1801. He married Anna Wilson, of Putney, who was born in Keene, N. H., 1801. They came to Northfield in 1823.

Mrs. Houghton died in 1848.

Mr. Houghton married for his second wife Eunice, the daughter of John Preston. Mr. Houghton and Anna had the following children, all but one born in Northfield:

Rosannah, b 1823; Oscar S., b 1823; Sarah O., b 1825; Lyman, b 1827; Matilda J., b 1829; Cynthia A., 1831; James W., b 1833; Charles S., b 1837; Adaline B., b 1839; Hannah, b 1842; Almond, b 1844.

Mr. Houghton died in 1867.

Mrs. Eunice Houghton died in 1877.

James Steele was born in Antrim, N. H., in 1793. He married Esther Smith, in East Roxbury, Vt., in 1815, and she was born in Randolph, in 1798. They had six children, all of whom are now living:

Fanny E., b 1818; Sylvanus, b 1820; Marcia, M., b 1825; James E., b 1829; S. Warren, b 1831; Frederick W., b 1838.

Mr. Steele died at the old homestead, April 16, 1869.

Mrs. Steele died December 29, 1875.

James Steele bought a farm of Nathan Morse, Esq., January 26, 1829, for $3,700, only one-half an acre being cleared, and moved on to it about the first of April following. He had to draw his goods on a hand sled about two miles, as there were no roads. His habitation consisted of a small log house, covered with hemlock bark, and no fire-place. He had to build a fire on the ground in the center of the house, and the smoke went through a hole left open in the roof; oiled paper was put up to holes in the side to admit light, and a blanket hung up for a door. They had three children at that time. He came from Brookfield to Northfield.

JOSEPH NEWTON was born in Grantham, N. H., in 1796. He married Rachel Rawson, who was born in Cornish, N. H., in 1799. They moved to Northfield in 1827, and located near the town line on the road to West Roxbury. They had nine children:

Lucinda M., b 1820; William S., b 1822; Calista P., b 1824; Mary Ann, b 1827; Harriet, b 1829; Adeline, b 1831; Francis, b 1833; Frank, b 1836; Francis T., b 1839.

NELL A. WHITTAKER was born in Plainfield, N. H., and when he came to Northfield in 1815 he settled on the Livermore farm, west of the railroad. He married Elvira Carpenter, and they had seven children:

Nancy, b 1816; Ira F., b 1818; Mary, b 1820; Lucy, b 1822; Lydia, b 1824; Benjamin, b 1825; Hannah, b 1827.

HENRY JONES was born in Claremont, N. H., in 1820, and when a lad worked for Harry Ainsworth on the West Hill. He bought the farm formerly owned by Deacon Parker, where he now resides. He married Jane Dunsmore, and had six children:

Elvira, b 1845; Susan, b 1845; Isabella, b 1850; Jenny, b 1853; Henry A., b 1859; Clara E., b 1863. All born in Northfield.

THOMAS COBURN was born in Buckstield, Me., in 1765. He came to Northfield in 1816, and with Isaac Hardin, who came with him from Maine, a young man whom he brought up from a three month's child, they bought a forty-five acre lot where Loran Fuller lives, built a log house and lived in it until they built the framed house in which Mr. Fuller now resides. Mr. Coburn married Rebecca Warren, of Monmouth, Me., who was born in 1774, and had one child:

Washington, born in Northfield in 1817.

Mr. Coburn died in 1842; Mrs. Coburn died in 1839.

Josiah P. Brooks was born in Alstead, N. H., in 1797. He married Betsey Robbins, of Hancock, Vt., who was born in 1799. He came to Northfield in 1840, and settled on the West Hill, beyond Knapp's Corners, on the old county road leading to Waitsfield. He had six children:

Prentice B., b 1825; Thomas S., b 1828; Ellen, b 1830; Martha and Mary, twins, b 1835; Harriet, b 1837. All but one born in Northfield.

James Houghton was born in Putney, Vt., in 1790, and came to Northfield in 1823. He located on the Waitsfield road a mile and a half from Depot village. He married Betsey Parker, and they had eleven children:

Mary E., b 1819; Jason D., b 1821; Harriet N., b 1823; Lucius W., b 1824; Fanny E., b 1827; Cyrenus E., b 1828; Julia M., b 1830; Dan A., b 1832; William S., b 1833; Stella, b 1835; Betsey, b 1838.

James Webster was born in Berlin, Vt., in 1796. He married Susan Edwards, of Roxbury, Vt., who was born in 1814. They lived on the West Hill, and had six children:

Aurora A., b 1833; Byron A., b 1835; Lucius C., b 1837; Eliza D., b 1839; Julia A., b 1841; Susan, b 1842.

Mrs. Webster died in 1842.

Mr. Webster married Lucy Kendall, of Hamilton, N. Y., for his second wife.

Mr. Webster died in 1870.

Loran G. Fuller was born in Braintree, Vt., in 1822, and came to Northfield in 1832, living when a lad with Deacon Parker, on the West Hill. He married Mary Rice in 1847, and had four children:

Emogene, b 1849; Sarah L., b 1852; Annie E., b 1854; Nellie M., b 1858. All born in Northfield.

Deacon CHARLES CLOSSON was born in Thetford, Vt., in 1799, and came to Northfield about 1821, and settled on the farm now owned by John Plastridge on the West Hill. He married Sarah Davis, who was born at West Fairlee, Vt., in 1802, and had three children:

Sarah Ann, b 1828; Infant Son, b 1830; Martha Jane, b 1831; Hannah Eliza, b 1833.

Mrs. Closson died January 12, 1835.

Mr. Closson married for his second wife Marcia Greeley, of Berlin, Vt., in 1835, and had one child:

Lucia P., born in Northfield in 1839.

Mr. Closson married for his third wife Mrs. Harriet Dunham, in 1865. He removed to Worcester in 1848, and died there in 1872.

SETH P. FIELDS was born in 1791, and settled on the mountain, near its height, on the road to Waitsfield, in 1819. He married Sarah Closson, of Thetford, and they had seven children:

Caroline S., b 1817; Simon C., b 1820; Elizabeth, b 1824; Lucy P., b 1828; Sarah W., b 1832; Hannah M., b 1834; David D., b 1836. All but the first one born in Northfield.

Mr. Field married for his second wife Nancy Lane, of Strafford, and they had one child:

Moses, b 1840.

NATHAN ROYCE came to Northfield from Williamstown about 1818, and settled near the Center village. At the time of his death he resided on the Reuben Smith farm, now owned by Calvin Farnsworth. He married Sarah Gault, of New Hampshire, and they had ten children:

Polly, b 1794; Patty, b 1796; Lucinda, b 1799; Lavisa, b 1800; Sophia, b 1802; Luis, b 1804; Harris, b 1806; Prudence, b 1808; Elijah, b 1811; Sarah Ann, b 1812.

Zebedee Briggs came from Pittsfield, Vt., and settled in Northfield in 1825, on some of the land where his son Horace B. now lives. Mr. Briggs was born in Pittsfield in 1799, and his wife, Hannah Stockwell, was born in Williamstown, Vt., in 1800. They were married in 1823, and had nine children:

Charles C., b 1823; Abigail M., b 1825; Daniel S., b 1827; Lydia A., b 1830; Cynthia, b 1831; Sophia, b 1834; Horace B., b 1838; Orrin, b 1840; Arlette, L., b 1842. All but two born in Northfield.

Mr. Briggs died in 1867; Mrs. Briggs died in 1872.

Edward Eastman was born in Salisbury, N. H., in 1787. He married Susan Cheney, of Newbury, Mass., who was born in 1793. They were married in Bristol, N. H., September 4, 1811. They came to Northfield in January, 1834, and settled on Waitsfield mountain, near the line between the two towns. It was a very forbidding place, especially in winters, and we do not wonder that it was abandoned, and is now used only for a pasture. No one as we can learn has ever tried to *stay* there since. It developed one thing worthy of note, that it must have been a healthy place, for Mr. Eastman and wife are now living, at a good old age, and the children are hard working, healthy, industrious people. They had eight children:

H. W. Eastman, b 1817; John W., b 1819; Phebe E., b 1821; Charles L., b 1825; Edward J., b 1827; Hannah S., b 1832; Philania S., b 1834; Sarah J., b 1836. All but two born in Salisbury, N. H.

Zadock Williams was from Thetford, Vt., and came into town about 1827, and settled on the West Hill, not far from the four corners, on the Waitsfield road. He married Savaih Closson, and had one son:

Simon C., born in Lyons, N. Y., in 1825.

JACOB AMIDON was born in Randolph, Vt., in 1793, and came to Northfield in 1824. He married Mercy C. Whitten in 1816, and they had six children:

Olivia, b 1817; Samuel, b 1818; Marshall, b 1823; John W., b 1825; Clarissa, M., b 1829; George, b 1831.

Mr. Amidon married for his second wife Armania Richmond, in 1834, and they had four children:

Mercy C., b 1838; Numan D., b 1840; Joan A., b 1841; Adaline F., b 1843. All born in Northfield.

ASAHEL BLAKE was born in Keene, N. H., April 11, 1784. His wife, Elizabeth Dwinell, was born in Keene, January 30, 1805. They came to Northfield from Roxbury in 1809, and settled on the West Hill, on the William Dunsmore farm. They had ten children:

George W., b 1806; Olive, b 1808; Sarah N., b 1809; Charles F., b 1812; Ashael H., b 1815; Nelson, b 1818; Rual, b 1819; William, b 1821; Harriet, b 1823; Almira M., b 1829.

Mrs. Blake died in 1860; Mr. Blake died in 1867.

WARREN RICE was born in Claremont, N. H., December 24, 1794. He married Judith Johnson, who was born in Cornish, N. H., May 19, 1801. They moved into Northfield in 1821, and they had four children:

Ruhama P., b 1824; Almira T., b 1825; Arial K., b 1830; Willard A., b 1832. All born in Northfield.

Mr. Rice lived in the west part of the town, and died November 29, 1845.

Edward Ingalls, Esq., writing in the *Argus and Patriot* of this family, says:

Mrs. Rice's mother lived to be ninety-eight years old, and could read without spectacles when at that age. At one time the men folks were all gone, and Mrs. Rice was left alone with Mr. Rice's father and mother, they being infirm and unable to do anything for themselves, and an invalid son of her own, who was also helpless. The wind was blowing strong from the north-west at the time. Mrs. Rice thought she heard a crackling like fire. Looking about to see what it was, she found the roof of the house in flames, and burning smartly. She carried water quite a distance into the attic, and put the fire out in the inside so she could open the scuttle, when she climbed out on the roof and put it out.

DANIEL STEVENS was born in Hartford, Vt., December 7, 1775. He came to Northfield in 1820, and settled on the West Hill, on what was known for many years after as the Stevens farm. He married Polly Loomis, who was born in Hartland, October 15, 1776. They had eleven children:

Francis M., b 1799; Rachael, b 1800; Daniel, Jr., b 1802; Albert, b 1804; Amasa, b 1806; Mary, b 1808; Annis, b 1811; Lurenda, b 1813; Isaac S., 1815; Rodolphus, b 1817; Francis M., b 1822. All born in Hartland.

Mr. Stevens died in Northfield April 21, 1851.

Mrs Stevens died in Waterville, Vt., January 19, 1860.

ECCLESIASTICAL

AND

MISCELLANEOUS.

PART III.

Religious Societies.

To show how the different societies in Northfield stood in point of numbers when the law required the legal voters to express their preference where the ministerial money should be distributed, we take from the town records the report of the committee, made for the years 1823 and 1825.

June 3, 1823, Division of Ministerial Money as follows:

Methodist Society,	$12 85
Congregationalist Society,	8 42
Restorationist Society,	17 24
Free Will Baptist Society,	13 23
Christian Society,	5 61

Division for 1825, as follows:

Free Will Baptist Society,	$7 62
Congregationalist Society,	6 11
Restorationist Society,	11 33
Christian Society,	1 27
Methodist Society,	25 00

OLIVER AVERILL,
NATHAN GREEN,
VIRGIL WASHBURN, } Committee.
JOEL WINCH,
HARRY EMERSON,

ELIJAH SMITH, *Town Clerk.*

THE FIRST MEETING HOUSE

BUILT IN NORTHFIELD.

The Union Meeting House at the Center village was the first one built in this town, and was completed in 1820. The following named persons were chosen as a building committee, viz.: Amos Robinson, Charles Jones, Freedom Edson, Nathaniel Jones, and Oliver Averill.

At a meeting of the Proprietors, held April 6, 1820, for the purpose of selling the pews, it was voted that one quarter part of the value of the pews be paid in money, and the other three quarters in stock or grain, and that the house should be completed by the first day of November, and at that time a payment of money and stock to be made. The whole number of pews, fifty in number, were all sold at public auction save twelve, and brought $760.00.

The following Constitution was adopted:

ARTICLE I The Proprietors have a right to occupy it according to the property that each denomination have therein.

ARTICLE II. The division of the time shall be divided to each denomination by a committee appointed for that purpose on the first Tuesday of March in each year.

ARTICLE III. That if any denomination cannot or are not disposed to occupy the house on the day belonging to them, then in that case it shall belong to the denomination that is set next in order, and if they do not, it shall fall to the next, and so on, that the house may by that means be occupied.

ARTICLE IV. It is understood that said house is to be free for all denominations in all week days and evenings according to the division made by the committee mentioned in the second article of this Constitution, that each denomination shall have a right on their own days to hold their own meetings in said house according to their own discipline.

ARTICLE V. It is understood that the meeting house shall be free on all funeral occasions for *one* service.

The division of time for each denomination reported by the committee was as follows:

The Methodist Society, first Sabbath in each month except February and March; the Restorationist Society, the third Sabbath in each month and fifth in August; the Congregational Society, fourth Sabbath in each month except March and August; the remainder to the Free Will Baptist Society.

JOSIAH B. STRONG,
OLIVER AVERILL,
NATHANIEL JONES,
JOEL WINCH,
} Committee.

This first house built in Northfield for *religious worship* was one of humble pretensions and style. It was painted *yellow*, and there being no steeple or cupola upon it, it resembled a *barn* very much, and hence it became a bye-word, and was called by the irreligious "God's yellow barn." In process of time other churches, more expensive and desirable, were built in town, and this plain but comfortable old fashioned meeting house was sold to the Catholics, and placed upon the land in the Depot village given them by Governor Paine, where with some new improvements it made a respectable appearance. In the summer of 1876 it was consumed by fire, having been struck with lightning.

UNIVERSALISM

IN NORTHFIELD.

At an early day many prominent men manifested a desire to have Universalist meetings in town, and consequently an occasional meeting was held, as a preacher of that faith came along and desired to address the people. School houses, private houses, barns and groves were used by the early pioneers of Universalism, the friends feeling it a blessed privilege to occupy such humble places, where they could listen to the preached words. Timothy Bigelow was the first man we have any account of addressing the citizens of Northfield, on the subject of Universalism. We learn by the town records that he was ordained in Barnard, Vt., September 21, 1809, by the Universalist Convention, Thomas Barnes being Moderator, and Hosea Ballou clerk. He commenced preaching in Northfield about that time, and there are those now living who remember him.

No record has been preserved of the Universalist preachers who labored in this section up to 1821, when the union meeting house was built in the Center village, and the members of that order, by contributing to its erection, claimed as large if not the largest portion of it for holding their public ministrations. We learn that Father Palmer, who had formerly been connected with the Christian denomination, became a believer in "the restitution of all things," and preached with great unction and power in different parts of this town. Father Farewell, of Barre, a devout man, preached as opportunity presented in Northfield and vicinity, and had great success in making proselytes to that faith.

On dwelling on the love of God, he would frequently be so carried away with his feelings that he would cry and laugh at the same time, and men and women of other names were lead to admit that he was honest in his feelings; that he believed his doctrine was the power of God unto salvation.

This good father, so sincere, so devout, was a great controversalist, and delighted to place his opponents in a dilemma from which they could not extricate themselves. At one time it so happened that he had an interview with a brother of Armenian principles, and the question became interesting whether all would be saved for whom Christ died, when a brother of Calvinistic proclivities came in and joined in the discussion. Soon things became lively and interesting, when Father Farewell, seeing an opportunity for getting his brethren into a little pleasant difficulty, remarked, in reply to their assault upon his Universalism, "You, Brother Free Will, believe that Christ died for all men, do you not?" "O, yes," was the reply. "You, Brother Calvin, believe Christ will save all for whom he died, do you not?" "O, yes," was the response. "Now," said the Universalist father, "you discuss this subject while I am eating my supper, and see how near you can agree."

The Universalist church in the Center Village was built in the summer of 1811, Jesse Averill, Harvey Tilden and Joel Parker, being the building committee. Fathers Streeter, Palmer, Sampson, E. Ballou, A. Scott, and other Universalist clergymen took part in the dedicatory services. For the time it was quite a substantial building, and although up to this day a majority of the pews are held by this order, others of weaker means are allowed to use it for *funeral* occasions, and occasionally on the Sabbath, without charge. But time, the great leveller, has written decay upon its walls, and soon it will be numbered with the things that were.

Rev. L. H. Tabor was the first preacher employed

after this house was built, and he labored here but half the time, being engaged the other half at Plainfield. Rev. Alanson Scott followed him in 1843, and was the first clergyman of that order that resided here. Rev. R. S. Sanborn succeeded him, preaching a short time, and since him other preachers supplied the desk one-half or one quarter of the time, until the new church was built at the Depot Village, when the old one was abandoned entirely by those who built it.

Among the prominent Universalists who contributed liberally to the erection of the one or both churches at the Center Village, were Amos Robinson, Jesse and Oliver Averill, Lebbeus Bennett, Elijah Burnham, Isaac P. Jenks, John West, John Starkweather, Heman Carpenter, Roswell Carpenter, Judge Robinson, David R. Tilden, Thomas S. Mayo, Samuel Fisk, Sidney Hatch, Moses Robinson, Sherman Gold, Harvey Tilden, I. W. Brown, Lewis Hassam, Volney H. Averill, Joel Parker, Elijah Pride, William Wales, Mrs. Hurlburt, and others.

After repeated efforts to get a vote to build a new church in the Depot Village, for the railroad was drawing business, the post-office and a majority of the citizens to that place, a vote was passed to take measures to purchase the land and proceed with the building. In November, 1858, at a society meeting, fifty-one votes were cast to locate said church on the H. M. Bates lot, north of the common, and H. Tenny, T. A. Miles, J. C. Gault, Sherman Gold and John Gregory were appointed a building committee. The church was completed the following summer, dedicated to God in the usual form December, 1859, and the Rev. O. H. Tillotson selected as pastor, and commenced his labors the first Sunday in January, 1860, at a salary of $1,000 per year. The society prospered under his ministration, for he was well liked, honoring his profession as he did by a well ordered life and a good conversation. He died in Northfield in 1863, aged 47 years, lamented by a large parish, leaving a devoted wife and one son to lament their loss. Of him it might have been said: "A good man has fallen." His faith sustained him through a long and distressing illness, and with heavenly serenity and blissful hope, he could say with the poet Browning—

If all our hopes and all our fears
  Were prisoned in life's narrow bound;
If, travelers through this vale of tears,
  We see no better world beyond—
O who could check the rising sigh;
  What earthly thing could pleasure give?
O who could venture then to die?
  Or who could venture then to live?

His remains were interred in our beautiful Elmwood, and many a tear has fallen upon his grave, at the recollection of his manly bearing and Christian usefulness.

Rev. Eli Ballou supplied the pulpit until the Rev. C. W. Emerson was settled as Pastor, who labored with them three years. Then followed the Rev. Stacy Haines Matlack, who, although in rather feeble health, preached to the society nearly one year, but was compelled to resign his pastorate on account of continued infirmity. The *Star*, published in Cincinnati, O., gave the particulars of the early death of this young and excellent brother:

He departed this life at the house of his parents at Eaton, Ohio, on Monday, April 15, 1878, aged 30 years, 8 months, and 11 days * * * He was the son of Samuel G. and Mary Matlack, and was born in Dixon township, Preble county, O., Aug. 8, 1847. His father and mother were originally Quakers, but for many years they have rejoiced in the full blessedness of the Universal Hope. Born of this parentage, Stacy was naturally modest and unassuming. Conscientious in a very high degree, he was incapable of wronging any one. And his sensitive nature felt most keenly the wrongs of others. Reared in a Christian home, by Christian parents, he early manifested a predisposition in favor of the ministry. On attaining his majority he entered the theological department of St. Lawrence University at Canton, N. Y., in the fall of 1868. Completing the regular course of three years, he graduated in the class of '71. Soon after, receiving a call from Northfield, Vt., he entered immediately upon the active work of the ministry. * * * For five long, weary years Bro. Matlack was confined to his parents' house in Eaton, O., suffering greatly from inflammation of the spine, and died at last of consumption. Through all he was remarkably patient and cheerful, bearing his affliction with true Christian fortitude, as becomes a true soldier of Christ. Not once was he known to murmur or complain, and though he desired sincerely to get well, he could say, "O my Father, if it be possible, let this cup pass from me; nevertheless, not as I will, but as thou wilt." With a bright future before him of usefulness in the world, we do not wonder that it might be his desire to be restored to health once more. Nor did he give up this hope till a few hours before his death. When he realized that his end was very near, he bade his parents and sister an affectionate adieu, and soon after expired without a struggle.

The Rev. R. A. Green followed Mr. Matlack, remaining five years. Since then the hard times and the removal of many friends, have greatly embarrassed the society. Rev. William Madison Kimmell, of Ohio, commenced his labors as Pastor the first Sunday in May, 1878.

METHODISM.

By Rev. W. J. KIDDER.

In the year 1804, eight years after the introduction of Methodism into Vermont, Barre circuit was formed, and Northfield was included in this circuit, and the circuit preachers (as they were called) had regular appointments in the town, preaching in school houses, private houses, barns, and groves. Oliver Beal was the first regularly appointed minister. How often he preached in town we have no means of knowing.

In 1805 Elijah Hedding, afterwards one of the Bishops of the Church, and Dan Young, were appointed to the circuit. These were young men of superior quality and of great piety. A gracious revival prevailed, and many were added to the Church. This year an incident occurred which showed the skill of Mr. Hedding in the administration of discipline—exceeding kind and forbearing toward the penitent, the unfortunate, and the ignorant. On the other hand he was alike decided and vigorous towards the willfully stubborn and wicked. A dispute had for a long while existed between two members of the church, who were brothers-in-law, concerning some property, which not only increased in violence, but at length involved most of the members of the society. Mr. Hedding called the society together to have the dispute between them settled. Both of them were fiery, impulsive, ungovernable men. The object of the meeting was to procure an amicable and brotherly adjustment of the long-pending dispute, or at least devise some method of settlement. Mr. Hedding sat between the two men, and the wife of each sat beside her husband. They began to talk over the subject of dispute, when one of them warmed up and called the other a liar. Instantly both started to their feet and rushed at each other, the females screamed, and a general alarm ensued. Mr. Hedding proved himself equal to the awkward emergency. He rushed between them, seized each of them by the collar of his coat, and with his herculean frame and strength held them at arms length face to face, but unable to strike each other. They struggled for a moment, but found themselves as though clutched in the jaws of a vice. Holding them thus, he commenced to lecture them in round terms; shamed them about the meanness and wickedness of the act their unbridled passions had prompted them to commit in the presence of their wives, their family relatives, the religious society of which they were members, their pastor, and especially in the presence of God, whose servants they professed to be. He told them of the scandal they had brought upon the church, and the reproach cast upon the cause of God by the course they had pursued toward each other.

From the hearing of this entire lecture there was no escape, and they writhed under its withering power. After they had got somewhat calmed, Mr. Hedding suddenly exclaimed, "Let us pray," and kneeled down, bringing the two men with him to their knees upon the floor. Still retaining his grasp, he prayed for them in the most fervent and powerful manner. When he had closed, he shook the one he held by his right hand and said, "Pray brother, pray!" Soon he commenced praying and weeping, confessing his sins, and beseeching God and his brother to forgive him. When the first had closed, Mr. H. shook the other and called upon him to pray. He was the most pugnacious of the two, and it was hard work for him to clear his throat so as to give utterance to words. "A thousand frogs seemed clogging his speech," but he at length broke through his difficulty, and earnestly prayed God and his brother to forgive him. When he said amen, Mr. H. relinquished his grasp and they all arose to their feet. "Now shake hands" said he, "and live as brethren, and love each other as long as you live." They immediately embraced each other, and almost as quickly settled their dispute. The two men ever after lived on the best terms, in fraternal and christian fellowship.

The following named clergymen have acted as Pastors from 1806 to 1878;

NAMES.	TERM OF OFFICE.
Phillip Munger and Jonathan Cheney, - -	1806.
Sam Thompson and Eleazer Wells, - -	1807.
Solomon Sias, - - - - -	1808.
Warren Bannister and George Gary, - -	1809.
Eleazer Wells and S. Streeter, - - -	1810.
N. W. Stearns and J. Jewett, - - -	1811.
E. F. Newhall and J. Dennett, - - -	1812
David Kilborn, - - - - - -	1813
David Kilborn and J. Walker, - - -	1814
Joel Steel, - - - -	1815
Joel Steel and Thomas C. Pierce, - - -	1816
Leonard Frost, - - - - - -	1817–18
Thomas C. Pierce, - - - - - -	1819
S. B. Haskell and E. Dunham, - - -	1820

This year a society was formed for the purpose of drawing their share of the public money, and forty-six gave their names as members, headed by Elijah Smith, Jr., who for many years was a prominent member of the Church. About this time they commenced holding their meetings in the yellow meeting-house their portion of the time.

Abraham Holway, - - - - - -	1821
J. F. Adams and D. David Leslie, - -	1822
Samuel Norris and Haskell Wheelock - -	1823
David Kilburn, H. Wheelock and A. H. Houghton,	1824
John Lord, David Leslie and Elihu Scott, -	1825

In 1826 Old Barre Circuit was divided, and a new circuit, called Brookfield Circuit, was formed, and Northfield was included in it, and this year David Leslie and George Sutherland were the preachers.

C. D. Cahoon and C. W. Leavings. - - 1827
William McCoy and E. Jordan. - - 1828
William McCoy and R. Harding, - - . 1829
John Nason and F. F. Daley, - - - 1830
E. J. Scott, W. Wilcox and H. Johnson, - - 1831
E. J. Scott, Z. Colburn and A. Fay, - - 1832
E. J. Scott and A Fay, - - - - 1833
C. Cowen and J. Smith, - - - 1834

This year Brookfield Circuit was divided, and Northfield Circuit was formed. A Parsonage was purchased, being the house where David Hassett now lives.

C. Cowen and J. Smith, - - - - 1835
J. A. Leavitt, - - - - - - 1836
Samuel Richardson, - - - - 1837
John G. Dow, - - - - - - 1838
A. T. Bullard, Nathan Howe and A. J. Copeland, 1839

February 2, of this year A. T. Bullard received the following letter from the Hon. Charles Paine:

NORTHFIELD, February 2, 1840.

Dear Sir:—The meeting-house which belongs to the owners of the Northfield Factory is now unoccupied. The owners are desirous that it should be so occupied as will best promote the welfare, not only of the people of the village in which it is situated, but also those of the town. They therefore tender the use of it, through you, to the Methodist society.

Respectfully your obt. servant,

CHAS. PAINE.

The Rev. A. T. BULLARD.

This offer was gratefully accepted by the society, and the next Sabbath they removed from the Center and commenced the occupancy of the house thus tendered, and continued to do so until the death of Governor Paine.

John Currier and John Perrin, - - - 1841–2

In 1843 Northfield was made a station.

James Patterson, - - - - - - 1843–4

After Northfield was made a station, the society

formed in 1820 and reorganized with two hundred members. Thomas Courser was chosen President, and Elijah Smith, Clerk.

Alonzo Webster, - - - - - -	1845-6
A. G. Button, - . - - - -	1847-8
John G. Dow, - - - - - -	1847-50
H. P. Cushing, - - - - -	1851-2

During Mr. Cushing's pastorate the congregation had become so large that it could not be accommodated, and Governor Paine had the house enlarged by the addition of sixteen pews. The society, also, during this time built a new parsonage—the one they now occupy—and sold the old one.

William J. Kidder, - - - -	1853-4

In 1854, Governor Paine having died, the Church was sold by his heirs, and went into the hands of the Congregationalists. The Methodists set about providing themselves with a place of worship, and the house they now occupy was built at an expense of $4,734, and dedicated to the worship of Almighty God the last week in December, 1854.

E. A. Rice, - - - - - -	1855-6
W. D. Malcolm, - - - - -	1857-8
I. McAnn, - - - - - -	1859-60

Through Mr. McAnn's efforts, seconded by many members of the society, especially the female portion, a debt which had rested like an incubus upon it was removed.

A. S. Cooper, . - - - - -	1861-2
J. A. Sherburne, - - - - -	1863-4
S. H. Colburn, - - - - - -	1865
Joshua Gill, - - - - - -	1866-7
Richard Morgan, - - - - -	1868-9

During Mr. Morgan's pastorate the Church was remodeled and enlarged and beautified; the old organ exchanged for a new one, at an expense of $1,200, Brother Joseph Gould generously paying the same.

A. C. Stevens, - - - - - -	1870-71-2
W. R. Puffer, - - - - - -	1773
W. D. Malcolm, - - - - - -	1874
A. B. Truax, - - - - - -	1875-76-7
O. M. Boutwell, - - - - - -	1878

For many years there has been a flourishing Sunday-school connected with the Church. H. R. Brown is the Superintendent, with a corps of twenty-three officers and teachers. There are 200 scholars, and 300 volumes in the library.

The present membership of the Church is as follows:

Probationers, - - - - - - -	24
In full membership, - - - - -	320
Total, - - - - - - -	344

Several Ministers have been raised up in the Church, and gone out as heralds of salvation. Prominent among them them was Paul C. Richmond, who for many years was a prominent member of the Maine Conference, and who, after a long, successful, and laborious ministry, a few years since crossed the dark river, and went triumphantly to his reward. Others are still in the field gathering sheaves for their Master in the Vermont, New England, and Providence Conferences. In the year 1870 a perpetual lease of a piece of ground was secured for camp meetings, and by an act of the Legislature the Central Vermont Camp Meeting Association was incorporated, with power to hold all the property necessary for the purpose of holding camp meetings, or any other meetings of a religious character, Sunday schools, picnics, or temperance meetings, and all such property to the amount of ten thousand dollars is to be free from taxation. This ground has been fitted up at an expense of some two thousand dollars. Several cottages have been erected thereon by the different societies of the Montpelier district, and by private individuals as family residences, and camp meetings have been held on the ground annually, we think, with good success.

CONGREGATIONALIST.

By Rev. WILLIAM S. HAZEN, A. M.

Most of the early inhabitants of Northfield were Universalists, and for a number of years after its settlement this was the prevailing religious influence in town. In 1804 the Methodists made a beginning, and about 1814 a Free Will Baptist church was organized. As the population of the town increased, a number of families were found who preferred the "Congregational way." Virgil Washburn, a devoted Christian, who came from Randolph, was especially active among them. Occasionally meetings were held in private houses or barns. The professing christians among this company, after repeated consultations as to how they could best prosecute their own spiritual interests and those of their friends, decided to form a church. Accordingly on the 27th of May, 1822, the "First Congregational church of Northfield" was organized, in what is known as "The Little Yellow Meeting House," which stood in the Center Village. It was composed of nine members, all of whom have passed to their heavenly reward.

The first record of the church reads as follows:

NORTHFIELD, May 27, 1822

This day was organized the First Congregational Church of Christ in this town, composed of the following members, viz Josiah B. Strong, Virgil Washburn, Moses R. Dole, Samuel Whitney, Thomas Houghton, Lucy Whitney, Clarissa Strong, Rizpah Whitney, and Betsey Houghton, by professing their faith in Christ and entering into Covenant bonds with God and each other. They then proceeded to choose Brother Josiah Strong, Moderator, Brother Samuel Whitney, Clerk, and Deacon Virgil Washburn, Deacon.

Attest,

ELIJAH LYMAN,
AMMI NICHOLS, } Ministers of the Gospel

Thus this small company of disciples of Christ were organized into a Church, and were ready for Christian work. But their condition and prospects were not flattering. They were without a home. The only right they had in any House of Worship was in the one in which the church was organized. They could occupy that the fifth Sabbath of every month in which there were five Sabbaths. They were not able to support the regular preaching of the Gospel. A part of the time they held services on the Lord's Day, which Deacon Cady usually conducted, Governor Paine frequently reading the sermon. Occasionally they had preaching, and the ordinances were administered by the pastors of neighboring churches.

When the church had increased in strength and influence so that it was thought advisable to hold public services every Sabbath, a school house in the Depot Village was occupied, and afterwards a room in Governor Paine's woolen factory.

During the winter of 1835 the question of building a house of worship was agitated, and a "subscription paper" was started to raise the necessary funds. But Governor Paine forestalled the necessity of such action by building the house now owned by the Congregational Society, and inviting the church to worship in it. It was dedicated to the worship of God, "the Father, Son, and Holy Ghost, on Thursday, December first, 1836." This house was occupied six years, when the members of the church and society decided to build a house of which they could have the entire control. Accordingly the work of building was undertaken in 1843. The house was located at the Center Village, and was dedicated "to the service of Almighty God, on Thursday, the third day of August, 1843." Thus, when twenty-one years old, the church had a local habitation as well as a name. It worshipped in this house till, through the influence of the railroad, business centered in the Depot Village, and it seemed advisable to hold Sabbath services there. The house now occupied by the church was purchased of the heirs of Governor Paine, and at a church meeting, held December, 1854, "Voted to change the place for worship on the Sabbath from the Center Meeting House to the Meeting House in the Depot Village." This house has since been the home of the church. It has been enlarged, and twice thoroughly repaired.

As already stated, for the first ten years of its existence the church was not favored with the services of a pastor. In September, 1833, Mr. James Furguson, a young man, commenced laboring with the church. He was called to be its pastor. The call was accepted, but Mr. Furguson died the very day he was to have been ordained. On the last Sabbath in May, 1834, Rev. Calvin Granger preached his first sermon here, and arrangements were made with him to become acting pastor. At a church meeting, held June 4th, 1836, "Voted to give Rev. Calvin Granger a call to become our pastor, with a salary from the church and society of two hundred dollars, the remainder of the salary to be supplied by the Home Missionary Society." This call was accepted, and on the first day of December following Mr. Granger was installed pastor of the church. Since then the church has been favored with the regular preaching of the Word, except during intervals incident to a change of pastors. The following is a list of the pastors, and acting pastors, with their term of office, as nearly as can be ascertained:

PASTORS.

NAMES.	TERM OF OFFICE.
Calvin Granger, - - - -	1836-42
Josiah H. Benton, - - - -	1847-49
Ambrose Smith, - - - -	1850-53
William S. Hazen, - - - -	1861.
ACTING PASTORS.	
Calvin Granger, - - - -	1834-36.

William Claggett, - - - - -	1843–45.
Caleb B. Tracy, - - - - -	1853–55.
Levi H. Stone, - - - - - -	1856–63.
William S. Hazen, - - - - -	1863–64.

The first Deacon was Virgil Washburn, who held the office from the day of the organization of the church till April 1st, 1832, when at his own request he was dismissed, and recommended to the fellowship of the Congregational church in Randolph. The following is a list of Deacons, with their term of office:

DEACONS.

NAMES.	TERM OF OFFICE.
Virgil Washburn, - - - - - -	1822–32.
Caleb Winch, - - - - - -	1832–43.
Calvin Cady, - - - - - -	1832–64.
Samuel Denny, - - - - -	1842–48,
Charles C. Closson, - - -	1845–48.
William Winch, - - - - -	1848.
Leonard Harrington, - - - - -	1849–55.
Lorenzo Belknap, - - - - -	1864.

There have been connected with the church three hundred and forty-five different persons, one hundred and twenty-one of whom are now members.

Though there had been something of a Sabbath School, or perhaps, better "Bible classes," connected with the church for several years, the school was not regularly organized till about the tenth of December, 1836. Then the following resolution was passed by the church:

Resolved, That we view a well regulated Sabbath School as a very important means of grace, and believe it our duty, as members of the church, to use our utmost endeavors to sustain one in this place, by causing the attendance of our children, and procuring the attendance of others as far as practicable.

Samuel Denny was chosen Superintendent.

While this church had enjoyed the preaching of the Word, it has done something through its members toward giving the preaching of that Word to others. Three who here first professed their faith in Christ have become ministers of the Gospel: Rev. Daniel Parker, who died some years since while living at Brookfield; Rev. C. M. Winch, who is now acting pastor of the church at Corinth, and Rev. George W. Winch, pastor of the first church in Enfield, Conn.

Such is a brief history of the Congregational church in this town. Some people on reading it may think Christian effort has been useless, or at least very inefficient, because after fifty-six years of labor there is so small a church numerically to show as the result of such labor. But it must be remembered that all the fruits of all moral or religious enterprise are never to be seen. "One soweth, and another reapeth." Aside from the influence on this community in sustaining a Christian church these years, the full value of which eternity alone will reveal, the church has been continually exerting a wider influence in sending forth to other parts of the land those nurtured in its bosom. Who will attempt to tell of the good it has thus been doing? Such country churches as this, gaining in numbers slowly, if at all, yet holding their ground, are like those mountain springs which are continually sending forth streams to irrigate and fertilize the plains below, rendering what would otherwise be a barren waste a fruitful garden.

EPISCOPAL.

By Rev. F. WIESTON BARTLETT, A. M.

The Parish of St. Mary's was first organized in 1851, under the auspices of the Rev. Dr. Josiah Perry, who died after a few months of faithful service. We ascertain from the records that an association was created April 10, 1851, to form a parish in the town of Northfield, for the purpose of supporting the Gospel ministry and maintaining public worship, in conformity with the Constitution and Canons of the Protestant Episcopal Church in the Diocese of Vermont. The name agreed upon was St. Mary's Parish, Northfield. The Articles of Association were signed by Samuel W. Thayer, Jr., Edward H. Williams, H. H. Camp, James Carey B. Thayer, F. E. Smith, E. G. Babcock, Perley Belknap, James Moore, H. L. Briggs, Isaiah Shaw, J. H. Glennie, Benjamin Cridland,. J. N. Mack, Riverius Camp, Jr., Ozro Foster, C. H. Finlay, Peyton Booth, John Pollock, D. P. Burns, and H. M. Bates.

The first service was conducted in what is now Judge Carpenter's law office, which was then a private school house. The parish organization was preserved; but after Dr. Perry's death no services were held until the winter of 1856-7, when clergymen from different parts of the State officiated, and worship was conducted at the Center village. At this time there were but four communicants. The summer following a change was made to the Depot village, and to the edifice at the corner of Elm and Main Streets, which is now occupied by the society for divine worship. This house was opened for service by the Rt. Rev. John Henry Hopkins, D.

D., LL. D., on Christmas day, 1857, and on the following day was solemnly set apart by him as a church. The Rev. Messrs. Shelton, Swett, Graves, and W. C. Hopkins were in attendance. To Mr. Swett the Parish had been greatly indebted for his zeal and interest in their behalf; and a resolution, passed subsequently by the Vestry, expressed their obligations, and their opinion of the great value his labors had been to them.

After the consecration of the church the parish was served by the clergymen named above, and also by the Rev. Messrs. Bachelder, Oliver, Herrick, and Randall, all of this Diocese. The last named organized a Sunday School, January 17, 1858. The church had hitherto been under the general supervision of the Clerical Convocation of Vermont; but on February 17, 1858, a call was extended by the Vestry to Rev. William C. Hopkins, a Deacon, doing duty in St. Albans. His acceptance having been approved by the Bishop, he entered upon his duties Easter Day, April 5, 1858. Almost as soon as Mr. Hopkins took charge, we find the subject of the free seat system considered by the Vestry, and on May 23, 1858, a resolution was passed at a Vestry meeting, declaring as the sense of the meeting that the Free Seat System, as proposed by Mr. Hopkins, was desirable. This system was not, however, at this time made the rule, but on New Year's day, 1862, the Vestry made the pews unconditionally free for one year, an arrangement which has ever since continued. Mr. Hopkins, having this year received from the Governor an appointment as Chaplain in the Grand Army of the Union, the Vestry passed resolutions congratulating him on the same, and, while consenting to part with him for a season, asking him to continue his connection with the church as Rector. Such an arrangement was made. For six months following the services were conducted by the Rev. J. Isham Bliss. Meantime the Rector wrote from Pensacola,

Florida, under date of February 27, 1863, resigning the rectorship, which the Vestry declined to accept. The Rev. Germont Graves became minister-in-charge in May, 1863, and continued in the position for one year. Charles Fay, D. D., of St. Albans, officiated on Sundays in the summer following, and services were thereafter conducted by Danforth H. Brown, as Lay Reader. The resignation of Mr. Hopkins as Rector was accepted November 27, 1864, with expressions of great regret. He had been a laborious pastor, and had continued during his absence to manifest his interest by sending gifts of money to the church from himself and the Seventh Regiment Vermont Volunteers, of which he was the Chaplain.

The Presbyter John B. Pitman, formerly of Fishkill, N. Y., became Rector in the Spring of 1865. His resignation was accepted November 13, 1866. The able and learned Edward Bourns, D. D., LL. D., the President of Norwich University, was engaged by the Vestry to conduct service until a Rector could be procured. He was made minister-in-charge Easter, 1867, and continued his official relations until Roger S. Howard, D. D., previously of St. James', Woodstock, became Rector, in the summer of 1869. Dr. Howard resigned the position to take effect the first of May, 1872. The Rev. A. D. McCoy thereupon officiated for a short time. Malcom Douglass, D. D., at this time President of the University, frequently officiated during the vacancy in the pastorate. The Rev. G. C. V. Eastman was next elected Rector, and entered upon his duties January 30, 1873. He resigned April 5, 1875. Dr. Philander D. Bradford and Dr. George Nichols, as Lay Readers, conducted the services of the church until the appointment of Mr. William Lloyd Himes, Deacon, in the Spring of 1876, who resigned the parish to take effect Easter, 1877, having meantime been ad-

FREE WILL BAPTISTS.

This denomination had quite a good society in 1823, so that they drew more public money than the Methodists that year. But *schisms* got in among them and so disturbed the flock, that they died out and have no longer a name to live in Northfield. Elder N. King was their prominent preacher. He was ordained on the first day of July, A. D. 1802, assisted by Elders John and Aaron Buzzell, Pelatiah Tingly and Nathaniel Brown.

Sylvanus, son of Colonel Ezekiel Robinson, was ordained as a Baptist Elder, by the laying on of hands, by Elders James Morgan, George Hackett, and Ziba Pope, on the twenty-seventh of February, A. D. 1821, and preached here and elsewhere as opportunity presented.

James Morgan was ordained as a Baptist Elder on the tenth day of June, 1822, by Elders Daniel Batchelder, and Thomas Moxley, and preached considerable in Northfield. Many years have passed since the Baptists gave up their organization, and the writer has not been able to find one of that order, that can give him a history of the rise and decline of this once prominent society. Deacon Nathaniel Jones was its principal lay member, and his zealous advocacy of Millerism not only tended to break up the Baptist society, but injured him in point of property.

THE CHRISTIAN SOCIETY.

This society had something of a following in 1823, but was the smallest of all, as we learn by the amount of public money they drew. After the yellow meeting house was removed from the Center, they ceased holding meetings, and became extinct as a religious society. Efforts have been made to find some one that would give a brief account of this order in Northfield, but in vain.

ROMAN CATHOLIC.

We would have been pleased to have received an account of the growth and prosperity of this Church in our town, as we wish to treat all *fairly* without *partiality,* but was not successful in inducing any one to undertake the task. And so we must forego the pleasure it would have given us to hand down to posterity the early beginnings of what has grown to be a large society, with the largest number of communicants, and the best church edifice in Northfield. Their zeal and devotion to their principles is worthy of emulation by other societies professing to be followers of the meek and lowly One.

MISCELLANEOUS.

GEOLOGY.

By Gen. ALONZO JACKMAN, LL. D.,

Professor in Norwich University, Northfield

REMARK.—In accordance with the character of this book as a history of Northfield, the following article is presented in historical form. It, therefore, enters into the bearings of the subject through the successive periods of remote years, and at the same time whatever is introduced pertains to Northfield. For the chronological order, reference will be made to Dana's Geology.

From a long series of critical observations upon the stratified rocks of the earth's crust, and a close study concerning their contained fossils, geologists have, pretty uniformly, come to the following conclusion, viz.:

That there was a time when no living substance existed upon the globe: when all the earth was under water; and, during ages of this chaos, the oceanic currents, at some places, wore away the earth's crust, and the resulting detritus, mixed with volcanic discharges, was spread out at other places upon the ocean bed, thereby forming immense stratified deposits to unknown depths. This duration of time is called the *Azoic Period*, toward the close of which the dry land began to appear, as "mere islets in the great continental sea." (Dana, p. 77.) After this there was a time when *life*, in its simplest forms, began in the *great deep*. And during the progress of ages the ocean became filled with animal life, as Radiates, Mollusks, Articulates, and Vertebrates.

and, in the same manner as above stated, vast stratified deposits, including fossils, accumulated to the depth of some seven miles. (Dana, p 144.) Further, the earth rose gradually above the water, the dry land became covered with vegetation, and animal life every where abounded. This portion of time is called the *Paleozoic Period.* After this there was a *Mesozoic Period,* whose deposits are some two miles deep. (Dana, p 198.) And after this there was a *Conozoic Period,* whose deposits are some one and a half miles deep. (Dana, p 244.) And then came the *Age of Man,* which is now in progress.

During the time pertaining to each of the above *grand periods,* the earth was many times convulsed, when its crust in some places was raised to mountain masses, and at other places depressed to sea-basins, thus, in a manner, separating those grand periods into several sub-divisions; but the *grand divisions,* at their closing epochs, were more emphatically marked, as if disturbed by *special* upheavals of such magnitude that at each time nearly all animal life upon the globe became extinct, then the following period received a new order of beings upon a higher scale of life. In this manner the earth progressed, from period to period, upward to the *Age of Man,* and onward to the condition in which we now behold it. (Dana, p 66.)

At the times and places of these terrestrial disturbances, mentioned above, the volcanic heat became so intense as to metamorphose those stratified deposits:—the sand, into *granite;* the clay, into *roofing slate;* and the coral-reefs and shell-banks, into *marble,* &c. (Dana, p. 312.) Further: When these deposits were being *broken-up* by upheavals, the oceanic currents, charged with gravel-drift, ground off their ragged edges, and moved the detritus to other places of deposit. Thus, the continents, from period to period, rose gradually above the water. And now we see the earth with its stratified outcropping rocks, *well water-worn*, even to the top of our highest mountains.

Large portions of the earth's surface are observed to be covered with unstratified deposits, which are confusedly mingled with gravel and boulders; and, sometimes, these deposits are in hillocks of small water-worn stones; as may be seen in Depot village, in the vicinity of School street. Also, on the tops of our highest mountains-peaks, we often see large granite boulders, and other rocks, which must have come from great distances: and, apparently, at a time *not very remote* in the *past*. Now the "*Glacier theory*" fails to account, consistently, for *all* these appearances; for, were there, west of the Green Mountains, a glacier, or ice-flow, from the North, it would naturally pass through the Hudson Valley opening; but, to suppose that this glacier would turn eastward, climb the western front of the Green Mountains, and, as the "drift marks" indicate, cross Vermont the *rough way* over hills and valleys, in nearly a horizontal path, is to suppose what involves a dynamical absurdity. If, now, we try the theory that there was a flood like the one described in Genesis (Chap. vii), all appearances at once wheel into a consistent line of argument, and are compatible with a complete solution of the mysterious problem: for such a flood would in the polar regions raise from their ancient beds large masses of ice, which had received from mountain ravines gravel and bowlders, by means of thaws and glaciers. Also, from the frozen tops of mountains, the ancient masses of accumulated ice would float, thereby tearing off their rocky scalps. These icebergs, moved by wind and current, would drift toward the equator, and on the thawing passage drop their rocky freight upon the submerged land. Further, icebergs, drawing a greater depth of water, would lodge on submerged mountain ridges, and there remain until sufficiently reduced to be pushed over by the elements, thereby making, in their rocky tops, the "drift marks," which are distinctly seen on the heights about Northfield. As our admitted flood should subside, hillocks of water-worn stones would be formed by the thawing of stranded icebergs. Also, *sandy terraces*, similar to those near the Methodist Camp Ground, the Fair Ground, and the Cemetery, would be formed. (Such terraces have, hitherto, been placed by Geologists in a "Champlain Period.") In fact, to account for the appearances every where seen upon the earth's surface, it seemingly requires what is identically the "flood." But whence came the water to make such a flood? It came in from the ocean, when "all the fountains of the great deep were broken up," as a consequent result of the ocean bed being upheaved and the dry land depressed. Thus the whole earth became again submerged, as it was in the Azoic Period. Further, the subsidence of the flood was caused by the same agency, in returning the continents and ocean beds —possibly in part—to their former conditions. *And all this is in complete accordance with admitted principles in the science of Geology.*

The "mere islets" of the *Azoic Period* in the ancient ages of the world, were the *first* dry land, (Dana, p 77), but the next land which rose out of the sea was the Green Mountains, (Dana, p 92), which is, therefore, about the oldest dry land upon the globe. When the Green Mountains began to show themselves above the water, the Paleozoic formation had in its structure only the Potsdam and Trenton deposits, (Dana, p 80, 91), which now rest on the mountain. As ages advanced the mountains gradually rose out of the ocean to completion, thereby bringing to the surface, in the order of their formation, the successive Paleozoic strata, thus causing an increase of dry land. Hence, from the mountain top eastward, these successive strata have an eastern *dip*, a western *outcrop*, and a *strike* generally parallel to the Green Mountain range. These several outcrops, in the order of their formations, have those of the upper formations considerably to the east of those belonging to the lower formations. Further, in the process of their rising, the Green Mountains were so irregularly pushed up that their stratified structure received many cross-breaks and contortions. The ocean currents then scooped out these cross-breaks and wore off their rough projections, thus grinding down Vermont into a grand system of high mountains and deep valleys. In this condition the Green Mountains finally came up out of the sea, and now present themselves as a kind of *High Backbone Ridge*, with large vertebral knobs, and long rib-like spurs, extending eastward to the Connecticut valley, and between these spurs flow the vein-like streams, as Black river, Quechee river, White river, etc.

To get a better idea of the stratified formations in the Green Mountain structure, conceive an explorer to walk from the mountain top eastward through Northfield, and to observe the rocks he passes. This person would first walk on the upper surface of some Paleozoic formation, down its dipping slope into Mad river valley, near Waitsfield. Here he would meet the high outcropping front of the next formation above, which he would climb, and having arrived at its top, where it is called "Bald Mountain," he would find himself two thousand six hundred and thirty-six feet above tide-water; but, on Waitsfield Mountain, at the highest point in the road between Waitsfield and Northfield, he would stand two thousand one hundred and thirty-five feet above tide-water, and upon a slaty formation of hard greenish stone highly charged with quartz. He would next, on the upper surface of this formation, pass down its dipping slope into Dog river valley at Northfield, where he would find himself seven hundred and twenty-eight feet above tide-water, and six hundred and thirty-eight feet above the surface of Lake Champlain. The hill northwest of Elmwood Cemetery one thousand three hundred and fifty-nine feet, and that just south of South village one thousand and nine hundred feet above tide water. Also, he would notice a stratum of light greenish talcose slate-rock, well charged with quartz grit, and locally called "*Jenkstone.*" It splits freely into desirable thicknesses, breaks handsomely into rectangular forms, and is doubtless a good building stone. For proof see Mr. Jenks' dwelling-house. Next in order he would notice a stratum of lightish gray micaceous sandstone, locally called "*Whetstone Ledge,*" from which whetstones, hones, and the like are manufactured by Wood & Son, and they are said to be good. Proceeding onward he would meet the high outcropping front of the *famous slate formation*, from which the noted roofing slate are taken by Adams & Co. Having climbed this high front—called Paine mountain—and standing on its top, he would find himself two thousand four hundred and thirty-five feet above tide-water, or one thousand seven hundred and seven feet above the Depot, and he would also get a magnificent view with a clear sweep around the whole circumference of the distant horizon. Thence, proceeding onward upon the upper surface of this formation, he would pass down its dipping slope into Berlin pond valley, where he would meet the outcropping front of a dark slaty limestone formation. Thence, proceeding over this elevation, he would descend into Williamstown valley, and so on he could travel up and down to the Connecticut valley, and to the sea.

At first sight this traveler would think that the rocky stratification over which he passed stood nearly perpendicular to the horizon; but, on closer inspection, he would discover that what he took for *stratification* was the *slaty cleavage* of the rock, which is always nearly perpendicular to the bed of stratification. (Dana, p 36.)

Now the town of Northfield is on an eastern spur of the Green Mountains, and at the centre of the State, for, by actual estimation, from maps and various surveys, the center of the town and the center of the State are both found to be upon the same town lot. (Lot number nine in range five. See town map.) The town being thus on the Green Mountains, Northfield farmers cultivate about the oldest land in the world where terrestial life first began. In fact

"The dust we tread upon was once alive."—*Byron.*

Dog river runs through the eastern part of the town in a direction a little east of north, taking in on both sides quite respectable tributaries, which drain the several minor valleys of the town. Thus, by the river, its tributaries, and their great number of feeding springs, the town is well watered.

Instead of the surface-soil rising abruptly from the banks of the river and brooks, these streams are skirted by handsome narrow meadows and terraced flats, from whose outer limits the ground rises into the highlands in such manner that nearly all the surface, even to the tops of the highest hills, is susceptible of cultivation. There is very little waste land in Northfield.

On the river the soil is generally light and sandy, but back from the river on the upland the soil is dark, strong, and good, suitable for all the crops generally raised in the State. The native timber growth of the town consists of fir, spruce, hemlock, maple, birch, ash, elm, and the like.

NORWICH UNIVERSITY.

By Capt. C. A. CURTIS, A. M., U. S. A., President.

Located in Northfield in 1866.

Norwich University was incorporated by act of the Legislature of Vermont, November 6, 1834, with all the powers and immunities of a college, and was opened for the reception of students on the first Monday in May, 1835. The buildings occupied by the University at Norwich had been previously built and used by the American Literary, Scientific, and Military Academy, a school established in 1820 by Captain Alden Partridge, formerly an officer of the United States Engineer Corps, and for some years Superintendent of the United States Military Academy at West Point. Captain Partridge had met with various vicissitudes in conducting his Academy, mostly through a restless opposition to West Point, which Institution he heartily opposed after his resignation from the army, on account of a personal grievance connected with his supercedure by another officer. This restless anxiety to build up a military school, which should be a formidable rival of the National school, led him to accept an invitation to move school and cadets to Middletown, Conn., where substantial buildings had been erected for a College, whose corporation disappointed the citizens by going to another town. The Captain thought that Middletown being in the center of a populous region would afford him greater facilities for carrying out his plan. Accordingly in the Fall of 1825 he marched his corps of cadets down the valley of the Connecticut to the new location.

There is a report that New York next proposed to Captain Partridge to move his school there, and that he abandoned Middletown with such intention. However that may be, it is certain that his connection was broken with Middletown, and he returned to Norwich in 1832 to re-open his school in the buildings he had abandoned in 1825. During these days he had lost prestige. When he left West Point he had a reputation as wide as the Union, and a large following looked upon him as a much abused man when Sylvanus Thayer was appointed to succeed him at the Point; but his abandonment of Norwich, his proposed abandonment of Middletown, and his arbitrary conduct in his position as Principal of the school had begun to lose for him the support and confidence of the public; accordingly he made a failure of his attempt to re-establish a school at Norwich.

In the year 1833 the Universalist denomination held a convention at Claremont, N. H., for the purpose of considering the practicability of founding a denominational college. They adjourned to Woodstock, Vt., and there Captain Partridge, through a delegate, invited the convention to visit Norwich and look at the military academy buildings. In April, 1834, the convention of Universalists met at Norwich, and, liking the place and the substantial buildings, voted to found their college there, and invited Captain Partridge to be its President. A charter was procured that winter, and the college opened in the Spring of 1835. Its course of study was peculiar in one respect—it allowed a student to omit the ancient languages and classics, and conferred upon him the degree of "Bachelor of Science." Norwich University was, therefore, the first institution to confer this now very common degree. Another peculiarity was the introduction of military science and tactics into the course, and require them to be taught under the act of incorporation. This last feature has, more than any other, given an excellent record to the Institution. In the late war the college furnished a larger proportion of officers according to the number of her graduates than any other college in the country. No graduate ever bore a musket in the ranks. There were thirteen General officers and forty Colonels who took their degrees from Norwich, and the efficiency of the Vermont regiments in the field may be ascribed to the officers drawn from this college, with which they were well sprinkled.

The University remained at Norwich until the building known as the "South Barracks" burned in March, 1866, when, upon invitation of this town, it was removed here. The college, owing to the policy of its first and fourth Presidents—Captain Partridge, and Rev. Edward Bourns, LL. D.—the incumbents who occupied the chair during the greater portion of its life, has never acquired an endowment. This has hampered its success to a great degree.

The Presidents since the foundation of the University have been the following gentlemen:

Capt. Alden Partridge, A. M., from 1834 to 1843, 9 years.

Gen. Truman B. Ransom, A. M.,	from 1843 to 1846, 3 years.
Gen. Henry S. Wheaton, A. M.,	from 1846 to 1849, 3 years.
Rev. Edward Bourns, LL. D.,	from 1849 to 1865, 16 years.
Major Thomas W. Walker, U. S. A.,	from 1866 to 1868, 2 years.
Rev. Roger S. Howard, D. D.,	from 1868 to 1870, 2 years.
Rev. Malcolm Douglass, D. D.,	from 1870 to 1874, 4 years.
Capt. C. A. Curtis, A. M., U. S. A.,	from 1874 to present time.

With the advent of Doctor Bourns, who was a presbyter of the Episcopal Church, the Universalist element was eliminated from the University, and the former body have since had the controlling influence.

The college since its foundation has conferred the following number of degrees:

Bachelor of Arts,	107	Master of Civil Engineering,	13
Bachelor of Science,	131	Doctor of Medicine,	3
Bachelor of Philosophy,	2	Doctor of Divinity,	15
Civil Engineer,	2	Doctor of Laws,	13
Master of Arts,	75		

There has been connected with the University as Professors and instructors fifty-seven gentlemen. Of these six were graduates of Dartmouth; twenty-eight, Norwich University; one, Middlebury; one, University of Vermont; one, Harvard; one, Trinity College, Dublin, Ireland; one, New York City College; two, Columbia; one, Cambridge, England; two, United States Military Academy; one, Bowdoin; one, Williams; one, Trinity; one, Brown; one, Michigan; one, Upsala, Sweden. The remaining nine were foreigners teaching modern languages, and their colleges are unknown.

The present members of the Corporation and Faculty are as follows:

Capt. Charles A. Curtis, A. M., U. S. A., *President.*
Rt. Rev. William H. A. Bissell, D. D., Burlington.
Hon. Dudley C. Denison, Royalton.
Rev. Josiah Swett, D. D., Fairfax.
Col. Henry O. Kent, Lancaster, N. H.
Hon. George Nichols, M. D., Northfield.
Hon. P. D. Bradford, A. M. M. D., Northfield.

Mr. Perley Belknap, Northfield.
Hon. Henry Clark, Rutland.
Gen. Levi G. Kingsley, Rutland.
Col. Charles B. Stoughton, New York.
Mr. Hiram Atkins, Montpelier.
George M. Fisk, Esq., Northfield.
Col. Thomas J. Lasier, Claremont, N. H.
Col. Kittredge Haskins, Brattleboro.
Rev. Malcolm Douglass, D. D., Andover, Mass.
James A. L. Whittier, Esq., Boston, Mass.
Col. Robert Grosvenor, Providence, R. I.
Charles H. Reed, Esq., Boston, Mass.
Maj. Henry E. Alvord. East Hampton, Mass.
Clinton S. Averill, Esq., Milford, N. H.
Col. Fred. E. Smith, Montpelier, *Secretary*.
Joseph Stedman, M. D., Boston, Mass.
Mr. Thomas H. Canfield, Burlington.
Rev. Thomas J. Taylor, Windsor.

FACULTY.

Captain Charles A. Curtis, A. M., U. S. Army, *President*,
and Professor of Military Science by appointment of U. S Government.

Alonzo Jackman, LL. D.,
Professor of Mathematics, Natural Philosophy and Civil Engineering.

Charles Dole, A. M.,
Professor of Rhetoric, History, English Literature, and Assistant Instructor in Tactics.

Charles E. H. Gestrin, Ph. D.,
Professor of the Latin, French, and German Languages.

William M. Rumbaugh, B. S.,
Professor of Drawing and Assistant Instructor in Mathematics and Tactics.

Philander D. Bradford, M. D.,
Lecturer in Natural History and Physiology.

Rev. F. Weston Bartlett, A. M.,
Professor of Moral and Intellectual Philosophy.

GRADED AND HIGH SCHOOL.

By JAMES N. JOHNSON, Esq.

The Northfield Graded and High School is the chief and most important public school in the valley of Dog River. It was established nearly in its present form in 1870. The High School is the successor of the Northfield Institution formerly the Northfield Academy. This Academy was chartered by the Legislature in 1846. Previous to that time there has been no regular high school in this valley. Governor Paine donated the grounds for the Academy site in 1850, upon an eminence between the river and the Central Vermont railroad, and not far from the geographical center of the village of Northfield.

Through the exertions of Governor Paine, Heman Carpenter, John L. Buck, James Palmer, George R. Cobleigh, Benjamin Porter, Leander Foster, and quite a number of other public spirited citizens, a subscription of about $2,400 was raised for the purpose of erecting the school building, and another smaller subscription was raised to pay for furniture and apparatus. About a hundred men signed the main subscription, donating sums ranging from $5.00 to $500. The following are the main subscribers to the fund, with the respective amount of their subscriptions:

Charles Paine,	$500	James Moore,	$50
Heman Carpenter,	100	H. R. Campbell,	50
N. W. Lincoln,	25	A. Wetherbee,	25
Elijah Smith,	25	P. Belknap & Co.,	50
H. H. Camp,	50	N. C. & C. S. Munson,	50
Stephen Cochran,	25	G. P. Randall,	25

Dr. S. W. Thayer,	$50	H. L. Briggs,	$12.50
George M. Cady,	50	James Gould,	50
William Nichols,	75	Thomas Connor,	50
James Palmer,	75	William R. Tucker,	20
J. C. Cady,	40	R. H. Little,	50
William Rogers,	35	A. S. Braman,	20
E. A. Webb.	30	H. Nye,	20
George K. Cobleigh,	20	Leander Foster,	25
C. S. Dole,	25	Theophilus Cass,	20

The first meeting of the Trustees of the corporation was held at the Northfield House in the (then) "Factory village," March 6, 1847. The following named Trustees were present and formed by-laws, etc., viz.: Charles Paine, John L. Buck, Leander Foster, James Gould, James Palmer, and Heman Carpenter. John L. Buck, Esq., was chosen President, James Gould Vice President, and Heman Carpenter Secretary and Treasurer. Judge Carpenter filled these last positions continuously from that time till 1868. The Academy building was erected in 1851, by William H. H. Dunham and E. K. Jones, at a cost of about $2,600, and was dedicated and the school opened in the month of September, 1851, with C. C. Webster, A. M., as Principal. It flourished well. Rev. R. M. Manly succeeded as Principal in 1852-3. In 1854 the name of the school was changed by the Legislature to Northfield Institution, and after that time the following successive gentlemen were Principals of the school, viz.; John H. Graham, A. R. Bissell, George Brooks, J. G. McIntire, George F. Beard, and Charles G. Tarbell. Under their able teachers the Institution was well patronized, and acquired marked success. Having no separate fund for its support like more favored institutions, the school deteriorated to some extent during the War of the Rebellion.

After the decease of Northfield's benefactor, Governor Charles Paine, the following resolutions were unanimously adopted by the Board of Trustees of the Academy, January 30, 1854:

WHEREAS, The Trustees of the Northfield Academy have heard with deep grief the melancholy intelligence of the death of the Hon. Charles Paine, one of the Trustees of this Institution, who died at Waco, Texas, on the sixth day of July, A. D. 1853: therefore,

Resolved, That in his death this Institution has lost one of its first friends, and one whose aid contributed largely to the establishment and success of the same.

Resolved, That the friends of this Institution will ever hold in grateful remembrance the many public and private virtues of our deceased friend, and the services he has rendered the cause of education in our midst, and the advancement of the growth and prosperity of our State.

This Institution will perpetuate its organization, the following named gentlemen being the present Trustees:

P. D. Bradford, *President*,
Lorenzo Belknap, *Vice President*,
J. H. Orcutt, *Secretary and Treasurer*.

P. D. Bradford,
George Nichols,
J. H. Orcutt,
L. Belknap,
George M. Fisk,
} *Executive Committee*.

Perley Belknap, P. D. Bradford, J. C. Cady, Lorenzo Belknap, George Nichols, J. H. Orcutt, W. S. Hazen, E. K. Jones, J. C. B. Thayer, George M. Fisk, Charles Dole.

In the year of 1870 the village school district made a permanent arrangement with the Trustees of the Institution to take the building, repair it, and occupy it as a Graded and High School building, free for all pupils of the village. This was accomplished through the efforts of the friends of popular education, notably Hon. Heman Carpenter, James N. Johnson, Esq., Rev William S. Hazen, Thomas L. Salisbury, Esq., A. S. Braman, Esq., and J. H. Richardson, Esq. The Graded and High School opened in September, 1870, with three hundred and thirty-one pupils, Marshal R. Peck,

A. B., Principal. It took years of patient hard labor to mould and grade the several departments into good running order. Mr. Peck remained two years, and performed a herculean task for the school, for which he should ever be gratefully remembered by the public. Succeeding him as Principal have been A. R. Savage, Esq., Eben C. Smith, A. W. Blair, and W. W. Prescott, all efficient teachers, and the many lady teachers who have taught in the graded departments have not been less efficient. It received its charter by act of the Legislature in 1872.

The old Academy building was accidentally consumed by fire, January 13, 1876, and during the following season the present large, well built, and commodious school building was erected for the District at a cost of about $11,000, by J. C. Rice, upon the same site. Its dimensions are sixty by ninety feet, two stories high, modern build. The interior has seven main rooms, or Departments. The school is at present in a flourishing condition, and stands well among similar institutions of the State. It costs from $2,500 to $3,000 a year to run it.

The Directors of the school for 1878 are as follows:

Rev. William J. Kidder, *President*
James N. Johnson, Esq., *Vice President.*
Charles A. Edgerton, Esq., *Secretary.*
Hon. George Nichols.
George H. Crane, Esq.
Dr. O. O. Davis.
Edward Ingalls, Esq., *Clerk.*

MASONIC RECORD IN NORTHFIELD.

The first record of De Witt Clinton Lodge, No. 15, F. and A. M., was November 8, A. L. 5848, working under a Dispensation from the Grand Lodge of Vermont.

The Record does not show where they met, but it is believed they held their meeting in I. W. Brown's Hall at the Center village. The officers were as follows:

Joel Winch, *W. M.*,
H. W. Carpenter, *S. W.*,
Walter Little, *J. W.*,
Elijah Smith, Jr., *Secretary*.

Date of charter January 10, A. L. 5849.

CHARTER MEMBERS.

H. W. Carpenter, Joel Winch, Samuel L. Adams, Oramel Williams, Walter Little, Joshua Lane, Joseph Bean, John Fisk, Zeno Crocker, S. B. Holden, Phillip Staples, John Leonard, and Jesse Averill.

The first officers appointed by the Grand Lodge were as follows:

Joel Winch, *W. M.*,
Oramel Williams, *S. W.*,
Walter Little, *J. W.*,
Phillip C. Tucker, *Grand Master*,
J. B Hollenbeck, *Grand Secretary*

Rev. John Gregory received the first Degree August, A. L. 5849.

Joel Winch was Master from 1849 to 1851. Joel Winch, Jr., was elected Master, February 12, A. L. 5851, and held the office to 1853.

A. V. H. Carpenter was elected Master for the year 1853, and held the office one year.

Joel Winch, Jr., was again elected Master for the year 1854, and held the office for one year.

A. H. Proctor was elected Master for the year 1855, and held the office one year.

David L. Howe was elected Master for the year 1856.

A. H. Proctor was again elected for the year 1857, and held the office for two years, 1857 and 1858.

E. G. Babcock was elected Master for the year 1859, and held the office for two years.

C. N. Carpenter was elected Master for the year 1861, and held the office for two years.

E. G. Babcock was elected Master for the year 1863, and held the office one year.

James P. Warner was elected Master for the year 1864, and held the office for one year.

E. G. Babcock was again elected Master for the year 1865, and held the office one year.

J. L. Mack was elected Master for the year 1866, and held the office for six successive years—from the year 1866 to 1872.

J. G. Somerville was elected Master for the year 1872, and held the office two years.

George W. Kingsbury was elected Master for the year 1874, and held the office one year.

Henry Ferris was elected Master for the year 1875, and held the office two years.

J. L. Mack was elected Master for the year 1877, and is yet in that office.

H. L. Kenyon was elected Secretary in 1875, and has held the office since that time.

Masonic Relief Association of Vermont,

ESTABLISHED IN NORTHFIELD.

This popular and growing institution is located in Northfield, and its principal officers are citizens of this town. It was organized in February, 1875. Hon. George Nichols was elected President; J. L. Mack, Vice President; G. B. B. Denny, Secretary, and J. C. B. Thayer, Treasurer, and the same gentlemen continue to hold these several offices at the present time.

The expediency of establishing an association for the relief of families, and legal representatives of deceased masonic brethren in good and regular standing, was for a considerable time a subject of reflection and consideration on the part of the leading members of the craft in Vermont. The initiative steps were taken in Northfield by the brethren residents. The object of the Association commended itself at once to the true hearted craftsmen as every way worthy and feasible, and as offering a plan within the reach of every brother in the State, whereby he could provide for the family a safe policy, at the cheapest possible rates.

Experience has already taught us that this is a noble, praiseworthy Association. Like other charitable societies that are founded on the great principle of brotherhood, it seems a legitimate outgrowth of *free masonry*, and as such commends itself to all who have covenanted together in Masonic fellowship. A moment's careful reflection will convince the most bigoted that this institution was conceived in the spirit of true charity and wisdom, promising to bless those who are weak and dependent. Many of those who have joined the order are of the laboring class, and it is to them a great joy and relief to know that they have made provision for their families should Providence remove them from the loving presence of those who are dependent upon them. The old saying that "poverty is no disgrace, but very inconvenient" is felt to be true by those who are dependent upon every day's labor for a comfortable living. As long as health and strength exists the laboring man can keep up a buoyant spirit and labor manfully, but sickness comes, and frequently poverty with it, and then to whom can he go for relief?

Now there is a kind of pride which we can hardly condemn, that urges many of the poor to conceal their real condition from the curiosity of a well meaning benevolence. There are those who cannot bear *poverty*. They know the world well, or at least they suspect it. Many of them have seen better days. They know, as things are, it is too often the case that poverty is accounted a stigma. It is hard, it wrings the spirit with bitterness to say to those whom we have loved as friends and as equals, "I am poor, I am almost destitute, with wife and children to support, can you give me a little help?" Decently the growing poverty has been hidden from the most familiar friend. With an honest pride we have patched the old weather beaten garment, and eaten in secret the scanty meal. With an anxiety for *self* and *family*, that no one knows but God and ourselves, we have husbanded the failing fuel, and denied ourselves many of the comforts of life. But a time comes when it must be made known. *We must declare it*: not for *ourselves*, perhaps. We had almost rather lie down, and let the white kind snow be our winding sheet, and bid adieu to the world with frozen tears! We are bound to others by tender chords, and we cannot—no, we must not see them suffer!

Here comes the angel, Relief, and says, "cheer up, my brother man!" Associations are formed all over the land to help the needy and destitute, founded on the

Heaven born principles of "Friendship, Love and Truth," providing by weekly instalments for the sick, and making provision for those who are made widows and orphans by the relentless hand of death!

We rejoice that Northfield is not backward in these *relief movements*, and trust the day will come when the great heart of society shall be pervaded by a true Christian charity, when a system of mutual relief shall every where be established, and all be exercised by the spirit of a genial brotherhood, and not as a mechanical *alms* giving, or *alms* receiving.

We give two articles from the Association illustrating its principles:

PREMIUM AND ASSESSMENTS.

The premium to be paid on admission to the Association shall be for all applicants under thirty years of age $2.00; from thirty to thirty-five years $2.50; thirty-five to forty $3.00; forty to forty five $3.50; forty-five to fifty $4.00; fifty to sixty $5.00; all over sixty years of age $1.00 for each succeeding year.

DISPOSITION OF THE RELIEF FUND.

SECTION 1. When a member of the Association dies, a sum amounting to as many dollars as there are members in the class or classes to which he belongs, will become payable from the Treasury.

According to the Secretary's report for 1878 there were on the nineteenth of June four hundred and thirty-eight members, a gain during the year of two hundred, with cash on hand deposited in Savings Bank, $942.61. The following are the officers for 1878:

George Nichols, President; J. L. Mack, Vice President; G. B B. Denny, Secretary; J. C. B. Thayer, Treasurer; J. L. Moseley, C. D. Williams, Auditors.

DIRECTORS AT LARGE: H. H. Smith, Rutland, Vt.; James Holloway, St. Albans; M. O. Pingree, Montpelier; John Gregory, Northfield; Frank C. Churchill, Lebanon, N. H.

COUNTY DIRECTORS: G. N. Williston, St. Albans; C. H. Forbes, Brandon; A. H. Cobb, Rutland; L. M. Reed, Bellows Falls; J S. Batchelder, Waterbury; E. D. Strong, West Randolph, L. J Flint, Derby Line; E. B. True, Newport; J. D. Wilkins, Stowe Lewis Graham, St. Johnsbury; George W. Soper, H. L. Kenyon H. Ferris, and J. L. Moseley, Northfield, Vt.

MOUNT ZION COMMANDERY,

No. 9, Knight Templars.

A dispensation was granted by the Right Eminent Grand Commander to the following Sir Knights: J. L. Mack, Joel Winch, Henry D. Bean, Stephen Thomas, Frank H. Bascom, L. Bart Cross, Emory Towne, G. C. V. Eastman, George W. Tilden, Charles E. Abbott, J. M. Poland, and Allen McGilvery, to open a Commandery of Knights Templars at Northfield, and to confer the orders of knighthood.

The first meeting under this dispensation was held Wednesday, April 9, A. D. 1873, A. O. 755, and the following officers were appointed:

Jona. L. Mack, *Eminent Commander.*
Henry D. Bean, *Generalissimo.*
Frank H. Bascom, *Captain General.*
George C. V. Eastman, *Prelate.*
Charles E. Abbott, *Senior Warden.*
Allen McGilvery, *Junior Warden.*
Joel Winch, *Treasurer.*
J. Munroe Poland, *Recorder.*
Emory Towne, *Standard Bearer.*
L. Bart Cross, *Sword Bearer.*
George W. Tilden, *Warder.*

A charter was granted them by the Grand Commandery, June 10, A. D. 1873, A. O. 755, and August twenty-seventh of the same year they were formally constituted with appropriate ceremonies by the Right Eminent Grand Commander, Joseph L. Perkins, and other grand officers. This interesting occasion was graced by the presence of Burlington Commandery, No. 2, and the street parade of the two commanderies is remembered by citizens of the village as being most beautiful and imposing.

During the entire five years that the Commandery has existed Messrs. Mack and Bean have held respectively the offices of Eminent Commander and Generalissimo. The office of Captain General has been held by F. H. Bascom, Emory Towne, and Fred E. Smith. The commandery has been uniformly prosperous. The rolls have constantly increased, and as yet no name has been stricken out by death. At present there are forty-six Sir Knights.

LILY OF THE VALLEY,

CONCLAVE No. 5,

Knights of the Red Cross of Constantine.

A charter having been granted to Henry D. Bean, George C. V. Eastman, Joel Winch, George W. Kingsbury, Charles E. Abbott, and Allen McGilvery, by the Grand Imperial Council of the State of Michigan, to form and hold a Conclave of the RED CROSS and Appendant Orders at Northfield, in the State of Vermont, the above named Sir Knights on the ninth day of April, A. D. 1875, A. O. 1562, organized Lily of the Valley, Conclave No. 21, Knights of the Red Cross of Constantine, by electing

Henry D. Bean, *M. P. Sovereign.*
George C. V Eastman, *Viceroy.*
Allen McGilvery, *Sir General.*
Charles E. Abbott, Jr., *General.*
Joel Winch, *Treasurer.*
George W. Kingsbury, *Recorder.*

A convention of the several Conclaves of the Order in this State having been called met at Burlington, Vt., on the thirtieth day of April, A. D. 1875, and organized the Grand Imperial Council of Vermont under the direction of Sir D. Burnham Tracy, 33°, Grand Sovereign of Michigan. The organization being completed, the above named charter, No. 21, issued by the Grand Imperial Council of Michigan, was surrendered for endorsement, and was re-issued by the new Grand Council as No. 5 on its roll of subordinates, by the authority of which charter Lily of the Valley Conclave has continued to convene regularly for the transaction of the business of the Order until the present time.

ODD FELLOWSHIP.

In the fall of 1849, and in the early part of the winter of 1850, a few members of the order conceived the idea of forming a Lodge in Northfield. Accordingly after much consultation Brothers Dr. Samuel W. Thayer, J. C. B. Thayer, Dr. Edward A. Williams, Isaac L. Stevens, and Thomas J. Nutter sent a petition to the Grand Master, asking to be instituted as a Lodge. Their request was cheerfully granted, and in accordance therewith the Grand Master granted them a dispensation. On the twenty-fifth of March, 1850, the grand officers visited Northfield, and instituted the Lodge, with the above named brethren as charter members. The same evening the following named gentlemen became members: T. A. C. Beard, S. S. Cady, James Palmer, and J. S. Abbott, making in all ten members. The first Noble Grand was Dr. S. W. Thayer, and the first Vice Grand J. C. B. Thayer, and Dr. Edward H. Williams the first Secretary.

Prosperity attended this Lodge, and at the end of three months they had a membership of thirty. At the end of two years they had sixty members, and but one death occurred up to that time. About the first of May, 1852, their hall was burned, with all their books and Lodge property, except the Secretary's book. The loss in Regalia $140; a Library worth $50; charter $30; Lodge Books and fixtures $70; carpet, hall, trimmings, lamps, etc., $150; money in Widow and Orphan's Fund Box $15, amounting in all to $350, on which there was no insurance. The Lodge had at that time a debt outstanding of $100, also claims for sick benefits for $50. With a debt of $150, without a penny to pay it with, and no Lodge room, the members scattered. Had it not been for the faithfulness of those who loved Odd Fellowship, it must have gone down never to rise again.

The first meeting after the fire was held in the Hall of the Northfield House, when measures were taken to revive the work. After a time a Hall was procured on Central Street, in the house now occupied by General Jackman. The next Hall was in Union Block.

Prosperity again dawned upon this noble institution, so that by January 1, 1859, they had in the Treasury $508.29, and were free from debt. But this state of things did not long remain. Sickness and death made inroads upon them, and soon their Treasury was depleted. About this time the railroad works were removed to St. Albans, and as a matter of course many of the members went with them. Again those left became disheartened, and the good work ceased, after paying all their debts.

In the summer of 1871, Past Grand Master, P. D. Bradford, proposed a meeting of the faithful at his office, and at that meeting a petition was drawn up and signed by a goodly number petitioning the Grand Master to be again recognized. The request was granted, and on the evening of August 1, 1871, the grand officers came to Northfield, and restored the Lodge to life. After a few months they began to recuperate, and have gained steadily in funds and members until the present time, with a good working Lodge, and a determination to make it a success. So that to-day they have one hundred members, and $1200 in the Treasury, and are *free from debt*.

The amount of relief paid by the Lodge cannot be told, as the records were burned. But since 1871 they have paid $150 for *funeral expenses*, have buried two brothers, and two hundred members have been admitted to this institution since its first organization.

EUREKA ENCAMPMENT

Of the Patriarchal Branch of Independent Order Odd Fellows was instituted January 7, 1874, and now numbers thirty-two members, have $100 in Bank, with good furniture and fixtures, and are free from debt. They meet first and third Mondays of each month, at seven and a half o'clock P. M.

Odd Fellows Relief Association,

WAS ORGANIZED IN NORTHFIELD FEBRUARY 2, 1875

Hon. P. D. Bradford was elected President, and O. D. Edgerton, Esq., Clerk. Since then one hundred and eighty-eight persons have become members, and it is permanently established as one of the institutions of Northfield that is destined to do great good. Its principles are the same as those of the Masonic Relief Association, and we refer the reader to the comment made upon the latter institution as appropriate for both.

GOULDSVILLE LODGE, No. 166.

INDEPENDENT ORDER OF GOOD TEMPLARS.

This organization is the pioneer Lodge of the town, being formed December 20, 1871, with 13 charter members, there being just a sufficient number to obtain a charter. July 31st, 1872, the Lodge had a membership of 100, having gained 87 members in a few days over seven months. October 11th, of the same year, received notice of the death of Brother Charles Grant. This was the first death of a member. March 18, 1873, Brother E. N. Chandler, a worthy member, was instantly killed by an engine; also, the same month, Brother Sherman Gold, a charter member, and a life-long Temperance man, was called to a higher life. The same spring the Lodge was again called to mourn the death of a worthy member, Sister Myra Bowen; also, January 13, 1876, the Lodge lost our esteemed and worthy Brother, Joseph Gould, who was also a charter member. December 1, Sister Ella Simons died, and was shortly followed by her sister, Mrs. Harriet Thrasher, another worthy member.

The highest number of members at any one time was one hundred and thirty-nine. The lowest since the first quarter was sixty-eight, and at the present time has a membership of 74, in good standing, and doing a good work. The finances are sound; the Lodge is free from debt, and an amount of over $80 in the treasury. As an auxiliary of the Lodge, there is also a Juvenile Temple, consisting of over 40 members, mostly children between the ages of 5 and 16 years, well organized, and doing a good work for Temperance, and in connection with the Lodge, may be considered one of the permanent institutions of the place.

LIST OF WORTHY GOOD TEMPLARS LODGE FROM THE TIME IT WAS ORGANIZED TO THE PRESENT.

H. H. Perkins, George Carter, A. F. Andrews, Charles F. Beard, H. S. Thrasher, D. R. Fisk, Charles McIntosh, H. L. Rich, E. F. Sisco, H. P. Flint, D. R. Fisk, A. Rich, A. F. Andrews, S. L. Gilder, H. L. Rich, Charles Benedict.

MOUNTAIN GEM LODGE,

INDEPENDENT ORDER OF GOOD TEMPLARS.

This Lodge was organized 20th March, 1873, at South Northfield, and was the second Lodge of Good Templars in the town. It has numbered among its members the best citizens of that part of the town, and has always exerted a good healthful moral influence, as well as Temperance sentiments. It started with 28 charter members.

The following were the first officers:

W. W. Holden, *Worthy Chief Templar.*
Dora L. Holden, *Worthy Vice Templar.*
E. K. Jones, *Worthy Secretary*
Harriet E. Jones, *Worthy Assistant Secretary.*
George H. Denny, *Worthy Financial Secretary*
Martin Cobleigh, *Worthy Treasurer.*
Wm. Slade, *Worthy Chaplain.*
Frank S. Mead, *Past Worthy Chief Templar.*
F. A. Jones, *Worthy Marshal.*
Olive A. Howe, *Worthy Deputy Marshal.*
Matilda J. Howe, *Worthy Right Hand Supporter*
Delia Mead, *Worthy Left Hand Supporter.*
Elra M. Slade, *Worthy Guard*
O. A. Slade, *Worthy Sentinel.*

The Worthy Chief Templars, since the organization of the Lodge, have been as follows:

W. W. Holden, Thomas Slade, E. K. Jones, Martin Cobleigh, E. Kimball, Allen Slade, Herman T. J. Howe, Dan. Derby, Frank W. Gold, Fred. A. Jones, Jeff. E. House, Albert Steele, Elra M. Slade, S. P. Orcutt and F. E. Steele.

The following have been Worthy Vice Templars:

Dora L. Holden, Elva M. Steele, Harriet E. Jones, Carrie Cobleigh, Celia Gold, Nellie Kimball, Emma A. Wright, Aurora M. Edson, Clara Cobleigh, Anna Fuller, Etta Briggs, Susie Jones, Abbie Kimball, Anna Jones and Roxana Orcutt.

The Lodge Deputies have been Thomas Slade, W. W. Holden, S. P. Orcutt and Dan. Derby.

The following have been Delegates to the Grand Lodge: W. W. Holden, E. K. Jones, S. P. Orcutt, Thomas Slade, and Dan. Derby.

The Lodge now numbers about fifty members. It is numerically the smallest Lodge of the town, but it has always numbered among its members more of the eligible inhabitants of its jurisdiction than either of the other Lodges; and, although its field of labor has not been as hard as the others, yet it has always exerted a good influence and done a good work.

NORTHFIELD LODGE, No. 175.

Independent Order of Good Templars.

Was organized in the village of Northfield, at Concert Hall, April 3, 1873, by Colonel John B. Mead, of Randolph, Grand Worthy Chief Templar, assisted by Rev. E. Folsom, Deputy Grand Worthy Chief Templar for Washington County, and by large delegations from the Lodges at Gouldsville, and the South village.

Over one hundred names were on the application for a charter, and of them eighty presented themselves for initiation, on the evening of institution. Starting with so large a membership, comprising many of our best citizens and representing all branches of industry, it stepped at once into the front ranks among the Lodges of the State, and in January, 1875, a little more than a year and a half, it had a membership of two hundred and one, making it the Banner Lodge of the County and of the State, which position it has since held. The largest membership was in August, 1877, when it numbered two hundred and ninety members in good standing. At the occasion of its Fifth anniversary the report shows that there had been initiated into the Lodge over five hundred members; one half that number have severed their connection with the Lodge, by removals, withdrawals etc., leaving the present number two hundred and fifty. In January, 1875, this Lodge, assisted by the cotemporary Lodges of the town, entertained the Grand Lodge of the State; and in January, 1879, will again have the same pleasure The officers at the organization of the Lodge, were

Frank Plumley, *Worthy Chief Templar.*
Altha Dutton, *Worthy Vice Templar.*
Ladoit Derby, *Worthy Secretary.*
Mrs. L. W. Avery, *Worthy Financial Secretary.*

L. W. Avery, *Worthy Treasurer.*
J. F. Davis. *Worthy Chaplain.*
S. B. Spaulding, *Worthy Marshal.*
Hattie Clifford, *Worthy Deputy Marshal.*
Lizzie Knapp, *Worthy Guard.*
H. W. Davis. *Worthy Sentinel.*
Mrs. L. L. Plumley. *Worthy Right Hand Supporter.*
Clara Maxham, *Worthy Left Hand Supporter.*
A. R. Savage. *Lodge Deputy.*

Succeeding Worthy Chief Templars,

Rev. R. A. Greene. Frank Plumley. J. F. Davis, O. D. Edgerton, Dr. P. D. Bradford. L. W. Avery. W. H. H. Claflin. Dr. W. H. Bryant. C. M. Johnston. and F. R. Bates.

Succeeding Worthy Vice Templars.

Mrs. L. L. Plumley. Mrs. L. W. Avery, Mrs. Carrie M. Smith. E. Nellie Chase, Ellen Davis, Mrs. A. Buckley Emerson. Cora Bacon. Nettie Braley, Alice Sylvester. Emma Thomas, and Lillie Rumrill.

Lodge Deputies—1873-4, A. R. Savage; 1874-5, L. W. Avery; 1876-7, O. D. Edgerton; 1878, Dr. P. D. Bradford; he resigning, Dr. W. H. Bryant.

Representatives to Grand Lodge—1874, A. R. Savage, Frank Plumley; 1875, W. H. H. Claflin, Ella Dutton; 1876, O. D. Edgerton, Mrs. L. W. Avery, Washington Coburn; 1877, J. F. Davis, C. M. Johnston, Mrs. Carrie Smith; 1878, Rev. A. B. Truax, Dr. W. H. Bryant, Mrs. W, H. H. Claflin.

Members of the Lodge honored by the Grand Lodge—1874, F. Plumley, Alternate Delegate to Right Worthy Grand Lodge; 1874, A. R. Savage, District Deputy for Washington County; 1875, and since F. Plumley. Grand Worthy Secretary, by annual elections; Mrs. F. Plumley, Assistant Grand Secretary two years; 1876, O. D. Edgerton. Member Finance Committee three years; 1876, Mrs. L. W. Avery, Delegate to Right Worthy Grand Lodge; 1877, C. M. Johnston, Assistant Grand Secretary; 1877, O. D. Edgerton, Delegate to Right Worthy Grand Lodge; 1877, J. F. Davis, and Dr. P. D. Bradford, State Deputies; 1878, O. D. Edgerton, State Deputy; 1878, Rev. A. B. Truax, Grand Worthy Chaplain; 1878, Frank Plumley, Chairman, and O. D. Edgerton, served upon special mission Committee.

Without giving this Lodge more credit than is its due, it may justly be said that it has done and is doing a good work in the temperance reformation of the town. The Lodge and its members very properly feel a just pride in the position it has taken in the councils of the Grand Lodge, where its influence is by no means inconsiderable. May all the Good Templars of this town take "excelsior" for their motto, "vigilance" for their watchword, and with "envy toward none, but with charity for all," ever press onward and upward in their noble work of rescuing the fallen and saving others from falling, until all the inhabitants of the town shall be redeemed from intemperance, and alcohol banished from our midst.

THE DEGREE TEMPLE,

Independent Order of Good Templars.

In 1873 the Degree members of Gouldsville, Mountain Gem, Roxbury, Brookfield and Northfield Lodges organized Union Degree Temple, No. 12, with the following officers:

A. R. Savage, *Degree Templar.*
Helen Flint, *Degree Vice Templar.*

meetings were permanently established at Good Templar's Hall with Northfield Lodge. On account of the same reasons for the change of place of meetings most of the members of the other Lodges withdrew, and the Temple is now confined largely to Northfield Lodge. There has been about one hundred and fifty members in all, of which there now remains about sixty. The Temple is intermediate between the subordinate and Grand Lodges, and when well sustained and worked, it is quite as enjoyable as anything in Good Templary.

Northfield Juvenile Temple, No. 1.

Not least among our valuable institutions, and means of doing good, is Northfield Juvenile Temple, No. 1. Some of our people, realizing the benefit of a thorough temperance education for our children, met April 3, 1875, in Good Templar's Hall, with Miss Lucy Bradshaw, of Montpelier, then State Superintendent of Juvenile Temple, who organized the first Temple in the State, with 53 members, 15 honorary and 38 children. Rev. R. A. Greene was chosen Superintendent, and held that office nearly two years, as long as he remained in town, when Mrs. L. E. Pope was appointed, and served five months, until she resigned. Mrs. C. M. Persons was appointed, and has held the office the last year, and is doing a noble work. Their pledge, the best one in the temperance organization, is as follows:

"I do most solemnly promise that I will never, so long as I live, make, buy, sell, or use as a beverage, any spirituous or malt liquors, wine, beer or cider. I also promise to abstain from the use of tobacco in any form. I also promise that I will never take the name of God in vain, or use profane or wicked words. I also promise to do all I can to honor this pledge by a good example, and that I will obey the laws of the Juvenile Templars.

This Temple has increased in numbers and usefulness, and now has more than one hundred and fifty members, working zealously for Temperance.

SONS OF TEMPERANCE.

CENTRAL DIVISION, NO. 80, INSTITUTED FEBRUARY 16, 1858.

This noble institution had its day of working great good in Northfield in the cause of Temperance. The best minds in this town were its warmest supporters, and many addicted to their cups were rescued from a drunkard's doom by their instrumentality. The elevation of the race, the salvation of the inebriate from temporal ruin and disgrace, the rescue of the moderate drinker from a debasing and corrupting habit, and the relief of the widow and the fatherless, were the primary objects of this institution. Men of all religious proclivities engaged in this work, and unitedly labored for the good of humanity. But, like other benevolent associations for the suppression of vice, it *declined*, and made room for what seemed to be more practicable temperance organizations. Still, we know its existence was a blessing to many, and should have honorable mention in this history.

CARSWELL TEMPLE OF HONOR

Was a temperance organization, and was instituted December 28, 1868. It took for its title the above name, and was short-lived. The expense of running it seemed too high for those in moderate circumstances.

BANKS.

The Northfield Bank was chartered by an act of the Legislature, November 23, 1854, with a capital of $100,000. The first meeting for the election of officers was held January 9, 1855, and the following Directors were chosen:

Calvin Ainsworth, Perley Belknap, Reuben Peck, John B. Hutchinson, and Alvin Braley. The same day Calvin Ainsworth was elected President by the Directors, and H. M. Bates, Cashier

In 1865, at a stockholders' meeting, it was voted to organize the Northfield National Bank, under the laws of the United States. H. C. Ely was appointed Assistant Cashier in November, 1864.

In 1878, January 8, at the annual meeting, George Nichols, John Lamson, Charles A. Edgerton, J. C. Gallup, and J. C. Cady were elected Directors, and George Nichols was elected President; since then, F. L. Ely Cashier, having deceased, Charles A. Edgerton, Jr., was appointed in his place.

The Northfield Savings Bank was incorporated in 1867. This prosperous and well-conducted institution has a record of which its friends may be justly proud. By close attention to its interests, and an economical administration of its affairs, it has, in eleven years, become strong and successful, and vies in importance and stability with older institutions in our State. The citizens of Northfield may congratulate themselves upon having a Savings Bank that is a safe depository of their funds. The following is a list of officers for 1877–8:

George M. Fisk, President; George H. Crane, Vice-President; James Carey B. Thayer, Treasurer; Carlos D. Williams, Secretary; Board of Directors, Orvis D, Edgerton, Jasper H. Orcutt, Andrew E. Denny, John P. Davis, Edwin K. Jones.

Amount of deposits, $151,861.17. Last report.

GOVERNOR PAINE'S LOG CABIN.

Men are now living in Northfield who can well remember the time when a log cabin was put on wheels, improvised by Governor Paine, and drawn to Burlington, upon the 12th of July, 1840, in the days of "Tippecanoe and Tyler too." It was a unique affair, and attracted immense attention by its novelty, and one of our most esteemed citizens, whose likeness graces our history, remembers tapping a barrel of cider and dispensing it to the distinguished crowd who rode inside of this rustic vehicle. We take an extract from an article written by De Witt Clark, editor of the Burlington *Times*, giving a graphic description of the celebration. He says:

* * * * * "But what attracted most our attention, next to the imposing display of numbers, was a beautiful log cabin from Northfield, mounted on wheels and drawn by 12 superb grays, decorated with flags and festoons. This team, we are told, belongs to an honest yeoman in Brookfield, and is ordinarily engaged in transporting produce to Boston; but, said the patriotic owner, this is the proudest load that ever my team was attached to, and to the country the most profitable. Without rein or check, these noble steeds promptly responded to the 'Gee up!' 'Whoa, Dobbin!' of the brave mountaineer who directed them, and when we saw them proudly treading our streets and doubling the shortest corners, with a rural tenement large enough for a country school-house, we could not help exclaiming, in the language of the old song:

"I've often thought, if I were asked
Whose lot I envied most,
What one I thought most lightly tasked,
Of man's numbered host,
I'd say I'd be a mountain boy,
And drive a noble team, wo-hoy!
Wo-hoy! I'd cry;

Now by yon sky
I'd sooner drive those steeds
Than win renown,
Or wear a crown,
Won by victorious deeds."

The cabin itself was a very fine one, constructed of peeled logs, twenty feet by ten, covered with bark, fitted up with paper curtains, a rough door, and a *leather string*, which hung out. The antlers of a noble stag graced one peak, while the outer covering of some unlucky coon stretched upon the gable bespoke the fate of sub treasurers and cornfield poachers. This tenement, too, was well filled with the early tenants of log cabins, and bore this significant motto, "The people are coming!" Exclamations were heard from every rank by the surrounding thousands, with three times three for old Washington, Paine, and the Northfield cabin."

THE HARLOW BRIDGE TRAGEDY.

Never was there a tragedy in Vermont which equaled the one that took place on the eleventh of December, 1867, at "Harlow Bridge." It occurred just after noon, and sent a thrill of horror all over the land. About one hundred mechanics and laborers employed in rebuilding the "Harlow Bridge" on the Vermont Central railroad, about two miles from the depot, were boarding at the Northfield House. That day they took their dinner there as usual, and this repast finished, the last meal that many of them were ever again to partake, about sixty of them got into a passenger car, and started back for their work. The train, consisting of one car and locomotive and tender, was in charge of Francis B. Abbott, for fifteen years a faithful hand in the employ of the road. He was requested to hurry up, so as to get back and take the others, and the train started, backing up. Intent only upon obeying orders, and forgetting all else, he ran at a speed reprehensible under the circumstances. A number on the train felt that they were going to destruction, but nothing was done to stop it, and then came the culmination of this horrid disaster, which carried mourning and desolation into so many families. It is said that the fireman spoke to the engineer about slacking his speed, and at last hurled a stick of wood at his head, to awake him from his revery, telling him to reverse his engine, which he did, but too late. The passenger car first plunged into the frightful abyss. Going down about twenty-five feet it struck upon the bank, which projected something like a shelf, and then broke, one part of it stopping there, and one going to the bottom, over sixty feet further. The tender followed, crushing in among those who remained with that portion of the car which lodged on the bank, where the greatest mortality occurred, those going to the bottom escaping comparatively easy. Across those on the shelf a large timber had fallen, and on this the tender, pinning them to the earth and crushing out their very life. The reversing the engine suddenly prevented that from following, although it had gone so far that a perpendicular line dropped from the flange of the driver, carried it four feet beyond the abutment. Affrighted, the engineer jumped from his post, but seeing his engine did not go over he at once regained his position, and thus prevented the machine from tearing down the road with the velocity of a scared bird, with no one to control it. The following is a list of the casualties:

KILLED.

Almon Wetherbee, foreman of bridge gang; Cristopher Devine, laborer; Patrick Garvin, laborer: Edward Sweeney, trackman; Timothy McCarty, trackman; Louis Rock, bridge builder, citizens of Northfield, and nine others killed, most of whom lived in Canada.

WOUNDED.

George Randall, telegraphist; Horace Kingsbury, carpenter; J. Mulcahey, laborer, citizens of Northfield, and thirty-five others from towns in this State and Canada.

ELMWOOD CEMETERY.

By Hon. PHILANDER D. BRADFORD.

Within the corporate limits of the village of Northfield, just north of the same, upon a beautiful piece of table-land, is situated Elmwood Cemetery.

The ground originally comprised an area of six acres and thirty-six rods, and was donated to the people of Northfield by their late benefactor, ex-Governor Charles Paine.

On the first day of April, 1854, many of the citizens of the town met, in pursuance of a call, at the office of Hon. Heman Carpenter, for the purpose of effecting an organization under the general statutes, subsequently known as "The Northfield Cemetery Association." The meeting was organized by appointing Heman Carpenter chairman, and George Nichols clerk.

A committee of five were appointed to prepare articles of agreement, and a code of by-laws for the association. At an adjourned meeting, held at the same place, April 8, the committee presented a code of by-laws, which were adopted, and an organization was perfected by electing a President, Clerk, Treasurer, and five Curators.

Governor Paine having deceased, his administrators, James C. Dunn, of Boston, and Miss Caroline Paine, of New York, agreeable to his expressed wish, executed a deed of the above mentioned land to the Northfield Cemetery Association. The deed contains the following words: "In consideration of one dollar and good will paid to our full satisfaction, we grant, confirm, and convey to the Northfield Cemetery Association the following described land, etc., for the burial of the dead, and for no other purpose." The Curators proceeded at once to inclose the grounds, lay out lots, avenues, walks, and open areas, causing the lots to be numbered, and a chart to be made of the same. But death was faster than they, for on the twenty-sixth of the same month, even before the grounds were inclosed, the remains of Daniel Stevens were buried there, his being the first grave in the cemetery. In October, 1855, an act was passed by the Legislature of Vermont incorporating the Northfield Cemetery Association. The act provided that the affairs of the Association should be managed by Trustees in number not less than five, nor more than seven, and that they should elect from their number a President, Clerk, and Treasurer. The corporation were as follows: Royce Jones, William Rogers, H. M. Bates, William C. Woodbury, George Nichols, J. C. Cady, P. D. Bradford, J. C. B. Thayer, Perley Belknap, Heman Carpenter, E. A.

Webb, E. G. Babcock, G. N. Cady, Calvin Cady, and W. F. Woodworth. In November, 1866, the Legislature passed an act in amendment of an act of 1855, "called an act incorporating the Northfield Cemetery Association," authorizing the Association formed under the General Statutes to accept the charter passed at the session of 1856, and that all rights, both in law and equity, be secured to and enjoyed by the association formed under the General Statutes that are secured to and enjoyed by the members of the association formed under the act aforesaid. At a meeting duly warned and held August 12, 1857, the association voted to accept the charter and amendment, and organized under the act of 1855 by electing five Trustees, viz.: William C. Woodbury, E. A. Webb, George Nichols, L. D. Gilchrist, and Jefferson Marsh. E. A. Webb was elected President, George Nichols, Clerk and Treasurer.

In November, 1867, an act was passed by the Legislature in amendment of an act passed November, 1855, changing the name of the Northfield Cemetery Association to "Elmwood Cemetery;" also authorizing the Trustees to contract with individuals for the perpetual care and improvement of any lot or lots in said cemetery. In November, 1876, the Legislature passed an act in amendment of the foregoing, giving full power and control to the Trustees as to the burial of the dead; also full power to control and prevent the burial and removal of bodies buried in said cemetery, as fully and to the same extent that Selectmen have in the burial grounds of the State, and to the extent necessary to protect said cemetery from encroachment or trespass by any person or persons. The cemetery contains at the present time the remains of five hundred and seventy-five persons. It has long been apparent that the grounds were not adequate to the increasing and prospective wants of the community, and the Trustees added to the same in 1877 by the purchase of additional land.

The site selected for this cemetery is beautifully adapted to that purpose, and shows the good judgment and taste of the donor. It is withdrawn a little distance from the busy thoroughfare, yet easy of access, and affords a pleasant walk, which appears a favorite one with citizens and strangers. If the character of a people for refinement and religion is indicated by the care of and taste displayed in beautifying the burial places of the dead, it is a matter of congratulation that our cemetery, with its beautiful monuments, its mementoes of affection, and numerous emblems of the Christian hope lighting up the darkness of this world, contrasts so strongly with the cheerless and unattractive burial grounds of fifty years ago. If this cemetery shall be beautified in years to come as it may be beautified, if art shall vie with nature in adding to its attractions, if affection, not avarice, take the lead in questions of expenditures, it will soon become one of the most attractive spots within the limits of our Green Mountain State.

The Association at its annual meeting, which was held on the first Tuesday in May, 1878, re-elected the former Trustees, viz.: P. D. Bradford, J. H. Orcutt, C. D. Williams, J. C. Gallup, and E. G. Pierce, who subsequently elected P. D. Bradford President, C. D. Williams, Clerk and Treasurer, G. B. B. Denny, Auditor, and James Evans, Sexton.

In connection with and belonging to said cemetery, is a substantial and commodious tomb, mention of which should not be omitted. At the annual town meeting in the spring of 1867, the Selectmen were instructed by a vote of the town to build a tomb for temporary deposit of the dead, to be located at such place as would best accommodate the town. During the following summer the Selectmen (Marvin Simons, William Winch, and Dr. Samuel Keith,) agreeable to instructions, caused said tomb to be constructed at an expense of twelve hundred dollars, and located it within the cemetery grounds, the Association donating the site. The front of the tomb is of hewn granite from Berlin quarry, with panels of serpentine from Roxbury quarry, donated by the late Thomas L. Salisbury. It is surmounted by a heavy marble cross, (the emblem of the Christian's faith) upon which is the monogram I. H. S.

This tomb, bordering upon the highway at the head of North Street, has been found of great convenience in the winter season, and for both usefulness and artistic beauty reflects great credit upon the town, and especially upon the member of the Board (Dr. Keith) who had charge of its construction.

EAST HILL CEMETERY.

This cemetery is situated at the four corners on the East Hill, near the first settlement of the town, in what is called the Robinson district. It was the first burying ground in Northfield, and for a number of years the only one. The land belonged to the farm of Amos Robinson, and no organization as we can learn was ever formed to control it. All who desired it for the burial of their friends had the privilege, and here many of the early settlers rest from their labors. Among the prominent men that are here interred are Amos Robinson, Nathaniel Robinson, Abraham Shipman, Thomas Averill and Jesse Averill, Lebbeus Bennett, Parley Tyler, William Jones, and Samuel Buzzell, with their wives and many of their children.

CENTER CEMETERY.

On the eighteenth of September, 1823, Ezekiel Robinson, Oliver Averill, Joseph Keyes, Harry Emerson, and Nathan Green bought of E. Taylor, Jr., and G. R. Spalding one acre of land lying west of where the yellow meeting house stood for a burying ground, paying therefor sixty dollars. It was laid out in lots eleven and a half by twenty-five feet in size, with a drive-way running through from east to west. The lots were sold at seventy-five cents each, and in 1829 had all been disposed of except two lots in the southwest corner, which were reserved as a burial place for strangers.

From time to time additions have been made to each side of the lot: that of Jonathan Briggs on the east, where the first meeting house was built, and last on the west one acre and one hundred and twenty-seven rods of land bought of Timothy Reed, September 30, 1874, for $204.45.

Soon after this cemetery was established, the bodies that were buried on what was called "Richardson's Meadow," a little west of the railroad, began to be disinterred and re-committed to the earth at the Center, until it is now thought nearly all have been removed. From 1811 to 1823 Richardson's meadow was the general burial place in the vicinity. Some few were carried to the East Hill burying ground, and some to the west of Depot village, in a little burial place near the farm of F. A. Preston, Esq.

Nature has done much to make this ground "beautiful for situation," and a little labor in the right direction, placing around the entire lot rows of maples, and other ornamentations, would make it more in keeping with the spirit of the age, that is devising ways and means to make these resting places of our honored dead more attractive and pleasant. The improvement so auspiciously began in the front part of the cemetery is praiseworthy, and it is hoped will be continued until the whole enclosure shall present an agreeable appearance.

GOULDSVILLE CEMETERY.

This burying ground is located in the center of the village, and shows care and attention in the laying out of the lots, and keeping them clear from weeds and briers. A distinguished traveler once remarked: "Show me the *cemeteries* and *churches* of a town, and I will tell you the character of the people."

The Falls village burial ground association was organized according to chapter eighty-one of Revised Statutes. The first meeting was held at the school house in district number thirteen on the twenty-seventh of December, 1848, at which a constitution was adopted, and the following officers chosen:

A. S. Braman, *Moderator*; Marvin Simons, *Clerk*; Leander Foster, James Gould, Samuel Smith, Lotan Libbey, Anson Munson, *Executive Committee*.

The land for the cemetery formerly belonged to the farm of Luther S. Burnham, and was bought and laid out in seventy-nine lots, and sold at $4.00 cash each. The grounds have since been enlarged by an addition of about one half an acre laid out by the Selectmen in 1877, which still belongs to the town, but will be deeded to the association when paid for.

Dog River Valley Association.

In the summer of 1873 a meeting was called to take into consideration the propriety of forming an association to benefit the farmers of Northfield, and it resulted in the formation of the above named society. In October first and second of the same season the first Fair was held, on Frank W. Gold's trotting park, known as the "Dog River Valley Fair," which was so great a success that they have been continued each year since. It proved that the resources of Northfield and vicinity were equal to the occasion. Calling in the aid of Williamstown, Brookfield, Braintree, Roxbury, and Berlin, the Fair was as good as any ever held in the County. Every department was well represented, and Floral Hall was the center of attraction not surpassed by any in the State, and elicited applause from thousands of people. The following were the officers:

John Gregory, *President*; Frank W. Gold, Northfield, George Crane, Williamstown, W. C. Clark, Brookfield, William Orcutt, Roxbury, and C. E. Andrews, Berlin, *Vice Presidents*; James Morse, *Secretary*; J. F. Davis, *Auditor*; William Winch, *Treasurer*.

After serving as President three years, Mr. Gregory declined a re-election, and J. H. Orcutt was chosen to fill that position, which he has creditably held since. C. D. Williams is now the acting Secretary.

THE GREAT REBELLION OF 1861.

The world never before witnessed such an uprising of the people! It was as though the whole current of thought and feeling had been changed in a day. Men met on the marts to forget all about stocks and market quotations, to prove their loyalty to the Government. Congregations gathered in the churches to forget creeds and theological differences in their absorbing devotion to the salvation of their country. Women gathered, to forget small talk and social tribulations in the noble enthusiasm ever awakened in woman's bosom when great emergencies arise. Schools were listless, and the eyes of both teachers and pupils turned longingly to the streets where the people were gathering. The solemn tread of regiments was answered by the acclamations of the gathered thousands who everywhere thronged the highways. Men met friends changed to soldiers, and with a benediction bade them adieu. Fathers, mothers, and sisters sat down to the evening meal to find one chair vacant, and the prayers which went up from that family circle called down God's blessing on the absent one. It was indeed the season of sorrow, but it was also the carnival of patriotism. This world may never witness its like again. Let us pray that an overruling Providence may spare the country from another such a visitation of *treason,* when citizens shall fly to arms to protect with their lives and fortunes their beloved country.

When the call came booming over the mountains for help to stay the giant rebellion that was grasping at the very throat of the nation, did Northfield hesitate? No! In that hour it was not found wanting! True to its loyalty, it responded, "We are coming, father Abraham," and amid tears and partings it sent its brave boys to the front. O, it will be long remembered, when amid the ringing of bells, the boom of cannon, and the shouts of the populace, the train moved out of the depot carrying loved ones who might never, never return. It was indeed a day to try men's souls; but love of country prevailed over all other considerations, and with a heroic and manly firmness they went forward. All honor to the brave men who, in that hour of tribulation and sorrow, rallied around the old flag, "Shouting the battle cry of freedom." Honor to the noble women, who bade their husbands, sons, and brothers go and save their country! May we never forget them.

"When thee, Jerusalem, I forget, skill part from my right hand!"

The citizens of Northfield, through the Rev. William C. Hopkins, presented Captain Boynton a purse of gold containing $500.00, to assist those who should need help in their new calling South, showing by their works that they were not only patriotic but generous and just! "By their fruits ye shall know them."

Sunday, April 28, 1861, "The New England Guards" attended services in all the churches in Northfield, viz: In the morning at the Universalist, at one o'clock at the Methodist, at three o'clock at the Episcopal, and at five o'clock at the Congregational. All the churches had special services appropriate to the great occasion.

New England Guards of Northfield.

First Regiment of *three months men* mustered into the service of the United States, May 2, 1861; mustered out of service, August 15, 1861:

Captain, William H. Boynton; *First Lieutenant*, Charles A. Webb; *Second Lieutenant*, Francis B. Gove; *Sergeants*, Charles C. Stearns, Joseph C. Bates, John Randall, Silas B. Tucker; *Corporals*, Wesley C. Howes, John H. Hurley, John L. Moseley, Adin D. Smith; Thirty-two Privates.

According to the Adjutant General's Report, Northfield furnished the following men during the war:

Nine months men, seventy-four; three years men, one hundred and eighty-eight; one year men, three; re-enlisted, thirty-nine; furnished under draft, twenty-one; procured as substitutes, seven; entered service. two; United States Navy, seven.

The names, with company and regiment, of each of the above had been carefully prepared by the editor, but was found too long for publication, and was reluctantly omitted.

List of Killed and Died of Disease.

A. D. Smith, killed at the Wilderness, May 5, 1864.
William J. Howe, died December 7, 1862.
Washington Hunt, died January 26, 1862.
Newman Amidon, died December 19, 1861.
Franklin Averill, died in Andersonville.
Kneeland Badger, killed at Cedar Creek, October 19, 1864.
William Balch, died October 12, 1862.
Orrin O. Blodgett, died March 5, 1862.
Charles W. Blood, died October 6, 1862.
Gilbert E. Fisk, missing in action, July 3, 1863.
Van. L. Fisk, died —— 28, 1863.
William P. Fisk, died in Andersonville.
John Fitzgerald, died September 1, 1862.
L. L. Fowler, died October 6, 1862.
Alfred Jacobs, died September 2, 1864.
Lester Patterson, died December 25, 1863.
E. F. Smith, died October 1, 1864.
G. Smith, died February 1, 1864.
A. Woodworth, died October 28, 1864.
C. Woodworth, died August 28, 1864.
Oscar Maxham, died January 28, 1865.
A. O. Ralph, died July 21, 1864.
John Norton, died July 21, 1864.
Charles Roulston, died January 6, 1862.
S. M. Russell, died October 21, 1864.
William H. Sturtevant, died May 11, 1863.
John Dutton, died August 12, 1862.
George N. Willey, died March 22, 1862.
S. P. Woodward, died August 15, 1864.
C. E. Woodbury, died December 2, 1862.
George Young, died February 23, 1863.
Heman Dole, died in Rebel Prison.
John Dutton, died in Rebel Prison.
D. A. Houston, died October 13, 1862.
L. H. King, died March 11, 1865.
M. A. Locklin, died September 22, 1864.
John Taggard, died October 14, 1862.
C. Webster, died May 29, 1863.
William Murphy, died in 1863.
George Rumney, died in 1864.
Levi Smith, died in March, 1863.

Officers and Business Firms in 1878.

POPULATION IN 1820, - - - - [illegible]
POPULATION IN 1840, - - - 2,[illegible]
POPULATION IN 1870, - - - - [illegible]

OFFICERS—*Clerk*, George B. B. Denny; *Treasurer*, C. S. Richmond; *1st Selectman*, George Nichols, *2d*, R. W. Clark, *3d*, James Morse; *Constable*, O. O. Davis; *Superintendent of Schools*, Charles Dole; *Listers*, John L. Mosely, C. A. Tracy, J. C. Gallup, *Overseer of the Poor*, F. A. Preston; *Agent*, John P. Davis.

POSTMASTERS—Northfield, J. H. Orcutt, Gouldsville, A. J. Andrews, South Northfield, F. Jones.

JUSTICES—George H. Crane, Andrew Howarth, Martin Cobleigh, Howard Davis, George B. Loomis, A. O. Smith, C. A. Tracey, A. L. Smalley, D. T. Averill, Charles Dole, S. D. Horner, James Morse.

BANKS—Northfield National, President, George Nichols, Cashier, C. A. Edgerton, Jr.; Northfield Savings, President, George M. Fisk; Treasurer, J. C. B. Thayer.

CHURCHES—Congregationalist, Rev. W. S. Hazen; Episcopalian, Rev. F. W. Bartlett; Methodist, Rev. A. B. Truax; Universalist, Rev. W. M. Kimmell; Catholic, Rev. J. Galligan.

LAWYERS—Heman Carpenter, George M. Fisk, James N. Johnson, Frank Plumley, Cyrus M. Johnston.

PHYSICIANS—P. D. Bradford, Clifton Claggett, Edwin Porter, W. N. Bryant, Leonard Thrasher, William B. Mayo.

DENTISTS—S. L. Wellington, N. W. Gilbert.

EXPRESS AND TELEGRAPH AGENT—C. A. Webb.

LITERARY INSTITUTIONS—Norwich University, President, C. A. Curtis; Northfield Graded and High School, Principal, W. W. Prescott.

LIVERY STABLES—Lewis W. Avery, W. H. Morrie.

MANUFACTURERS—*Coffins*, G. W. Maxham, J. L. Abbott, W. W. Holden; *Doors, Sash and Blinds*, Martin Cobleigh, George W. Kingsbury; *Flannels*, A. Howarth, J. W. Gould; *Leather*, Smith, Denny & Brown; *Lumber*, Denny & Brown, D. R. [illegible], J. C. Rice; *Roofing Slate, and Flagging for Sidewalks*, [illegible] Company, J. H. Orcutt, Agent; *United States Artificial Stone Company*, D. T. Averill, President.

MECHANICS—*Blacksmiths*, Frank Gosley & Son, V. W. Smith, Joseph Davis, Warren C. Briggs, V. W. Smith, L. Knapp, R. Pinney; *Carpenters*, W. H. H. Claflin, A. D. Metcalf, L. W. Adams, J. L. Abbott, C. Bennett, F. S. Newton; *Cooper*, S. O. Emerson; *Founders and Machinists*, C. R. Ely, A. F. Spalding; *Barbers*, A. E. Downing, D. E. Vayett; *Mill-wrights*, H. D. Bean, W. W. Rumrill; *Marble Workers*, E. L. Soper & Co., J. H. Hurley; *Masons*, George Dole, S. C. Davis, L. R. Robinson; *Millers*, Jonas Rich, Thomas Slade, Denny & Brown, Lewis G. Wood; *Painters*, S. F. Gibbs, E. Huntley, W. R. Bean, Fred Carlton, Asa Strong, E. Ingalls, W. Coburn; *Photographers*, R. M. McIntosh, L. H. Newell; *Shoemakers*, L. S. Wellington, S. P. Grow, David P. Holt, Frank Larose, E. Tatro; *Slaters*, George F. Rich. A. K. Knapp, E. P. Kelley; *Tailors*, J. L. Mack, Joseph K. Egerton; *Wheelwrights*, A. C. Chase, R. T. Eastman, J. B. Shortridge, Mead & Wardner; *Wool Carder and Cloth Dresser*, S. D. Dodge.

MERCHANTS—Edgerton Brothers, George H. Crane, E. K. Jones & Co., Davis & Ward, C. Denny & Co., A. F. Andrews, E. W. Robbins; *Clothing*, J. C. B. Thayer; *Boots and Shoes*, E. G Sanborn, G. B. B. Denny; *Clocks and Watches*, W. F. Cushman, Lewis Dodge; *Clothing, Hats, Caps, and Gents' Furnishing Goods*, G. B. B. Denny; *Drugs, Paints, and Fancy Goods*, Nichols & Williams, E. Porter; *Fancy Goods and Notions*, E. L. Soper; *Flour and Grain*, Smith & Goodspeed, Denny & Brown, Thomas Slade; *Groceries*, N. N. Chase, S. F. Judd, W. A. Blake, Denny & Brown, Stebbins & Richmond, Elbridge G. Pierce; *Meat Markets*, Boynton & Moseley, D. Bacon; *Stoves and Hardware*, N. Huntley, George W. Briggs, S. W. Steele; *Paints and Wall Paper*, E. Huntley; *Millinery*, Mrs. Slack, Mrs. M. S. Gilchrist, Mrs. M. B. Jones, Miss C. H. Mead, Miss R. Fletcher, Miss Maria M. Howes.

EATING SALOONS—H. L. Kenyon, T. A. Wiley.

HOTELS—Northfield House, J. H. Ransom: Center House, William Blood.

CONTENTS.

A FEW ANTIQUARIAN RELICS

EXHIBITED AT THE CENTENNIAL, NORTHFIELD, JULY 4, 1876

One BALLOT BOX, used at the first town meeting in 1794. Dug out of a block of wood by Seth Smith, and presented to the town by Eleazer Nichols, Esq.

Two MILL STONES, brought into Northfield by Elijah Paine before any settlement was made, and used in the "Mill Woods" on the East Hill. Taken from their original bed in the stream of water where they had fallen when the "old mill" went down, and exhibited on the *common*, where they will in all probability remain for ages to come, serving as one of the landmarks of Northfield's first beginnings. By Messrs. John L. Moseley, C. W. Williams, Charles Reed, Lewis Avery, and Dr. P. D. Bradford.

One DRUM, taken from the British at the battle of Bunker Hill by Mr. Cady, and used during the Revolution; also used during the War of 1812 by Major Leonard Persons, of Windsor, and in the War of the Rebellion by Leonard Persons, of Northfield; made in London in 1712. By Lyman Holden.

One DUNLAP ADVERTISER, one NEW ENGLAND COURIER, first papers ever printed in America; one ENGRAVING OF FIRST LOCOMOTIVE ever built: three pieces of CONTINENTAL MONEY; one CEDAR CANE, from the first house built in America, at St. Augustine, Florida. By John Gregory.

One BED SPREAD, carded and spun by Maria Belknap eighty-two years ago, when she was sixteen years old. By Rev. Ira Beard.

One GLASS MUG, two hundred years old; one EARTHEN SUGAR BOWL, two hundred years old; one SCOTCH PRINT, two hundred years old; one SCOTCH PRINT, one hundred and fifty years old, one BOOK OF SERMONS, printed in 1774. By Allen B. Kelt.

One JO AND MOLLOY'S MILK PAN, Indians; CUP AND SAUCER one hundred years old; one BOWL, one hundred years old; one PEPPER BOX, one hundred years old; one WINE GLASS, one hundred years old; one POWDER HORN, one hundred years old. By the greatest curiosity on exhibition, Perry Marsh, who played on a Fife for General Winfield Scott at the battle of Lundy's Lane in the War of 1812, and who now is as "good as new" on that shrill piercing instrument of "*ye olden time*."

One SPADE used by Governor Paine in breaking ground at Northfield for the Central Vermont railroad, preserved in a glass case, and kept securely by the railroad officials at St. Albans. By John Gregory.

One BIBLE that was given to Joseph Thompson in 1785, Thompson being the man that fought with Colonel Sherman for the name of Barre, Vt. By John H. Blodgett.

One BOOK OF OBSERVATIONS in all the Greek words, etc , 1646; one BOOK ON SANCTIFICATION OF THE LORD'S DAY, MDCCXXXV; one ARITHMETIC, 1779; CONFESSION OF FAITH, 1793; READY RECKONER, 1790. By Allen McGillveray.

One SILVER SPOON, one PINT CUP, one TEA POT, and one small cup. Susanna Phinney was born in Connecticut in 1749, and married Samuel Richardson in 1768. The first cup was given to her at her marriage, and was an old cup then. The tea-pot is over one hundred years old, and the small cup Samuel Richardson carried in his knapsack in the old French War. The silver tea-spoon was Mrs. Phinney's at her marriage in 1790. Two SMALL TUMBLERS, one PIECE OF PRINT. The largest one was brought from Connecticut by Mrs. Richardson about 1770. The smallest was given to P. S. P. Staples by his grandmother, and is one hundred and fifty years old. The piece of print was Susannah Phinnes's dress when eighteen years old. All the above are now the property of Mrs. Jane F. Briggs.

One THREAD CASE, two hundred years old: one WORK POCKET, two hundred years old; one SHAWL, one hundred years old: one HANDKERCHIEF, one hundred years old: one HANDKERCHIEF, one hundred years old: one STAND SPREAD, seventy-five years old; one EATHERN TEA-POT, one hundred years old; one SALT-DISH, one hundred years old; one TIN GILL CUP, one hundred years old. Presented by Mrs. Serviah Williams.

One SUGAR BOWL. By Mrs. Simon Williams.

One PEWTER MUG. By Mrs. Lester Martyn.

Two POD AUGERS, made in Connecticut, over two hundred years old; one PINE TREE SIXPENCE; two POD AUGERS, made in Connecticut, one hundred years old. By H. W. Buzzell.

One GLASS MUG AND EATHERN BOWL, supposed to be one hundred and fifty years old. By Le Geer.

One PIECE OF WEDDING DRESS of Mrs. Jason Dole's grandmother: also a PORTRAIT; one NARRATIVE of the captivity of Mrs. Johnson by the Indians in 1814. By Mrs. Jason Dole.

One BED SPREAD, made in the West India Islands, Nassau, one hundred and fifty years old. By Allen McGillveray.

One CHAIR, over two hundred years old. By S. H. Curtis.

One BIBLE HISTORY OF 1641. By John Moseley.

One POCKET BOOK, seventy-five years old; one PEWTER PLATTER, one hundred years old; one HANDKERCHIEF, one PIN KNITTING SHEATH, one hundred years old, two SAMPLERS, one hundred years old; one SHIRT, one hundred years old, one BELT, one hundred years old; one SNUFF BOX, eighty years old; one SPOON, one hundred years old. By Miss Hatch.

H. D. Bean, to whom we are indebted for so large an exhibition of antiquarian articles, presented specimens of ancient coin, among which were Egyptian, Roman, Greek, and Indian; also the following articles: One HISTORY OF THE TURKS, published in 1621; one COLLECTION OF SERMONS, written in 17[illegible], one MASSACHUSETTS REGISTER, published in 1785, when John Hancock was Governor of the State; one BOSTON GAZETTE AND COUNTY JOURNAL, printed March 12, 1770; one VERMONT WATCHMAN, published in Montpelier by Walton & Goss, February 21, 1815, containing "A Treaty of Peace" between Great Britain and America; one POST BOY, published at Windsor, September 23, 1806; one VERMONT REGISTER of 1812; one NARRATIVE OF THE SHIPWRECK of the Nottingham galley of one hundred and twenty tons, ten guns, on her passage from London to New England on the twenty-fifth of September, 1810; one work entitled the REPUBLIC OF PLATO in ten books, published in Glasgow, Scotland, in 1763; one CONE from the Cedars of Lebanon in the Holy Land; one SYRIAN LAMP from Holy Land, such as was spoken of by Christ in His Parable of the Ten Virgins; one KNIFE left in a stump in Northfield by the Indians on returning from the burning of Royalton

CONCLUSION.

Titles.—In closing this work, having completed it so far as we are able, permit us to say that we have used no titles that do not justly belong to the individuals represented; none are used for compliment's sake. The reader might think the profuse number of titles that abound were put on for effect, but it is not so; it only completes a part of Northfield history, and would be incomplete without them.

Errors.—It would be impossible to write a history of nearly two hundred families, and have it free from errors, and hence we do not claim this work free from them. Many have died leaving no record of their families, others have moved away, and we can learn nothing of their present whereabouts, while others have left but a partial record of names and dates that are necessary to make a history reliable and interesting. But as a general thing our citizens have with great unanimity responded to our request for information, and if errors are found, either of omission or commission, the reader will please charge it to the circumstances under which the writer was placed, the shortness of time allowed for writing the history, and pardon all mistakes.

Our Plates.—When it was concluded to introduce Portraits into this work of such of our citizens as felt disposed to furnish them, the thought never occurred to us that more than twenty would be furnished. But we have been surprised, "yea, moved with joy," to have so many of our enterprising citizens avail themselves of this privilege. After consulting artists in Albany, Boston, and New York, we concluded to give the job to the Photo Engraving Company, of New York, who are working under the "Moss patent," a new style of engraving, which in the main is satisfactory, and speaks for itself. The elegant and truthful portrait of Governor Paine is worth many times the price of the book, and that it is correct beyond a doubt is verified by Hon. E. P. Walton, who remembers distinctly that when it was engraved on steel for Bank bills it was submitted to the Board of Directors of the Vermont Central railroad, Governor Paine being present, and met with their decided approval. Our artist has happily preserved its characteristics, for which we are very thankful. The Portraits are much lower in price than any firms we consulted, and $3.00 each less than their standard rate.

THANKS.—The author wishes to express his thanks for efficient aid to Dr's George Nichols and P. D. Bradford, O. D. Edgerton, Esq., James N. Johnson, Esq., and Rev. W. S. Hazen; also to R. M. McIntosh for the gratuitous stereoscopic views used for our monumental engravings, and to L. H. Newell for his generosity in furnishing portraits for the engravings, which show him to be a young artist of the first rank. With these remarks we close, wishing we had made a work more attractive and acceptable, which we believe we could have done had we more time and the "sinews of war" to aid us.

THE AUTHOR.

www.ingramcontent.com/pod-product-compliance
Lightning Source LLC
Chambersburg PA
CBHW031828270326
41932CB00008B/586

9783337425579